Watchdogs' Tales

The District Audit Service – the first 138 years

Trafalgar Square
showing Morley's
Hotel c. 1857; a
favourite place for
meetings of District
Auditors' Society from
1854–1881.

THE DISTRICT AUDITORS' SOCIETY

Watchdogs' Tales

The District Audit Service – the first 138 years

Foreword by HRH The Duke of Edinburgh

Edited by R U Davies

LONDON: HER MAJESTY'S STATIONERY OFFICE

Foreword

HRH The Duke of Edinburgh

The use, or misuse, of public funds has always attracted public attention. Financial scandals can be relied upon to cause acute embarrassment for governments. With the introduction of a formal system of local government, it was appreciated that there was a need for an independent auditing body. Such was the old District Audit Service. Set up in 1846, it was only superseded by the present Audit Commission in 1982.

The fact that the District Audit Service lasted 138 years suggests that it performed its very important and valuable task with reasonable competence. However this book also shows that standards tend to vary with the accepted attitudes and ethics of the time. Some of the stories might appear rather odd - not to say bizarre - by modern ideas, but, in spite of these occasional aberrations, the Service stuck to its basic purpose of checking that no unlawful use was made of public funds.

This book is in the nature of a tribute by the Audit Commission to its predecessor. The structure and the powers may have changed but the basic purpose has remained the same. The task is still to ensure that public funds are not wasted and that the services, for which they are voted, are managed effectively, efficiently and economically. In these days, when local authorities have responsibilities for so many services to the public, the task of the Audit Commission has become even more important. Its great strength is that it can concentrate on trying to get value for money while keeping out of the political arena.

We owe a debt of gratitude to the District Audit Service for laying such firm foundations for this vital function. I am sure that the Audit Commission will maintain all that is best in the traditions established by their predecessors.

1986

Acknowledgements

The editor and authors wish to express their thanks to the following people who contributed in many different ways to the preparation of this book.

Patricia A Church

Caroline Fryer

Mary Gharbi

Deborah Harvey

Gillian Holland

Kate Moore-Scott

Isobel Saville

Mandy Swindells

Contents

Preface

Apart from an interesting backward glance to Norman times to speculate on the origins of the district auditor's one-time peculiar duty to 'allow' or 'disallow' accounts, this book sets out to cover the 138 years from the Poor Law Amendment Act 1844, which first provided for the appointment of district auditors, to the Local Government Finance Act 1982 which saw the disappearance of the office of "district auditor" from the statute books. The first 138 years . . . for happily district auditors and the District Audit Service flourish and continue to serve local government as auditors appointed by the Audit Commission.

The book is not intended to be a formal history of the Service. The historical facts are ably recounted in L M Helmore's "The District Auditor" (MacDonald Evans Ltd 1961) and, more recently, in the opening chapters of "Local Government Audit Law" by R Jones (HMSO, second edition 1985). It is a collection of essays written by past and present members of the Service which it is hoped will convey to future members an appreciation of their inheritance and something of the spirit and characters of their predecessors and of their endeavours for the good of local government.

The genesis of this book owes much to Cliff Nicholson, CBE, Deputy Controller and Director of Operations of the Audit Commission. Moreover, without his continued support and guidance the project could not have been brought to a successful conclusion.

I am grateful to all the members of the District Auditors' Society who sent me material for this book and especially to those who allowed me to badger them into making major contributions.

November 1986   R U Davies

The Antecedents of the District Auditor

E J Burdon

It would be misleading to begin any sort of account of the District Audit Service by looking at the state of local government immediately before the creation of the office of district auditor in 1844. Certainly, the unsatisfactory audit provisions of the Poor Law Amendment Act 1834 demonstrated the need for his existence, but the powers with which the district auditor appeared do not derive from anything in the local government of the 18th and early 19th centuries, of which the Webbs said in their book *The Parish and the County*:

> "If we were asked to name a period in English history during which the country possessed the largest measure of self government, when its local administrators were most effectively free from superior control, either of the National Executive, Parliament, or the Law Courts, we should suggest the years between 1689 and 1835, or more precisely the century which elapsed between the accession of the House of Hanover and the close of the Napoleonic Wars".

To find the origin of the auditor's powers, and indeed of many of our accepted ideas of financial control, it is necessary to cast at least as far back as Norman England in the 12th century. Even at that distant time we find a well-developed organisation. Local government under the Normans and Angevins was in the hands of sheriffs, appointed by the King and operating with the local customary courts which had existed from before the Conquest. Membership of these courts seems usually to have been an obligation arising from tenure of land in the area.

The sheriff collected royal income arising within the shire – rents of manors, levies such as Danegeld, scutage, and aids, and debts due to the King. In practice, the periodic manorial rents were usually commuted into a lump sum, the 'farm', from which the sheriff had to account whatever the actual amount of his collections.

He was not the only person liable to the King for periodic income; there were also stewards and bailiffs of honours, bailiffs and reeves of towns, guardians of the affairs of vacant bishoprics and abbacies and of escheated feudal fiefs, and also craftsmen's guilds which paid a yearly licence duty. But it seems that the sheriff acted for many of these minor accountants and in any event his proceedings were typical.

His account was rendered at the Exchequer to the King's

representatives before a number of royal officers who acted as auditors. They were so-called not because the accounts were unwritten, but because they heard and determined disputes arising out of accountings. Written accounts – the Pipe Rolls – existed very early on; there is an incomplete specimen from 1130, and an almost complete series survives from 1156 to 1833.

A surprising amount is known about the procedure at these audits – for audits these accountings were. The Exchequer was the first department of state to appear as a distinct entity, long before the Royal Courts of Justice, and its practice was described in authoritative detail by Richard of London in the *Dialogus de Scaccario* written about 1180.

The audit was held yearly, usually at Westminster with an interim settlement at the half year. The sheriff sat at one side of a large table, the Lord High Treasurer or his representative at the other, while the barons of the Exchequer, persons of substance such as the justiciar or those appointed for their skills or integrity, sat round and watched the proceedings. These were the 'auditors' already mentioned.

The table between the sheriff and the treasurer was marked out in squares like a chequer board. Hence the chamber in which the audit was held came to be called the Exchequer or Scaccarium (Latin – scaccarius – a chequer board).

This squared board was used, with counters, as a kind of calculator. The subordinate officers responsible set up counters in positions denoting the expenses met by the sheriff on the King's behalf, first periodical payments vouched from the Exchequer records, and then other expenses which the sheriff could prove. These were

called the sheriff's 'allowances'.

If the Treasurer rejected any expense claimed and the auditors agreed, the allowance was refused – hence 'disallowance' of items of account and 'allowance' of account as the terms were used by district auditors until recently.

Next, the amount due from the sheriff as shown by the Exchequer records, of which the 'Domesday Book' was the best known, was set up by moving the counters in the opposite sense on the board.

The amount of cash brought in by the sheriff (after an adjustment for clipped or debased silver coins, arrived at after a sample assay actually carried out under supervision on the premises) was next deducted by moving the counters, and the balance due to or from the sheriff read off the board. Details of the accounting were then entered in the Pipe Roll in the presence of the parties and of the auditors.

There is so much fascinating detail available about the procedure at these audits that it is difficult to confine oneself to essentials. For instance, in the 12th century arabic numerals were unknown in western Europe, though the abacus was certainly available. Arithmetic on paper with Roman numerals but no zero, while possible, was not easy.

The Exchequer invented a system, which can be regarded as a method of working the abacus principle on paper, which allowed them to calculate with demonstrable accuracy. This was a prodigy, the more clearly so that when the arabic system with zero was introduced following the writings of Alhazen after 1250, the Exchequer system held its ground, and indeed continued to be favoured by those who understood it, for centuries. There is a marginal calculation by Lord Burleigh from the time of Elizabeth I, in which he uses the Exchequer system.

The counterfoil receipt system also deserves notice. It involved the use of tally sticks, each consisting of a square length of wood with opposite sides smoothed. The amount of money involved was entered in duplicate on opposite corners by a code of notches. The nature of the transaction was written, again in duplicate on the two smooth sides, and the stick was then split lengthways so that full details of the transaction appeared on each piece.

One party to the transaction took one piece (the 'feuille'), the other party keeping the other (the 'contrefeuille'). When the transaction was discharged, as by payment of money due or by production of the 'feuille' as a voucher in an accounting, the two pieces were clipped together by a strip of tin – a forgery would not fit – and stored in the Exchequer.

At first, the sticks were about 8″ long, but the larger sums involved in later centuries made lengths of up to 3′6″ necessary.

This system continued in use for six centuries, but in 1783 a statute abolished tallysticks, introducing an 'indented cheque receipt' instead. This was to have effect only on the death or resignation of the chamberlains then in office, which did not occur until 1826.

In 1833 and 1834, statutes swept away the rest of the ancient procedure, and on 16 October 1834 the tallies accumulated over the centuries were fed into the furnaces which warmed the House of Lords. As a result the Houses of Parliament were burned down, apparently because the flues overheated. The matter is thought worth mentioning, as coming as near as any accounting system ever has done to setting the Thames on fire.

In fact, the professional competence of the 12th century auditors commands the respect of any modern practitioner. They had a clear grasp of the importance of the separation of duties, of independent verification of each step in accounting, of the use of counterfoil receipts, and of the cardinal principle that irresponsible local government shows up in the accounts.

With the coming of the Plantagenets at the end of the 13th century the sheriff and his court-leet began to decline in importance. Nevertheless they bequeathed a persistent tradition to later local government of voluntary service, local knowledge, local patriotism and an indefinable capacity for educating members in the art of administration while they practised it. Whether this can survive the era of paid members and overriding ideological loyalties remains to be seen. But it has outlasted turbulent periods in the past.

With the decline of the sheriff, local government funds ceased to be subject to the Exchequer audit, and a suggestion that, upwards of four centuries later, the powers of that audit suddenly reappeared on the local government scene certainly needs support. This it is hoped will appear below.

In fact, at the national level the uses of audit were not lost to sight. The Parliaments of the 14th century experimented with audit of the affairs of Royal ministers after they lost office as a means of enforcing responsible government.

From the mid-14th century, the justice of the peace, originally created to relieve the Assize Courts of an increasing load of criminal work, became increasingly important in local administration, and such funds as he controlled were not subject to any central audit.

In Tudor times, the introduction by Henry VIII of Lord Lieutenants and the activity of such offshoots of the Royal Council as the Court of Star Chamber caused the sheriffs' importance to dwindle still further. In this reign also, the growing need to provide for the relief of poverty caused a metamorphosis of the ecclesiastical parish into a unit of secular local government.

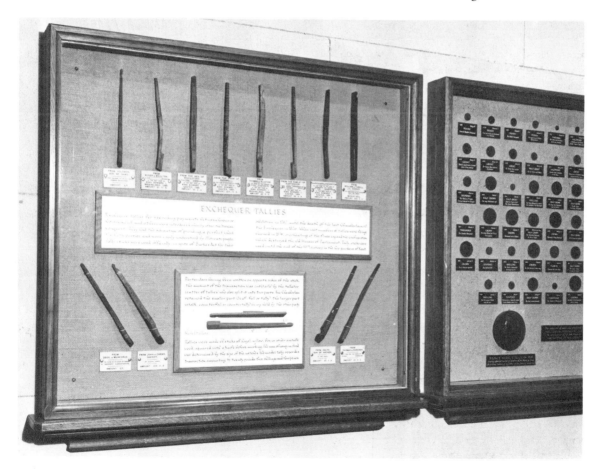

1/1 Some examples of the Tally Sticks used by early auditors.

At first, voluntary donations to the church were relied upon for the local finance of poor relief, but it soon became necessary to invoke compulsion by authorising churchwardens to make assessments on parishioners. After the Poor Law Act 1601 this became the poor rate, and the relief of poverty was made the duty of churchwardens and the newly created overseers of the poor.

Thereafter, constables and surveyors of highways became associated with the parish, and it exercised other duties inherited from the earlier manorial courts, but its principal business was the administration of the poor law. This became, during the next two centuries, increasingly disorderly and burdensome. Various statutes were passed from time to time to remedy specific abuses, or to authorise local combinations of parishes, but the only control lay with the magistrates and it was inadequate.

Parish sued parish in attempts to use the law of settlement to unload the maintenance of individual paupers upon one another. Poor relief was given to the able-bodied to supplement inadequate wages, naturally driving wage rates down and poor rates up. The principles of the Act of 1601 were widely disregarded.

The long neglect by the central power of this subject was only one product of the great constitutional conflicts between the monarch, the executive and the legislative which took place during the 17th and 18th centuries, and also distracted central attention from other developments in local government in the counties and boroughs, allowing the near autonomy to develop in this field upon which the comments of the Webbs were quoted earlier.

Throughout this period, the control of national finance by the Exchequer continued but became increasingly inadequate for the continually growing size of the task. New officers were added to its establishment to meet new circumstances and no doubt some of its methods changed.

It seems likely, for example, that a better way of striking the balance than the movement of counters on a board may have been adopted, though it must be remembered that the ancient Exchequer had quite extraordinary reserves of immutability. Thus when in 1731 the Courts were required by statute to abandon their peculiar Court handwritings and to conduct proceedings in English, the Exchequer obtained exemption and was still using Roman numerals and Latin for its records until 1834. Then, too, the sheriffs were still brought in to audit almost to the end, though their 'allowances' by this time often exceeded any income collected.

Even in the 12th century procedures, though effective, had often been protracted. In the 18th century they had become impossibly dilatory. Chatham, for instance, ceased to be Paymaster in 1755, but did not get quittance until 1769; the elder Fox relinquished the same office in 1765, but got his accounts settled only in 1783; and delays of these orders were far from exceptional.

Inevitably, such immoderate deliberation in settling accounts caused the retention in the hands of functionaries or ex-functionaries of large sums of public money, especially as it was usually considered quite proper to invest such balances and retain the profit, and no doubt also because the era of universal banking was not yet come.

The practice was attacked, but an easy defence was that the Exchequer's medieval methods of accounting and rigid technical formality were the reasons for retaining large balances. Those accounting for public monies, it was argued, could not fairly be asked to pay all the balances without final quittance from the Exchequer. If they did, their estates might be held liable for large sums at a distant date, and their heirs might well face ruin long after the person accounting was dead.

The scale of the problem may be judged from Holdsworth's statement in Volume X of his *History of English Law* that in 1783 the unaudited sums issued to persons accountable amounted to £44 million.

Moreover, during the centuries of growth of the machinery of government, a great number of offices had been created. Many were profitable sinecures; many others were remunerated by fees but could be profitably delegated to modestly salaried deputies. The Exchequer, being the oldest of the great departments of state, had more of these remunerative anachronisms than most.

So long as the Crown and the great Whig gentry worked together, little was likely to be done about these defects. The vast patronage which the gift of profitable offices in government conferred upon the Crown was controlled by the Whigs, enabling them to consolidate their hold on both executive and legislature during the reigns of George I and II.

George III, however, began to use his patronage for his own ends, to create his own party in Parliament, and from that moment reform became inevitable. In 1780, the great Whig orator, Edmund Burke opened a campaign for redress of such abuses. His immediate

1/2 The burning of Parliament; The House of Commons ablaze, 16 October 1834.

object was party advantage, but his immense historical knowledge and analytical powers translated his ends to a higher plane.

One of his earliest targets was the Exchequer, and in the early 1780s he secured the abolition of many sinecures. The Paymaster of the Army and the Treasurer of the Navy were no longer allowed to retain large sums. In 1782 commissioners were appointed to audit public accounts, at fixed salaries, and other reforms were effected, diminishing the powers of both aristocracy and executive. But they were far from sufficient.

Had Pitt been able to continue gradual reform, both the legislative and the executive might have adapted to changing conditions, new needs, and new political ideas. But the Napoleonic wars brought reform almost to a standstill with the result that after 1830 it was resumed in so drastic a form as to shatter the 18th century constitution of balanced powers.

At this point, we may revert to the Poor Law. A Royal Commission examined the abuses in this field from 1831, reporting in 1834 with such effect that the Poor Law Amendment Act of that year was passed almost unopposed.

Its audit provisions were, however, defective in that auditors were appointed and paid by the local Guardians of the Poor and their powers undefined, and although central regulations as to audit were issued by the Poor Law Commissioners, the resulting control was unsatisfactory.

The district auditor was therefore created in 1844, with statutory powers designed to make his audit effective.

In view of the then recent extinction of the ancient Exchequer audit, which had finally transferred its functions to the Comptroller and Auditor-General only in 1834, it seems reasonable to suppose that the draughtsmen of the 1844 Poor Law Act knew the strengths of Exchequer practice as well as its weaknesses and deliberately gave the district auditor powers whose effectiveness had been proved over the centuries. Use of the Exchequer terminology has already been noticed.

If the foregoing summary of the constitutional paroxysms of the 18th century appear laboured, it is because there seems no other way to account for the sudden appearance in 1844 of an officer with the powers of the district auditor. They cannot be traced to any other source than the Exchequer, and it has seemed necessary to show that, ancient as these powers were, they would have been freshly in the minds of the legislators of 1844.

E J BURDON LLB

Died on St George's Day 1986 shortly after completing the final corrections to his two contributions to this book. His main interest was the law, but he played a leading part in developing "Reappraisal". Enjoyed riding fast motor-cycles and skin-diving up to the last.

The District Auditors' Society

R U Davies

I   The first 50 years (1844–1894)

The Poor Law Amendment Act 1844 received Royal Assent on 9 August 1844. Section 32 of the Act provided for the formation of audit districts and the appointment of district auditors, and on 19 March 1846 the inaugural meeting of the District Auditors' Society was held at the Sussex Hotel, Bouverie Street, London. The meeting was attended by 21 district auditors and letters of support were received from another seven.

It was resolved that 'the district auditors present enrol their names to form a Society for the discussion of their practice and that the other auditors be requested to join them'. A committee of five was appointed to draw up rules for the guidance of the Society, to watch over the interests of members and with the power to call a special meeting in addition to the Society's annual meeting if they deemed it necessary.

Mr John Clark Meymott, the district auditor for the South-West Metropolitan district was appointed the Society's first Honorary Secretary and Treasurer and served the Society in that capacity for twenty-six years until his death in 1872 following a serious illness.

AUDITOR OF THE DISTRICT

2/1 1840's: "He should be removed from any local influence and above any temptation".

The Committee got to work quickly and the Rules of the Society were settled at their meeting on 30 April 1846. The opening paragraph epitomises the spirit which has continued to imbue the Society:

"The objects of the Society are to provide a medium of communication among the district auditors on matters relating to their office for the purpose of promoting uniformity of practice, of obtaining mutual advice on difficult questions, of preserving a store of information on matters concerning their office and also for promoting the interests of the members."

The Rules provided that each member should pay an initial subscription of £1 'and such future sums as the general meetings shall from time to time consider necessary'. The Honorary Treasurer's accounts showed then, as even to this day, that the Society has always managed its affairs thriftily.

2/2 1850: "An audit . . . the bridle by which local administrators could be guided to what was right, and restrained from what was wrong".

In the early years district auditors had to be of independent means for the appointments were part-time and the remuneration modest. As early as 1847, the Society made representations to the Poor Law Commissioners regarding the inadequacies of their salaries, and in their annual report to Parliament that year the Commissioners publicly acknowledged that 'we are of the opinion that these representations are entitled to consideration'.

In 1867 there were 49 district auditors. A report to the Society records that their average salary was £250 (after paying all expenses), 'which for the six and a half days which was the average time it took to audit the accounts of each Union gave auditors an average remuneration of £2.15s.0d (two pounds fifteen shillings) per day.'

Auditors had great difficulties in securing adequate remuneration and the Society often made representations to departments and Ministers, when Bills were introduced creating new authorities and making their accounts subject to audit by the district auditor, that the Bills ought to include provision for the remuneration of the district auditor. The minutes of the March 1887 meeting recorded in considering what action to take in relation to the Highways Bill:

"The Meeting considered that it would be unwise to repeat the course of action adopted in the case of the creation of the Rural Sanitary Authorities when the District Auditors were left to wait nearly three years for compensation and then only obtained it by a degree of urgency which was distasteful to themselves".

At the same meeting the new Burials Bill was considered:

"It appeared that under section 15 while existing Burial Boards would probably continue to defray the expenses of the Audit of their Accounts no remuneration was contemplated by the Act for the newly imposed examination and Audit of the Accounts of the Burial Authorities to be created thereunder."

The minutes record that:

"Several members renewed their complaints of the total inadequacy of the fees for School Board Audits which at 10s. 6d per Audit frequently left the Auditor not only unremunerated for his trouble but considerably out of pocket in the performance of a duty not voluntarily undertaken by him but compulsorily imposed by the Legislature a result which was felt to be opposed to all equity".

The Poor Law Amendment Act 1868 improved matters as regards remuneration for the audits of the Poor Law authorities – the Unions – by providing that henceforth district auditors should not only be appointed by the Poor Law Board but paid by them and deemed to be civil servants.

Later extensions of district audit to newly created authorities such as School Boards, Highway and Rural and Urban Sanitary authorities left the district auditors to collect their remuneration for those audits from the authorities themselves. For example, the Public Health Act 1875 provided that the auditor should receive from the authorities remuneration of not less than two guineas per day plus his travelling expenses. Eventually with the passing of the District Auditors Act 1879, new arrangements were introduced which lasted until the coming into force of the Local Government Act 1972.

Under the 1879 Act all the salaries and expenses of the district auditor were to be paid out of monies provided by Parliament and a stamp duty was to be charged on every local authority whose accounts were subject to audit for the purpose of contributing to the amount. The Local Government Board was made responsible for appointing district auditors and for fixing their salaries and expenses.

2/3 Deepening the Fleet Street Sewers, 1845.

As a result of these changes, the Society resolved in 1881 to delete from the Rules the words 'also for promoting the interests of members', and questions of their terms and conditions of service were henceforth pursued through other avenues.

It seems that the district auditors were left largely to fend for themselves, providing their own offices and staff and as late as 1871, the Society resolved that:

2/4 1860: "Careful selection of persons appointed as mobile, full time auditors with the devotion by them of their complete and undivided attention to the duties of auditing".

"The Poor Law Board be respectfully requested to supply the District Auditors with the Statutes, Books and Stationery required in the Execution of their duties".

Early on, in 1847, the Society sent a Memorial to the Commissioners drawing attention to 'the difficulties and serious inconveniences to the Auditor to recovering balances and disallowances from Parish Officers and others'. District auditors had to lay information before the Justices personally and attend hearings and there were problems in drafting the information. Many Justices were idiosyncratic on that score and rejected cases out of hand because of information which they considered to be defective. This, the Society pointed out, 'left the Auditor open to Action for Trespass to which he would have no defence'.

From their inception under the Poor Law Amendment Act 1844 district auditors had to exercise the powers of disallowance and surcharge and the recovery of sums due from persons accountable. The primary reason for their appointment was to stamp out abuse, unlawful use of public funds and fraud and, in the early years particularly, the meetings of the Society were almost wholly taken up with accounts of disallowances and surcharges.

Disallowances and surcharges were numerous and the amounts were often small, but it was an effective way of bringing home to members and officers their responsibilities and instilling into local government a strong sense of probity which has since grown into a tradition which is the envy of the world.

Most of the disallowances are of little relevance today but among those reported to the Society were:

"At one of my workhouses where there had long existed an

excessive consumption of Beer and Porter, I allowed all that had been ordered by the Medical Officer and deducted that from the total consumption and charged the Master with payment of the value of the excess £35.12s. 3d."

"Disallowed Magistrate Clerk's charges for fees exceeding the Table of Fees sanctioned by the judges which is almost universally done."

"Disallowed a payment for goods supplied to the union house by the Treasurer who is a partner in the firm supplying them it being made penal for the Treasurer to supply them by the 55th Geo. IIIrd ch. 137 sec. 6 extended by 4 and 5 Wm IVth ch. 76 sec. 51. The parties aggrieved are appealing to the Commissioners against this disallowance on the ground that although the Treasurer is liable to a penalty yet the payment to him for the goods is not unlawful."

"Mr Hazlehurst also reported that he had disallowed the cost of *The Times* supplied to the Select Vestry of Liverpool, which disallowance had been reversed by the Local Government Board on appeal.

He had also disallowed the cost of the *Justice of the Peace* supplied to the West Derby Union, and the cost of *The Queen*, which disallowance had been confirmed by the Local Government board."

"Mr Floyd – among other persons excused on the grounds of poverty was the Duke of Sutherland. Mr Floyd surcharged, and the money was paid."

"Mr White mentioned that in a Parish in which the Lighting and Watching Act was in force he had disallowed the cost of tunics and epaulets, buttons and other accoutrements for the use of members of the Fire Brigade. He was reversed on appeal."

Very early on the district auditors ran into the vexed question of how far, if at all, were they entitled to question matters of policy and the exercise of discretion

2/5 1870: District Audit applied to School Boards.

by bodies under audit. Being fair-minded men, they could see all sides of the question, and in a manner which has characterised them since as a body, came out with a guarded reply. A typical example can be quoted from the first year of the Society's existence. The Executive Committee was asked to consider in January 1847:

"Whether under the 54th section of the 4th and 5th Wm. IV, Chap. 76, Boards of Guardians are so exclusively the judges of the objects of relief and of the destitution which brings an Applicant within the legal definition of 'Poor' as to prevent the revision of their judgement by the Auditor, except in cases contravening the Rules of the Poor Law Commissioners." The Members after some discussion resolved "that except in cases under the prohibitory Order the Committee are not disposed to express an Opinion that the Auditors have no power of supervision over the Order of Boards of Guardians, but they consider it would not be desirable to interfere unless an extreme case is presented to them".

The fostering of faithful and prompt accounting and the encouragement and development of good accounting practices were among the great achievements of the district auditors. There were no professional bodies in the early days (the Corporate Treasurers and Accountants Institute, the very first, was not established until 1885), and the district auditors came on a local government world largely ignorant of accounting matters where laxity, abuses of trust and downright fraud were commonplace.

Collectors thought nothing of keeping two sets of books, one for the auditor and the other recording the true facts of the sums they had collected. As late as 1886 the minutes of the Society record:

2/6 Feeding the hungry at the Nichol Street Ragged School, Shoreditch.

"Mr Green-Price having asked what means, if any, could be used for the prevention and detection of duplicate books by Collectors, in the course of the discussion which followed, it was suggested that all rate books and receipt check books should be stamped by the Clerk to the Guardians".

Frauds were prevalent in the early years, and the district auditors felt that they needed to know how they were perpetrated, the methods adopted to effect concealment and how they were discovered. The district auditors acknowledged they needed to pool their experiences and the Society's Executive Committee on 6 March 1851 called for the members of the Society to submit reports on frauds which came to their knowledge so that the details could be circulated to members in confidence. The reporting of frauds for the information of auditors continues to this day.

The district auditors often tackled doubtful accounting head on. One auditor reported to the Society:

"At two Unions I took Declarations of the Masters to the truth of their Books and Balances and then went and compared the stores in hand and charged them with the deficiency and they paid in the amount to the Treasurer."

"One Master claimed for the half year on enormous waste on cheese. I charged him with 1 cwt. 3qr. 14lb. of it and he paid in the money."

Despite their preoccupation with legality, probably justified by the waywardness of many of the authorities subject to their audit, the early district auditors did find time occasionally to discuss good accounting practice at Society meetings.

In August 1854 a lively discussion took place 'as to the principle on which the cost of clothing for each half-year should be ascertained whether upon the clothing actually paid for, or the clothing consumed during the half-year. The practice appeared to vary and there appeared to be no directions on the subject'. In those days, work houses had large stocks of ill-fitting garments of rough quality which were drawn on to clothe the inmates.

The advent of the Public Health Act code under the Public Health Act 1875, applied to urban and rural sanitary authorities, introduced income and expenditure accounting and the district auditors were quick to get to grips with the innovation. The minutes of 29 March 1876 recount that:

"Mr Gibson's exemplification of the Accounts of Urban Rural Sanitary Authorities was laid before the meeting and received the commendations of the Members present".

The Society was successful at an early date in establishing the principle that collecting officers should pay over or bank their collections intact whatever the circumstances, a golden rule which auditors seek to enforce to this day.

It seems that there were often difficulties between the parishes and the Union, and that some parish vestries appointed Assistant Overseers to collect the rates in the parish so that they could ensure that the parish expenses were promptly paid before the balance was handed over. In November 1851 the Secretary was instructed to write to the Poor Law Board asking for their opinion on:

"Whether an Assistant Overseer, duly appointed in Vestry, whose defined duty is to perform all the duties of Overseer, is bound to pay over all monies he collects for Rates to the Overseer, as a Collector under Article 8 of the General

Accounts Order; or whether he is to retain them and pay thereout the proper payments of the Overseers, which it is his defined duty to do, and which he may be prevented doing if he pays over the money to the Overseers.

It appears that in some Parishes an Assistant Overseer, who gives security, is appointed for the purpose of preventing the money getting into the Overseers hands".

The reply was unequivocable:

"The money collected by an Assistant Overseer is to be paid by him to the Overseers (or their Bankers), in the first place and the necessary expenditure on behalf of the Parish must be provided for afterwards."

The notions that public bodies might lawfully borrow in anticipation of revenues due in order to meet pressing claims or that a body might lawfully rate for a working balance appeared to be anathema to the early members of the Society. The minutes of a meeting as late in the last century as 25 March 1892 record that:

"The following reported case was considered satisfactory. Disallowance was made in Cash Book of amount of order on

2/7 A meeting of the London School Board in the Council Chamber, Guildhall.

Treasurer so far as he provided funds to meet it, the account being overdrawn, and the members signing order were surcharged, the reasons being that payment was not made out of funds legally in hands of School Board, but temporarily advanced by Bank without legal authority, and that School Board cannot legally take credit for any payments, except such as are made out of School Funds or other funds legally available, and that School Board had neglected either to enforce payment of Precept or to raise sufficient sum in default under 33 and 34 Vict. c. 75, s. 56 (1 and 2). Local Government Board, in reversing decision, state that it was improper to draw cheques in excess of amount to their credit, but members of School Board were not legally liable to be surcharged for payment of debt legally due. As to second reason, the question is not whether the payment was made out of moneys provided by School Board, but whether it was made in discharge of a lawful debt, and the point taken in the third reason would not constitute a sufficient ground for the Auditor's decision. There were no grounds for disallowance, and the validity of surcharge depends on whether or no payment was or was not illegal. In the Appeal, the School Board pointed out their action might be objected to, if the precept on Overseers was based on an estimate exceeding their actual requirements; and the Local Government Board replied that they see no objection why School Boards should ever overdraw their Account, the amount can be estimated, and such a margin can be allowed as will secure the School Board against a deficiency''.

The Society was active in considering proposed legislation and did not hesitate to send deputations to wait on Ministers or make representations to the Commissioners about changes which they thought desirable. At a meeting of the Executive Committee in July 1848, for example, three Bills were discussed at length – the Highways Bill, the Sanitary Bill and the new Poor Law Bill. The Committee decided that 'it did not appear desirable to take any measures relative to the

2/8 Instruction of pauper children in the South Metropolitan District School, Sutton.

first two but decided to send a deputation to the Commissioners to suggest changes and additions to the Poor Law Bill'. Again, in 1886 the Society decided to make representations to the Poor Law Board regarding a proposed revision of the Accounts Order which they felt to be undesirable.

The Society's members had from the beginning a real concern for encouraging economy in local government expenditure and were not slow to disallow and surcharge payments which they considered extravagant. But their efforts did not always meet with the approval of the appellate body, the Poor Law Board. In 1856 the minutes of the Society recount that 'a case was mentioned where the Auditor had disallowed some items of extravagant and costly furniture for the Master's use and that the Poor Law Board had reversed the Auditor's decision'.

The doctrine of *functus officio*, lately so ably expounded by Reg Jones in his *Local Government Audit Law*, was tentatively asserted by the Society early in its life. In

1861 the Society resolved that:

> "It appeared to be the opinion of the Meeting that at any time during the Audit, the Auditor may alter or reverse any decision or certificate he may have made in the union accounts. But that when a Parochial Account is closed it cannot be afterwards opened".

By the time of its Jubilee Dinner in 1894, the Society had grown in stature and the work and responsibilities of its members much extended. In 1891 the Society had extended its congratulations to its chairman and former Honorary Secretary, Mr Lloyd Roberts, on his appointment as Inspector of Audits, and, as the minutes record, 'the first to occupy the position of Inspector of Audits who had practical experience of the work of an Auditor'.

When the district audit system was first constituted the work was comparatively small, being confined merely to the Poor Law accounts with the auditors being appointed by the chairman and vice-chairman of the various Unions. This was soon changed to appointment by the Poor Law Commissioners and in 1848 district audit was extended to local boards of health, then in 1870 to school boards, in 1872 and 1875 to rural and urban sanitary authorities, and in 1878 to highway authorities. The new county councils created in 1888 were made subject to district audit, and with the addition of asylums and isolation hospitals in 1890 and 1893 the district audit service was responsible for the audits of a total of 10,600 authorities. The Local Government Act 1894 further increased the workload with the addition of 6,900 parish councils and 6,400 parish meetings.

The Jubilee Dinner celebrating the fiftieth anniversary of the appointment of district auditors was held on 19 December 1894 at the Grand Hotel, Charing Cross. The function was presided over by R A White (district auditor for Lincolnshire), and among those present were H Lloyd Roberts, Inspector of Audits, S B Tristam, Assistant Inspector, and a company of 33 district auditors and assistant district auditors. The guests were senior officials of the Local Government Board and the guest of honour was the President of the Board, the Rt Hon G J Shaw Lefevre MP, son of one of the three Commissioners who put into force the provisions of the Poor Law Act of 1834 – the Act which first provided for the appointment of auditors for Poor Law accounts in place of the Justices.

The District Auditors' Society

II   The middle years (1894–1938)

This period begins with a milestone in the history of local government, the Local Government Act 1894, which created urban and rural district councils, parish councils and parish meetings. Together with a previous enactment, the Local Government Act 1888, which created county councils including the London County Council, it largely shaped the organisation of English local government until the great consolidating Act of 1933.

The period concludes with the outbreak of the Second World War and the suspension of the Society's meetings for the duration of that conflict.

The Society was sensible of the importance of the 1894 Act and at its meeting in March 1894 appointed a committee to examine and report upon the Act:

"The operation of the Act is to create a very large number of new authorities whose expenditure will be audited by District Auditors; while a considerable number of existing authorities will be abolished and replaced by new bodies. . . . It must be presumed that no expenditure whatever is withdrawn from the District Auditor's jurisdiction by the operation of the Act; while an unknown, but certainly in the aggregate, a very considerable quantity of expenditure

3/1 1890: District Audit is given custody of the Infant Authorities in the 1894 LG Act.

by new authorities is brought within the Auditor's province."

Carson Roberts had been elected to the Society in 1892 and his influence was soon felt. In 1895 the Society formed a committee to consider forms of accounts and 'to report upon any forms in local use which appear to render accounts clearer or more concise, or which provide a more ready or efficient check, and to formulate suggestions which may relate to the new Orders for Accounts now under consideration'.

At the Society's meeting in October of the following year, Carson Roberts submitted a resolution, unanimously adopted, which embodied for the first time the advocacy of accounts kept on the basis of income and expenditure; and this became the main principle in the committee's report and recommendations on the form of local authority accounts:

> "That it is desirable that the accounts of Urban District Councils should punctually record, not only the payments, but also the expenditure incurred in each of the spending departments, and not only the receipts, but also the income accrued and the arrears left due in respect of each source of revenue."

Questions relating to disallowances and surcharges still occupied the greater part of the Society's debates. One such question seems now particularly bizarre although relevant at the time, and shows the district auditor in a caring and humane light. The minutes of 26 March 1897 contain the following passage:

> "If when a person is bitten by a mad dog, the Medical Officer of Health orders him to be sent to the Pasteur Institute in Paris, who becomes liable for his expenses?
>
> They might possibly be allowed under Section 131 of the Public Health Act 1875, but being so doubtful it would be better to obtain the sanction of the Local Government Board before passing them."

Carson Roberts was evidently keen to develop and advance the practice of accountancy in relation to local government, and in April 1905 at the end of a meeting which had been wholly devoted to the consideration of legal questions, disallowances and decisions of the Local Government Board, he suggested that 'at future meetings the morning should be given up to the discussion of legal points and decisions of the Local Government Board but that the afternoon should be left free for the discussion of points of practical interest in connection with the Audit and the method of keeping accounts.'

The suggestion was warmly welcomed, and on the proposal of Carson Roberts a small committee was appointed 'to assist the Society to fix and regulate the Agenda with a view to the inclusion of practical points for discussion'.

At the Society's next meeting in October 1905 Carson Roberts was in the chair and saw to it that the new resolve was put into effect. The whole of the afternoon was devoted to a discussion on the audit processes involved in checking rate and other income accounts and in detecting fraud.

The record of that afternoon's discussions include the first reference to the bank slip test which has proved instrumental over the years in unmasking hundreds of defaulting collectors and which today is still a powerful audit tool.

Other measures to improve security and provide internal checks were discussed and commended including:

– requiring a written claim for exemption for rates written off as 'empty' from the ratepayer or owner;

– the issue of notices from the central office to all persons returned as in arrears;

– the verification of pass books by the banks, or a return of balances held by the banks;

– the use of the consecutive receipt check system;

The general principles for dealing with income accounts set out as follows in the minutes met with the approval of the meeting then as it would today:

"(i) That is is more useful for an Auditor to devote attention to the completeness of the list of charges collectable and to the truth and propriety of the lists of items returned as written-off or uncollected, than to spend time on comparing receipt counterfoils with collection accounts.

(ii) The variation of process is valuable in checking any collecting officer's accounts as unexpected checks are often the most efficient; and every departure from the stereotyped system of professional audit, which relies chiefly on the receipt check books will tend to greater efficiency in detecting fraud.

(iii) That it is desirable in every case to work from the origin of the charge, eg in the case of private works from the accounts of the expenditure on such works, in the case of rents from the register of properties lettable, in the case of hall lettings from the diary of the hall-keeper, etc.

(iv) That, wherever credit is allowed, it is essential that a full register of the income, as well as a cash account of the collections should be kept, and that in most cases a

3/2 The report on the Audit of County and Urban Accounts, 1903.

Printed for Private Circulation only.

UPON THE

REPORT

DEALING WITH

THE AUDIT OF COUNTY AND URBAN ACCOUNTS

MADE IN JULY 1903, BY

THE JOINT SELECT COMMITTEE

OF THE HOUSE OF LORDS AND THE HOUSE OF COMMONS

ON MUNICIPAL TRADING.

A STATEMENT

· UNANIMOUSLY APPROVED

BY

THE DISTRICT AUDITORS OF ENGLAND AND WALES

IS REGARD TO

THE RECOMMENDATIONS CONTAINED IN THE
ABOVE-NAMED REPORT.

THE District Auditors of England and Wales met in London on the 16th of January 1904, to consider the Report from the Joint Select Committee to the Houses of Parliament on the subject of County and Urban Accounts and their Audit.

The following statement of their views on the opinions and recommendations contained in that Report has been prepared by a Committee appointed for that purpose, and has been unanimously accepted and approved at a further meeting held in London on the 8th of April 1904.

The Report consists of twenty-nine clauses, the first five of which concern the reference and the arrangements made for dealing with it.

In the sixth the Committee select Municipal Accounts and their Audit as the branch of the reference with which their Report shall deal. It will be observed, however, that the recommendations made apply to all " the major local authorities, " viz., the councils of counties, cities, towns, burghs, and of " urban districts."

Clauses 7 and 8 express opinions in regard to the special importance of a high and uniform standard of account keeping in the public accounts throughout the country, and of the system for giving to the ratepayers full and continuous information as to the success or failure of all trading undertakings carried out by rating authorities.

The District Auditors entirely concur in the opinions expressed.

A

columnar form is the best for this register, ie an income account of the rate-book pattern which will bring out a clear list of the arrears.

(v) That it is desirable that the debtors' balances should be fully recorded on the balance sheet of every local authority, and that this should particularly apply to odd items of uncollected income, as it is the only real safeguard against any of them being overlooked."

Evidently the afternoon's discussions met a real need and the new departure was given pride of place at later meetings, the members deciding, before the meeting broke up, that 'the discussions on practical points of audit work should in future be held in the morning before the other questions on the Agenda are discussed'.

The need for auditors to be concerned in encouraging economy and efficiency in the way local government bodies carried out their functions was addressed as long ago as 1906 when at the April meeting, the Society was honoured for the first time by the attendance of a Minister of the Crown, the President of the Local Government Board (Mr Burns), and the Permanent Secretary of the Board (Sir Samuel Provis).

During his address to the meeting, the President of the Local Government Board 'alluded to the difficulties and also to the great importance of the Auditor's work, and to the call for the exercise of tact and discretion which it involved. He dwelt at some length on the importance of using, not only the powers of disallowance, but also the great influence which the Auditors possess in restraining waste and extravagance, and always on the side of purity in Local Administration'.

The minutes record that the whole time for debate, both in the morning and afternoon, was taken up with discussion of the opinions and resolutions to be submitted to the Departmental Committee on Local Authority Accounts. The meeting adopted resolutions which called for the accounts of local authorities to be kept on the income and expenditure basis, with separate cash accounts for each collecting or disbursing officer and for ledger accounts on the double entry system.

The establishment of sound principles for local government accounting continued to concern the Society. In 1907, at the invitation of the Inspector of Audits, a committee of members was formed to put forward suggestions for a proposed Order of Accounts for Rural District Councils. Oddly enough, apart from the Accounts (Payment into Bank) Order – necessary for the universal application of the bank slip test – and the Rate Accounts Order, no Accounting Orders were ever made for rural or urban district councils, only for borough councils which were largely not subject to district audit. Proof enough that the members of the Society had become effective mentors of sound accounting practices.

At the same meeting, wide-ranging discussions took place on 'The Placing of Contracts' and the precepts enunciated then are as pertinent as ever.

"Discussion on 'The Placing of Contracts';

The Members present were unanimously of opinion:

(i) That the District Auditor has a duty to perform in dealing with cases of personal interest, undue favour or corruption in the placing of contracts, and that such steps as are possible should be taken at audit to detect improper procedure in the matter.

3/3 1910: The District
Auditor – His
champions and critics.

(ii) That he should not confine his attention to cases brought before him by persons interested in the accounts.

(iii) That he should call for the rejected tenders and for the tabular statements (if any) in regard to the tenders received, and compare them with the accepted tenders.

(iv) That he should to some extent apply the process of comparing the prices paid for like commodities by different authorities.

(v) That he should make what use he can of statistical records, whether prepared by himself or by the statistical department, and that this process is more particularly useful in comparing the average daily or weekly expenditure upon provisions, etc., in workhouses and other institutions of similar size and character.

A number of special matters which call for attention in this work were referred to and discussed, including:

(i) The admission of opportunity for rigging tenders by failure to secure that equal information in regard to quantities, conditions, etc., is supplied to all tenderers and by leaving it possible for some to obtain information not granted to all.

(ii) Or by failure to institute a proper comparison between the several tenders with due regard to the importance of each item on the schedule.

(iii) The inclusion in tender forms of practically dummy items.

(iv) The advantage of a reasonable application of the principle of dividing contracts with a view to obtaining the lowest prices for the several items or groups of items, and the usefulness of arranging tender schedules in sections for this purpose.

(v) The comparative advantages of the system of depositing standard samples, and of calling for samples from the tradesmen.

(vi) The advantages and disadvantages of the system of including standard prices on the schedules and calling for tenders based on percentage variation of the listed prices.

(vii) The methods of guarding against alteration after deposit.

(viii) The dangers of extending contract periods without further submission to open competition.

(ix) The objection to the nomination of special manufacturers, especially when, in the case of provisional items in building and similar contracts, no previous competition has been invited."

Until his retirement in 1928, Carson Roberts exercised a great influence on the Society. He was elected Chairman on four occasions (1896, 1905, 1906 and for his valedictory meeting in 1928), and chaired many of the committees set up by the Society to formulate advice on various matters for the Local Government Board. From the time of his election, the minutes show that he contributed greatly to the Society's discussions and there are some passing references in the minutes to his singular contributions both to the development of audit law and practice and to local government accountancy.

In April 1913, the Society's minutes record a request by members that the Society publish a new edition of his book on 'The District Auditor's Procedure in matters involving a recourse to the aid of HM Justices of the Peace' as the original edition was out of print. 'Mr Carson Roberts indicated that he would be willing to revise the text and it was agreed to approach the Local Government Board to ascertain whether they would be willing to meet the cost of publication and so relieve the Society.'

In the minutes of the May 1919 meeting the publication of his book, *Accounts of Local Authorities* is briefly noted. This was a first in its field and the forerunner of his classic work, *Local Administration – Finance and Accounts*, written some ten years later. In May 1925 the Society also formally congratulated him on his Poplar surcharge and on his courage in taking the case to the House of Lords.

Attendances at Society meetings had continued to increase. In 1897 eligibility for election as members of the Society had been extended to assistant district auditors and by 1908 it had become very difficult for all the members present to hear what was said in the room at the Westminster Palace Hotel which the Society had used as its meeting place for the previous 20 years. Prior to that, the Society had mostly favoured Morley's Hotel in Charing Cross. Carson Roberts rather grandly proposed that the Society move to the Savoy Hotel.

3/5 Crowds pack the streets of London at the announcement of World War 1.

The members agreed, but it would seem that they found it a bit hard on their pockets for in 1911 the Secretary reported that he had enquired about a simpler luncheon at a lower price, and that the manager of the Savoy had agreed to supply luncheon at three shillings per head, coffee to be an extra, but that he would have to increase the charge for the room from five guineas to eight guineas.

The Society continued to meet at the Savoy Hotel until 1938 except for a break in October 1912 and May 1913 and for the first meeting after the end of World War I, in May 1919, which was held in the Central Hall, Westminster. In 1912, the Society had succumbed to the blandishments of the then President of the Local Government Board, Mr Burns, who when attending a meeting of the Society offered them the free use of the Audience Chamber at the Board's Offices for future meetings. The invitation was accepted and it was resolved that members make their own arrangements for lunch.

Two meetings at the Local Government Board's premises were more than enough for the members. Maybe they missed the Savoy lunches, but certainly the minutes record that the accoustics in the Audience Chamber were so appalling that members could not hear speakers and follow discussions properly. Perhaps the members, jealous of their independence, felt too much under the thumb of the Board in the Board's office. Anyway it was back to the Savoy for the October meeting in 1913. This was the last biannual meeting. Thereafter, with breaks for the two world wars, meetings of the Society were held annually, but instead of being one day occasions, were extended from the 1927 meeting into two-day conferences.

The Agenda Committee with Carson Roberts as its chairman usually had a weighty list of matters for discussion at each meeting; but time was always reserved for individual members to air points of particular concern to them.

Among the many problems raised were the following two, one at the April 1911 meeting and the other in April 1913:

> "What do the District Auditors, as a body, consider to be reasonable average allowances for waste in meat in the accounts of a Master of a Workhouse? If a particular Master habitually charges waste largely in excess of that which the Auditor's experience leads him to regard as reasonable, without any exceptional circumstances being alleged, and there is no other evidence of either fraud or culpable negligence, has the Auditor any power to deal with the matter?"

> "A large shop in the main street in a County town is kept unoccupied. An amount equivalent to a yearly rent is paid by a Syndicate of 3 or 4 tradesmen to the Owner in order to keep the premises vacant and thus keep out competition. Should the Overseers treat the shop as void while purposely kept unoccupied? If not, can the Overseers successfully sue the Owner for the Rates due thereon?"

As is often the case, there were animated discussions of both these issues but no firm conclusions!

Auditors have always had to be alive to the possibility of undeclared transactions deliberately omitted from accounts presented for audit. Carson Roberts seems to have been particularly astute. Among a long list of matters which he reported to the April 1899 meeting of the Society appears the following:

"A group of decisions was submitted supporting disallowances and surcharges made in secret interest accounts. They appeared to establish the following points:

(i) That whether the interest be allowed by the Bank to the authority, to the Treasurer, or to the Chairman, or to any other person, those who are aware of its existence are responsible for its being brought into account to the credit of the authority.

(ii) That if the fund supplied by interest has been withheld from audit, it is liable to audit for any length of time and however many audits have been closed in the interval. (The total income of the funds submitted to audit in the cases reported exceeded £20,000.).

(iii) That it is not always sufficient to see an item of interest brought into account, as, in a number of cases, it was found that a portion had been brought into account and the remainder carried to the secret fund by an arrangement with the Bank."

Persuading authorities to make available reasonable accommodation and working conditions for his staff bedevils the external auditor and judging from the Society's minutes, has prevailed from the earliest days of audit. At the same meeting as that at which Carson Roberts held forth about secret funds, one evidently exasperated district auditor asked 'Has an Auditor a right to the use of the Guardian's Board Room as long as the audit continues?' The answer from Carson Roberts was uncomforting and terse: 'The Auditor does not appear to have a right to the use of the Board Room under any statute or order.'

In times of real trouble, the Society has always done its best to relieve the plight of a member or his family when disaster has struck, particularly in the line of duty. Today, the Society has a permanently established fund for this purpose, but in times past the minutes record many occasions on which members have done their best to mitigate the effects of a tragedy. One example will suffice. In 1900 the Society set up a Committee to raise by subscription a fund for the benefit of the widow and children of Mr C L Hockin who lost his life in an accident while travelling home from holding an audit. The total receipts were reported as £411.11s 0d, a considerable sum for those days.

In 1909 the Local Government Board suggested that district auditors should include in their statutory reports stock paragraphs setting out the more important totals of an authority's income and expenditure including comparisons with estimates and the previous year's figures and a summary of the authority's balance sheet. The Society debated this suggestion very fully but concluded 'that the Auditor can comply with the spirit of the Board's suggestion in a better manner by using his influence to so shape the accounts and their published abstracts that the results are brought out in the most useful, clear and uniform manner'.

The minutes continue to record rather more tartly the views of the members:

"That the more responsible audit under the Public Health Act should not be influenced by the practice of professional audit, especially as the function of the latter audit, and consequently its range of comment in report, is more restricted, and as some of the considerations which have led to the inclusion of these recapitulations in its reports are absent in the case of the more independent audit."

"That the inclusion of facts clearly brought out in the accounts would lay the Auditors open to the criticism of 'padding' their reports more particularly if the practice were only resorted to when other subject-matter failed."

At the same meeting, an early attempt to introduce an audit certificate incorporating the concept of 'true and fair view' was defeated:

> "It was proposed by Mr Simner, and seconded by Mr Farquhar that the following form of certificate should be adopted in all audits under the Public Health Act:
>
> 'I do hereby certify that I have audited the accounts of which the foregoing is the balance sheet, and that the entries therein appear to be correct, complete and lawful.'
>
> An amendment to this motion was proposed by Mr Wilkinson and seconded by Mr Boggis-Rolfe to omit the words after Public Health Act and substitute:
>
> 'I have examined the above balance sheet, and I hereby certify that (subject to the disallowances and surcharges noted above and (or) to the reservations contained in my report to the Council) such balance sheet is a full and fair balance sheet and properly drawn up so as to exhibit a true and correct view of the financial position of the Council at the 31st March 198?, as shown by their books and those of their officers.'"

After some further discussion, the original motion was put to the meeting and carried.

About this time, the use of comparative statistics for audit purposes came to the fore in the discussions of the Society. In 1910 Mr Boggis-Rolfe opened a debate on 'Audit by Comparative Tables' pointing out that 'the objects of this system were to ascertain by comparative tables whether there had been fraud or mismanagement, and, with the least possible amount of labour, where an auditor might most profitably look for any such irregularity'.

A few meetings later, the President of the Local Government Board in an address to the Society added his contribution to the argument by suggesting that:

> "Auditors should direct their attention to the value of a comparative examination of expenditure of a similar nature as between Local Authorities and in respect of different years. An examination of this kind should not be confined to the large items, as experience showed that peculation occurred less on the large amounts than on the small".

The advent of the First World War forced the issue of test auditing. At the Society's last meeting for the duration of the war in April 1915 the suggestion was made, because of the depletion of audit staffs on war service, that it was absolutely necessary to curtail audit work and that 'most of the reduction of work should be on the expenditure and legality side, and that full attention should still be given to checking the income of the authority and to guarding against fraud'.

The member propounding this point of view said that 'he could not accept the doctrine that the examination of payments must be exhaustive', and suggested that 'some classes of charges or payments need only be tested'. After much heart-searching, this point of view was accepted by the Society.

The immediate post-war years of 1919–20 saw the demise of the Local Government Board and its replacement by the Ministry of Health, and a reorganisation of the district audit service with new young recruits being brought in as assistant district auditors from the Civil Service Inspector of Taxes examinations. The old system of patronage appointments was ended. Among those who were elected members of the Society in 1920 was C R H Hobbs, better known in later life as Hurle-Hobbs and author of *The Law Relating to District Audit*, the standard work on the subject for more than 30 years.

3/4 District Audit Staff/Students Society at the Victoria restaurant in March 1938.

The new Minister of Health attended the meeting of the Society in 1920, and, in a speech congratulating the District Auditors on having successfully overtaken the arrears of work resulting from the war, said 'I attach the greatest importance to the fuller development of the expert services of auditors. While personally I shrink from anything to do with accounts, my conviction is that neither in business nor in Government Departments is sufficient use made of scientific auditing'.

3/6 'Your King and Country'; A World War 1 post box displays a poster with a call to arms.

G. R.

YOUR KING & COUNTRY
NEED YOU
A CALL TO ARMS

An addition of 100,000 men to His Majesty's Regular Army is immediately necessary in the present grave National Emergency.
LORD KITCHENER is confident that this appeal will be at once responded to by all those who have the safety of our Empire at heart.

TERMS OF SERVICE
General Service for the period of the war only.
Age on Enlistment, between 19 and 30.
Height, 5 ft. 3 in. and upwards. Chest, 34 in. at least.
Medically fit.
Married Men or Widowers with Children will be accepted, and will draw Separation Allowance under Army conditions.

MEN ENLISTING FOR THE DURATION OF THE WAR
will be discharged with all convenient speed, if they so desire, the moment the war is over.

HOW TO JOIN
Men wishing to join should apply at any Military Barrack or at any Recruiting Office: the addresses of the latter can be obtained from Post Offices or Labour Exchanges.
GOD SAVE THE KING

At this, and subsequent meetings, much time was spent discussing the question of the general organisation of audit work and the need for auditors to 'frame schemes of audit work so as to critically examine all possible fields for fraud'. Small committees were established to consider the questions of audit files and forms and to arrange for the preparation of schedules of audit processes.

In these activities, the Society was helping its members to respond to the new initiatives of the times. As one of its last acts, the Local Government Board had issued in 1919 fresh 'Instructions relating to the Duties of District Auditors' which has still quite a modern ring to it. In the introduction the objectives of the external auditor are set out:

> "The intention is that the audit should encourage sound methods in all financial transactions, should check illegality and extravagance, and should secure the proper realisation and application of all income, and above all, that it should as far as possible, prevent fraud or waste of public funds."

The 'Instructions' stress the importance of the auditor examining financial systems to ensure that:

> "No necessary check or safeguard is omitted and that there is no needless complication or waste of work. In particular, he should inquire into the distribution of the duties and responsibilities of officials and the separation of the account-keeping from the work of receiving and paying money".

Among other matters, the 'Instructions' discussed the questions of reviewing the work of and the extent of reliance on internal audit and emphasised the value of comparing 'expenditure under various heads with that of other authorities by reference to a unit of cost or otherwise'.

3/7 The opening of extraordinary audit of Bermondsey's accounts in November 1932.

The years immediately following the first world war saw the development of the practice for members of the Society, at the invitation of the Agenda Committee, to deliver learned and detailed papers to the annual meeting, which as already noted became two-day conferences from the year 1927.

Early on, Hurle-Hobbs delivered a paper on *The Liability of Members of Local Authorities and Architects in respect of Overpayments on Works Contracts* which gave evidence of his command of legal matters. C W O Gibson, later to become a Chief Inspector of Audit, gave a long paper on the 'Detection of Fraud' which included the following passage on 'Dummy Cheques' which may be of interest.

"'Dummy' Cheques

In the world of fraud today 'dummies' take a most prominent place. We have 'dummy' records of all kinds, but from the auditors' point of view perhaps the most disquieting and most difficult to detect is the 'dummy' cheque. In this connection it is of the utmost importance to appreciate the difference between a forged and a 'dummy' cheque. While it is unnecessary to define what a forged cheque is, it should be explained that the term 'dummy' as used here is meant to denote a cheque that while bearing every indication of being genuine has never in fact been presented for payment through a bank, but has been fabricated solely with a view to deceiving the auditor. Personally, I have had only one experience of this particular kind of fraud, on an occasion when some 50 cheques that had never passed through a bank, were produced to me by

3/8 No 1 Audit District Dinner, Newcastle, 1937.

an Assistant Overseer wherewith to vouch a forged cash account and pass book. They had been prepared with meticulous care, and in addition to forged signatures and endorsements, their apparent authenticity was accentuated by the use of a facsimile of the bank's stamp that the Assistant Overseer had himself had made.

Suspicion having been aroused a closer inspection showed that:

(i) certain cheques bore dates prior to that of the embossed Inland Revenue stamp.

(ii) cheques that, had they been genuine, would in the ordinary course of business, have passed through the post, bore no sign of having been folded.

(iii) the endorsement on one cheque had blotted on to the face of the succeeding one, leaving a faint impression thereon, easily decipherable with the aid of a mirror, showing that it must have been written before the cheques were detached from the counterfoils, and presumably by the person drawing the cheques."

At the first two-day conference held in 1927 the main topic of discussion was the Rating and Valuation Act 1925, which, in consolidating into one general rate the poor rate and all the diverse local rates and in making the boroughs and district councils the sole rating authorities, was the foundation of the modern rating system.

COUNTY HALL AND ITS CATACOMBS.

THOUSANDS OF BOROUGH RECORDS.

One of the greatest transfers of administrative power in recent years has been that of London's poor-law responsibilities under the Local Government Act of 1929. It has transferred to the L.C.C. the powers and faculties of nearly thirty boroughs, and for the past three or four years this has entailed the reception and assimilation of mountains of multifarious records, some of them going back two or three centuries.

When the County Hall was built, of course, there was no conception of its ever being invaded by so vast a consignment of records. But by means of a scheme of broadly vaulted corridors, herring-boned with roomy and connected muniment rooms, ample provision has been made for the Council's own archives and more.

There is probably no public building in existence where all kinds of referenda, however remote, are so easily and readily at command, and the far-sighted scale on which the building was designed has proved its salvation in the present instance. For a great part of the central building, two storeys below ground, has been given up to storing these acquisitions from all parts of the London area, and to make a tour of them is like threading the catacombs of history.

The first consignment, consisting of the records of the Metropolitan Asylums Board, arrived in fifteen giant pantechnicons. Every trolley-load wheeled in had to be dusted, sorted, and entered on the register; and one official has himself handled every volume, paper, or roll in this great array.

THE CHAPLIN BROTHERS.

The next consignment amounted to 7,000 volumes of minutes of the various ministering authorities of the past, many of them with quaint, old-fashioned, and half-supercilious names, like Trustees of the Poor of Shoreditch (these records date back to May, 1774), or Directors of the Poor of Marylebone (1775). All these had to be made fit to join their cleaner and smarter neighbours, and then indexed and card-catalogued.

There are over twenty poor-law schools, each with many hundreds of youngsters, and some of these grown to fame. Here, for instance, in a broad album-shaped volume, printed with many categoric headlines all across the page, is the name of the interesting Camberwell stripling known to an admiring world as "Charlie" Chaplin. He is entered as a pupil of the "Cuckoo School" at Hanwell—so called from the name of a previous farm on the site—as arriving on June 18, 1896. On the next line stands the name of his brother, Sydney, who was one of the many lads sent to the training ship Exmouth.

3/9 County Hall and its catacombs; A newspaper clipping from The Observer, October 1934 comments on the transfer of borough records to County Hall.

The Rt Hon Neville Chamberlain, Minister of Health, attended the first day's meeting and addressed the Society. The minutes record that he said that he attached considerable value to the important contribution which he was confident would be readily forthcoming from the Auditors to the work of bringing the Act into smooth operation throughout the country. There was one particular direction in which in the course of the discharge of their official duties, the Auditors could, by reason of their being in constant personal contact with those concerned, render him great assistance. Many problems and difficulties would doubtless be encountered by the Local Authorities in winding-up the old and in constructing the new systems. Advice and guidance given to them on the spot by the Auditors would obviate formal references to the Department and afford the Minister substantial personal relief.

In May 1928, 87 members attended the conference to bid farewell to Carson Roberts on his retirement. The main theme of the conference was the Audit (Local Authorities) Act 1927 which removed from the Minister's jurisdiction appeals against decisions of district auditors where the amount involved exceeded £500.

Carson Roberts, who had been elected Chairman of the Society for this his last meeting as a serving member, introduced the subject and the minutes record that he said that:

> "This measure had effected the most important changes in the law relating to district audit that had occurred in his experience, extending over a period of forty-two years. The Auditor's judicial functions were now rendered immensely more important. In regard to disallowances made to obtain an authoritative decision the only change is that many more will be referred to the High Court either on appeal or on a case stated. It is only by the High Court that the Auditor's decision can be reviewed if more than £500 is concerned, and this is so even though it is only a correcting disallowance, e.g. a transfer or a correction of account or balance where no question of surcharge is involved.

> It is where objection is taken to expenditure on the ground that it is unreasonable, extravagant or improper, or where a question in regard to avoidable loss is raised, that the great change arises; and this side of audit duty is one of ever-growing importance.

> Experience has already shown that here the effect of the new law is that to which the Auditor takes objection stops forthwith, unless the L.A. is strongly advised that the Courts would hold the objection to be unfounded or unreasonable.

> Hence it is with a far greater sense of responsibility that Auditors should select the cases in which they take, support, or overrule objections. Though the L.A. may by a majority decide to accept the Auditor's decision, the minority may be counted upon to pillory in the press any decision which they regard as frivolous or ill-founded, or any case in which they think they can show that the decision of one Auditor is opposed to that of another".

By 1930 the increasing introduction of mechanical accounting began to affect the way in which audits were conducted, and Mr Bates, who later became Chief Inspector of Audit and died tragically while making an inspection of No. 1 Audit District (North East England), presented a treatise on "Mechanical Accounting Methods and their Effect on Audit".

He welcomed their introduction and the advantages they presented in their accuracy and the consequent reduction in the need for arithmetical tests by the auditor and the fact that they made fraud more difficult; but he could not resist a backward glance at hand-written accounts abounding in narrative descriptions and concluded his address by saying:

> "In the case of mechanical analysis it certainly is rather disturbing to be presented with a large volume, containing nothing but columns of figures together with a few thousand vouchers and to be told that all the expenditure details are recorded there and nowhere else.
>
> It is difficult to obtain a mental picture of these details of the accounts".

The practicability of current auditing which even today presents problems was actively considered by members in the early thirties, and part of a paper presented to the Society reads:

> "Attention is directed particularly to the recent criticism of District Audit that it was held too long after the close of the year whereas professional Accountants acting as Municipal Auditors did work consecutively during the year and this enabled the audit to be completed soon after the end of the year.
>
> The increase of the functions of large authorities now including rating and public assistance is resulting in a heavy load being cast upon the second half-year as they are seldom ready in the first half, and whereas, formerly the larger local authorities could be taken in order as they were ready, this is no longer the case. The position is worse in those districts where already several large County Boroughs and Boroughs are fully under audit.
>
> The question of continuous or early audits was discussed, and it was realised that the difficulties were (i) that the financial years of all local authorities ended on the same day, (ii) the question of staffing. No decision was arrived at".

At the same Conference, a paper pressing for the "institution and extension of internal audit" and urging that "the spirit of co-operation with internal audit must be continually fostered" voiced for the first time what has continued to be the attitude and policy of district audit towards internal audit. The speaker stressed that "internal audit is complementary to and not a duplication of district audit" and that "the internal audit system must be sound, and the District Auditor must assess its merits by close investigation".

In the mid 1930s members expressed their concern about signs of increasing corruption and the emergence of "pressure selling". An interesting account was given of an investigation at audit triggered off by a realisation that prime cost allowances in certain housing contracts appeared to be unduly high coupled with the deduction, from the misplacement of letters, that many of the vouchers, estimates etc produced to support final statements of account had all been produced on the same typewriter. The architect was successfully prosecuted for having received bribes from several contractors, and in the ensuing discussion reference was also made to other cases, e.g. that of an officer in a supplies department receiving commission in relation to a contract for petrol; and also a member of a mental hospital farm committee receiving 5 shillings per ton commission on the purchase of seed potatoes.

It was suggested that there seemed to be an increase of such cases, and that it was probably due to a new race of salesmen paid on commission who were ready to ignore the law as to the prevention of corruption and share their commission in order to obtain orders.

Accounting for capital assets – a topic which is still of lively interest today – was broached and discussed in some detail at the meeting in November 1936. The speaker stated that:

> "In many Authorities the real estate acquisitions in recent years had been numerous and valuable and the problems of proper treatment in account had assumed major proportions. The Report of the Departmental Committee on Local Authorities Accounts of 1907 recommended that all capital assets having abiding or realistic value should be shown in the Balance Sheet at their original cost, loans and capital provisions being shown per contra."

He complained that, apart from the provisions of the Housing Accounts Order under the Housing Act 1919, no form of capital accounts had been prescribed.

The independence of the district auditor has been one of the greatest and most cherished strengths of the Service. A handsome acknowledgement of this independence was given in a paper to the Society at its meeting in November 1934, on "Statutory and other Audit Reports – The Question of Privilege".

The paper recounted how a firm wrote to the Minister asking to be informed whether, following the publication of a report by a district auditor subsequent to an extraordinary audit, a civil action could lie for damages against certain persons including the district auditor. According to the paper there was an exchange of correspondence and the Minister's final letter read as follows:

> "This is a matter upon which it seems obvious that the Minister cannot advise. It is a question, or series of questions, upon which you must form your own judgement with the help of such legal advice as you may think it necessary to obtain.

> It may, however, be of assistance to you if I point out that your question seems to be based upon a misconception of the position with regard to these extraordinary audits. Apart from directing upon application made to him, that such an audit shall be held, the Minister has no part in the matter. The District Auditor, in conducting the audit and making his report, is performing a duty imposed upon him by Statute and exercising powers similarly conferred upon him: his powers are quite independent and in no way derived from the Minister. His report is made to the Local Authority not to the Minister; it is their property and any question of general publication is for them to decide.

> I am to add that in pointing out that he has no responsibility for the procedure adopted by the District Auditor in conducting his audit, the Minister must not be taken as agreeing with your suggestion that the District Auditor acted in any way improperly or even indiscreetly."

The speaker said that nothing further was heard from the firm.

The idea of the cyclical audit was first mooted by Mr Moyle in a paper which he gave to the annual Conference in October 1938 on *The Practice of Auditing by "Tests"*. He was concerned about the limited time available for checking, in particular, the accounts of the numerous accounting officers employed by the major local authorities, and wished to explore the manner in which the best possible use of the time could be made. The minutes record his remarks and the ensuing discussion as follows:

> "If we tested the transactions of some only of the officers concerned and each officer had an equal chance of being included in that test, we were probably fulfilling the principles of a test audit, and were at least testing the efficiency of the Authority's accounting methods, their method of control and their internal audit. He did not feel happy, however, unless the accounts of every officer had

come under some sort of scrutiny, but if we tried to do something of every officer's accounts that something might be very little indeed. An alternative was suggested in which by the adoption of some sort of a three-year plan we concentrated on a third of such officers' accounts in each year, submitting them to every known audit check. Under this system the remaining two-thirds could be left entirely unchecked or submitted to a superficial examination for the purposes of finding any obvious irregularities. As this superficial check would be, however, very slight indeed, it would need concentration, diligence and ability of a high order to make it effective.

In the discussion which followed it seemed to be the general view that all officers' accounts should come under some sort of scrutiny. The Chairman suggested that the superficial examination might come first and, on the result of that, it would be decided as to which officers' transactions should receive the concentrated check."

By 1938 the numbers of members attending the Society's annual conferences had grown considerably. In that year 84 members were present with only two apologies for absence. Whether the Department were jibbing at the cost of such large attendances or whatever the reason, the Society resolved at that meeting that eligibility for membership was to be restricted henceforth to senior assistant district auditors and above.

This was to be the Society's last conference until November 1946, a year after the end of the Second World War. In these middle years between the two World Wars, the members of the Society had successfully met the challenges of change from the half-yearly audits of numerous small poor law authorities and ad hoc boards to the annual audits of large, multi-purpose authorities, and from the era of handwritten accounts to the widespread introduction of punch-card accounting machines, and, beginning with the introduction of housing subsidies in 1919, to coping with the examination and certification of an ever-increasing volume of local authority claims for government grants.

The District Auditors' Society

III   From its centenary to the advent of the Audit Commission (1946–1982)

4/1 1940: "The Institution of the District Auditor is unique, and is another expression of the British genius for government." – Rt. Hon. Aneurin Bevan MP.

The activities of the Society restarted in some style after their suspension during the Second World War.

The centenary of the District Audit Service fell on 9 August 1944, the 100th anniversary of Royal Assent to the Poor Law Amendment Act 1844, but as the holding of conferences and congresses of all kinds was discouraged during the war due to the difficulties of travel and catering, the holding of any celebration was postponed.

In a way this was fortunate, for when the Society held its first post-war annual conference in November 1946 it was possible to use the occasion to mark two centenaries, that of the Service, and that of the Society which had held its inaugural meeting in 1846.

The celebrations took the form of a luncheon held during the conference on 14 November at the Connaught Rooms, Great Queen Street, London, when the principal guest was the Minister of Health, the Rt Hon Aneurin Bevan MP. Other guests included senior officers of the Ministry of Health and of the Treasury and leading representatives of all the associations of local authorities and of the professional

bodies for clerks and treasurers of local authorities.

In proposing the toast of 'the Minister of Health', the Society's Vice-Chairman for that year, Mr Hurle-Hobbs, wittily remarked:

"I cannot help feeling that it is just a little presumptuous to pledge health to the Minister whose particular function it is to dispense health. It is akin to proposing godliness to the Archbishop or to presenting the brewer with a draught of his own brew. And, Sir, I cannot plead that it is the Minister's political health that needs stimulating; because, so far as I know, his political health is in excellent condition. And why should it not be? Compared with the District Auditor, who has reached the venerable age of 102, the Minister of Health is comparatively young. He, Sir, is only 99 for he was not born until 1847, when the first President of the Poor Law Board was allowed to sit in Parliament.

I am sure the Minister will forgive my referring to the superior antiquity of the District Auditor. Indeed, were it challenged I should not hesitate to suggest that the District Auditor was conceived in 1601, and although the time that elapsed between that year and his ultimate birth in 1844 constitutes a somewhat lengthy period of gestation, I would if I were not a District Auditor, point to the very excellent finished article and say that any time taken in its production was absolutely warranted."

Replying, the Minister looked back to his own earlier experiences as a member of a Welsh local authority:

"I have not always been on the most friendly terms with the District Auditors. I started in local government when I was about 20 years of age, in a Welsh constituency and such is the imagination and creative genius of the Welsh that it does not tolerate easily the austere discipline of arithmetic. It was not until I came to the Ministry of Health itself and met Mr George, the Accountant General,

4/2 Rt. Hon. Aneurin Bevan MP on the occasion of the centenary dinner of the District Auditors' Society in London, 1946.

that I learnt that a knowledge of mathematics was not a bad thing. That is the only explanation I can find for the fact that I cannot understand the same formula for two Sessions together.

It is true, I think everybody will agree, that the institution of the District Auditor is unique and is another expression of the British genius for government. We succeeded in putting the Local Authorities under the control of the Ministry of Health and at the same time we put their financial affairs under the Ministry of Health and the Judiciary. It is a very remarkable compromise and has succeeded admirably. Indeed there is no doubt at all that the Auditor is one of the most important institutions of a civilised society. He introduces quantitative measurement into the qualitative enthusiasm of partisan politicians."

The toast of 'the District Auditors' Society' was proposed by the Permanent Secretary of the Treasury, Sir Edward Bridges, who remarked:

"It would not be right to let the occasion pass without some word about the work of the District Auditor. One hundred years ago, when you started, you audited the accounts of the Poor Law Authorities, and the total expenditure of the Local Authorities then was £12,000,000 of which the Poor Law expenditure was £6,000,000. Today, I am told that you audit the accounts of 14,000 Authorities and that the total expenditure of the Local Authorities is £500,000,000. But even those figures, of course, can give no true picture of the immense increase in the variety and complexity and importance of the job that you have to do. And that is not to be wondered at when one realises that those 100 years of your existence cover the whole development of Local Authority Government as we know it today."

The Chairman of the Society, Mr E M Tuke, replied to the toast and in doing so recorded the contribution which the Roberts family had made to district audit:

"No celebration would be complete without reference to a family who served with great distinction on the District Audit staff for well over 80 years. I mean, of course, the Roberts family. Thomas Kyffin Roberts was appointed in 1844. Of his two sons, Lloyd and Howell, the former became Inspector of Audits, whilst the latter, himself a District Auditor, was the father of two sons, Arthur Carson and Hugh Douglas. This may sound like nepotism but I can assure you it was nepotism at its very best. Carson Roberts was in every way our GOM and it is a matter of the greatest regret to all of us that his death two years ago has robbed us of his presence here today. Our Minister will, no doubt, be gratified that Wales has played such an important part, but I must add for the benefit of our Permanent Secretary that Scotland too has a share, for the mother of Arthur Carson and Hugh Douglas was a Scotswoman."

The centenary luncheon was an undoubted success and there sprang from it the practice thereafter of inviting to luncheon, on the first day of each annual conference, representatives of the Ministry of Health (or its successors) and, in rotation, representatives of other government departments which were involved with local government affairs. On the second day of each conference, the Society usually entertained representatives of one or more of the local government associations and professional bodies.

In the immediate post-war years, members were addressed on such newly topical matters as war damage repairs, civic restaurants, Rushcliffe salary scales, school milk and meals and the explosion in council house building. In regard to the latter, the Society's attention was drawn to the problems being encountered by a rural district council with a penny rate product of £320 which had spent £500,000 on building 300 Council houses in four years! In those days, local authorities were subject to income tax and papers were delivered on the intricacies of internal and external set off and the hidden reserves accumulated in income tax accounts.

Hurle-Hobbs in a learned dissertation to the Society in 1953 on *What is 'Policy'?* at times tackled this vexing question in a very down to earth and explicit manner. Commenting on a speech of Lord Summer, when *Roberts v Hopwood and Others* was before the House of Lords in 1925, in which Lord Summer said that he understood questions of policy to mean such matters as the necessity for a urinal and the choice of its position, Hurle-Hobbs loftily remarked that such an example was not particularly apposite:

> "If, for instance, a local authority decided to build five public conveniences in one short street, in flagrant disregard of the real needs of other parts of their area, must the expenditure on four of such urinals be accepted on ground of policy and allowed as a reasonable and proper charge to the Rate Fund?"

Hurle-Hobbs then went on to make a sweeping proposition which might give food for thought today:

> "The learned law lord is more helpful when he distinguishes policy from politics, and makes it clear that local authorities when administering funds which they derive from the levying of rates must not be guided by the

4/3 Coventry after a Nazi raid, November, 1940.

4/4 1950: The advent of improvement grants.

1950 s

THE ADVENT OF IMPROVEMENT GRANTS

4/5 1960: The auditor and the computer.

were given on discovered frauds and the lessons to be learned, but one given by Mr Northey in 1954 on three expenditure frauds in his district is perhaps noteworthy.

The three expenditure frauds which he recounted were all large in amount and were all perpetrated by trusted officers who worked with very little supervision. The first concerned a deputy borough treasurer of a county borough council, where part of the accounts were audited by district audit and part by professional audit, who lined his pockets by cashing some of the cheques used to make transfers from the rate accounts (subject to district audit) to the borough fund (subject to professional audit). The second was a rural studies organiser for a county's education committee who, through an innocent middleman, sold their own goods back to the county council; and the third fraud was carried on for four and a half years by a fire brigade clerk who invented his own firm and submitted invoices to the brigade for non-existent goods.

personal opinions of their members on political, economic or social questions; but by this injunction he limits, almost to extinction, the field in which policy can be exercised by local authorities."

He concluded by slyly remarking:

"I always try to avoid suggesting to an authority that they should discontinue any particular course of action and confine myself to inviting them to consider whether or not they are justified in continuing it".

The members of the Society have always regarded the detection of fraud as being an important part of their duty and recognised that the public often regards it as the main reason for the auditor's existence. Many papers

4/6 An early attempt at electronic calculating at Manchester University c. 1949.

In his consideration of the lessons to be drawn from the circumstances of these frauds, the speaker advocated the value of a 'deep audit' of a selection of a small number of expenditure vouchers. For the application of numerous tests to a relatively small portion of the accounts did tend to produce results, particularly, he argued, in revealing defects in system and division of duties.

The following year, 1955, Dickie Edwards returned to a topic which had exercised the Society on a number of occasions and which is a matter of lively debate in local government circles today. His paper on the verification of real estate assets belonging to local authorities aroused the concern of members to the extent that a sub-committee was formed to research the problem.

The sub-committee's report was presented to and adopted by the Society in 1957. Drawing on the collective experience of members, the report's conclusions and recommendations were quite pragmatic. The report concluded that, as the risk of large-scale fraud in real estate was small and losses were few and confined to small, unused plots of land, there was insufficient evidence of abuse to support an approach to the Department for legislation, and recommended that, whilst all local authorities should be encouraged to keep terriers and maps and make periodic inspection of their unused land, balance sheet control of real estate would raise difficulties out of all proportion to the additional security to be obtained thereby.

The wide-ranging discussions which surrounded the paper and committee report on local authority real estates prompted Mr Barraclough in the following year to address the Society on the difference between the duties of a district auditor and of an auditor under the

4/7 The code of practice: "An auditor ought to undertake tests for the specific purpose of discovering fraud."

Companies Act. The speaker made some basic propositions which perhaps ought not to be lost sight of even today:

"The functions of a company are quite different from those of a local authority. They are not even opposite; they are different in kind. A company exists simply and solely to make profits; a local authority exists to provide services. From this difference everything else flows. On it is founded the reason for the different codes of audit. The first duty of the commercial auditor is to see whether the shareholder's capital is still there and to ascertain whether or not it has earned any profit. The first duty of a district auditor is to satisfy himself that all the money taken from the ratepayer has been properly spent, or is still available. The commercial auditor is concerned primarily to ensure that the statement of the company's financial position is correct or, in other words, that the balance sheet statement of assets and liabilities is correct. The district auditor is primarily concerned to see that the council's expenditure is within the law and is charged against the right fund or body of ratepayers or, in other words, that the revenue or fund accounts are correct. The district auditor is thus more concerned with the revenue account and less with the balance sheet than is the commercial auditor.

A local authority's balance sheet is a statement of public accountability rather than of net worth or solvency. It shows how much of the ratepayers' money is still left – or how much has still to be demanded of him, and how much long-term debt has been contracted in his name rather than his commercial assets and liabilities. Moreover, the fundamental asset of every local authority – its rateable value – can never appear on any balance sheet."

The late fifties and early sixties saw the Society turning its attention to the new developments being introduced in the local government world – electronic computers, organisation and method, work study, and investment in equities. In 1957, S V Collins gave a paper on computers and audit which was very modern in outlook and presaged district audit's pre-eminence in this field; whilst in 1958 John Speirs reported on an O and M study by district audit into the department of a city treasurer – the first carried out by the Service. In 1962, W Slingsby gave early warnings of the defects in hurriedly cobbled work study bonus schemes which were to plague authorities for decades.

During this same period, a significant change was inaugurated when in 1963 the Society invited the Director and other senior officers of the Metropolitan Boroughs and O and M Committee to address that year's annual conference. From then on, it became the practice to invite each year leading figures from the worlds of local and national government and commerce and from the universities to address the Society on their specialities. The subjects and speakers chosen lay generally outside the immediate spheres of auditing and accountancy. Among those who thus widened the areas of the Society's discussions were clerks and chief executives, engineers, supplies officers, planners, academics, advisers to government departments, industrial auditors and the odd speaker from abroad.

At the 1963 Conference, John Speirs continued the questioning begun at earlier conferences by Northey and others on the objectives, standards and methods of district audit. He recognised that the standards and methods of district audit had changed over the years, but feared that district auditors would go on attempting to give too high a protection against the risk of fraud and leave themselves far too little time for more useful work designed to strengthen systems and detect major sources of waste or extravagance. He suggested that there was, for example, great scope for the use of unit and other comparative costs and in the application generally of lessons in economy learnt at individual authorities.

These themes were to be developed and expanded at succeeding annual conferences, leading to the formulation of the ideas of the structured form of audit, statistical sampling, performance reviews, audits of management systems, value for money projects, computer auditing and financial profiles.

In the epoch from the mid-sixties to the advent of the Audit Commission, the Society's annual conferences provided a platform for the discussion and launching of a whole range of new ideas and initiatives which, taken as a whole, made for a leap forward in the concept of the

role of the external auditor. These ideas and concepts were not matched in the thinking and practice of the external auditor in commerce and industry, nor did they find a universal welcome from every section of local government.

Original research and thinking provided much of the foundation for these moves to extend and deepen the usefulness and effectiveness of audit. In 1965, Reg Elliston gave a long and detailed dissertation on the audit of incentive bonus schemes based on his own painstaking researches into the theory and practice of method study and work measurement and the way bonus schemes were in actuality being constructed and operated. His work was eventually published by the IMTA (now CIPFA) and provided the only standard text on the subject.

At the same meeting experiments in the audit of management (value for money) were reported; the need was argued for the auditor to concern himself with establishing the efficiency of direct labour organisations; and attention was directed to the audit aspects of and the internal controls needed for large, integrated computer schemes.

The theme of computers was continued at the 1966 conference when G F Morris gave a weighty and comprehensive paper raising the vital question of the level of knowledge of computing necessary for auditors to carry out an effective audit.

The year 1966 saw the establishment by the Agenda Committee of the Society of the first of many panels of members to research, consider and report on specific topics. Three panels were initially formed to report on

4/8 The Electronic Brain: Originally designed to solve ballistics problems during the 2nd World War, it now found itself being used for more peaceful problem solving.

respectively:

Post-qualification training
Works departments
Audit practice and procedures.

In the following year further panels were formed to study particular management techniques and their usefulness to audit:

Organisation and method
Network analysis
Cost-benefit analysis
Operational research
Work study
Statistical methods.

In 1969 further panels were established to consider:

Highways
Management accounting
Planned program budget systems.

All of these panels produced reports which were circulated to members and discussed at conferences. Two are perhaps particularly noteworthy. In 1969 the Secretary of the Institute of Municipal Treasurers and Accountants requested the Society's permission to publish the Statistical Methods Panel Report. The report went on to win (jointly) the Sir Harry Page Merit Award for 1970. The other report was that of the panel on audit practices and procedures – the Audit Review Panel Report.

The Audit Review Report was presented to Conference in 1968 and had perhaps the greatest impact and influence of all. It was all-embracing and far-sighted, drawing on the work of the other panels. The report had two distinct themes:

(i) an appraisal of the requirements of local government for 'traditional' or 'regularity' auditing; and

(ii) consideration of the areas in which district audit could contribute towards improving the efficiency of local authorities – 'management auditing'.

The report recognised that illegality and fraud were of diminishing importance and that considerable savings were to be achieved in management auditing 'directed to examining the efficiency of management control and basically involving the auditor in finding out whether maximum value is obtained for money spent'. To enable the auditor to direct his efforts and resources more to 'management auditing' yet without abdicating his other duties and responsibilities, the report examined and endorsed the ideas being discussed and experimented with by members of:

the structured form of audit;
auditing of current records;
system audits and the use of flow charts;
the development of a new relationship of partnership with internal audit.

Ahead of the presentation of the Audit Review Panel Report, Peter Kimmance delivered a paper at the 1967 Conference on *The Audit of Management* in which he postulated that 'the auditor has a function to examine the financial validity of management decisions', and recognised the problem of dealing with findings at a local level and the need for a means of voicing much of the criticism, which audit had and would have to make, at a national level in order to overcome purely parochial responses.

At the same conference Bert Harrison rehearsed means which had been adopted to improve value for money in local authority purchasing and these examples of best practice were emphasised in an address by a county supplies officer.

Along with the presentation of the Audit Review Panel's Report at the 1968 Conference, Reg Harris demonstrated how, in one district, current auditing had been introduced, bringing with it not only its own inherent advantages but also the added and much desired bonus of the early completion of the audits of the final accounts of all authorities in the district. It is interesting to note that the changes advocated then are now standard practice under the Audit Commission.

4/9 The code of practice: "An auditor must satisfy himself as to the legality of items of account."

Cliff Nicholson also gave a perceptive and far-sighted address looking forward to local government reorganisation and, with it, the emergence of large authorities with effective internal audit organisations with whom it would be possible to forge a partnership in the total audit effort.

The concern of members of the Society to come fully to terms with computers and to make the maximum use of them for audit purposes is reflected in the number of individual papers which were given to the Society on computer-related matters in this period, and, perhaps more particularly, by the 1970 Conference which was wholly given over to these matters, papers being given on computers in management, fraud and the computer, interrogating the computer, and teleprocessing (terminals and on-line computing).

The advent of the Local Government Act 1972 and the impending reorganisation of local government took up much of the time at the 1972 Conference when papers were given dealing with the auditor's responsibilities in relation to the old authorities, the problem of ensuring that all assets and important financial records found their proper home, and the steps which both the old and the new authorities should take in order to effect an orderly transfer of business. Reg Jones returned to the subject of the 1972 Act at the 1974 Conference when he led the discussions on the audit provisions of the Act and the new Audit Code of Practice. This latter theme was taken up again the following year when a panel of speakers opened discussions on a number of points of concern. It emerged that the structured form would serve well the requirements of the new Code. 'Losses by

4/10 The code of practice: "An auditor has a duty to verify that different sections of the public have been fairly treated".

fraud are still relatively very small. Public concern, and hence the need for audit assurances, lies more on the "value for money" side.' The new right given under the Act to local government electors to question the auditor caused some concern to members.

The swiftly changing circumstances of the times prompted Jack Teesdale in 1977 to give a challenging address to the Society questioning its future continuance – 'unless we find a more positive role for the Society the danger is that it will become little more than an ageing luncheon club'. The minutes record that 'the predominant feature of the [ensuing] discussion was the undoubted enthusiasm for the continuance of the Society in an active role which would ensure the position of the Service in the forefront of local government auditing'.

There is no doubt that the Society met this challenge. In the following years the Society continued not only to discuss newly developing techniques and methods in finance, management and computing, but also took active steps to promote changes in audit objectives and practices. In 1978 the Society set up three new panels to research respectively,

The functions, objectives and form of local government external audit

Use and limitations of published statistics

Development of management systems questionnaires.

The Statistics Panel continued the development, compilation and circulation of statistics for audit use; questionnaires were produced for use in the audit of management systems; and in 1980 the Society set up jointly with CIPFA a working party under the chairmanship of Laurence Tovell to produce a set of standards for the external audit of local authorities. The standards were published in 1982 and had an influence on the Audit Commission's Code of Local Government Audit Practice.

During these years devoted to the rethinking of the role of the external auditor, the Society did not neglect its unique function of providing a forum for its members of all ranks to discuss together and explore in open debate the everyday problems peculiar to their work. Matters debated included, for example, the practical problems of investigating fraud and corruption; dealing with objectors, the conduct of hearings and multiple challenges to the accounts; judicial considerations of 'items of account contrary to law'; the effect of criminal convictions on audit proceedings; audit records and filing systems; the application of SSAPs to local authority accounts; and problems in complying with the 1972 Audit Code.

In 1981 the Government published its proposals for establishing an audit commission to be responsible for the external audit of the accounts of local authorities in England and Wales. The Society responded to the general invitation to submit comments on these proposals. Whilst welcoming much that was in the proposals, the Society felt constrained quietly to voice the current standing and achievement of the District Audit Service:

> "District auditors are the recognised specialists in local government auditing. As a result of research which we have carried out over the years we have adapted audit objectives and methods to meet the needs of the times. To this end a structured form of audit was developed during the 1960s

which resulted in greater attention being paid to value for money matters without detracting from the auditor's financial and regularity audit responsibilities. The Local Government Audit Code of Practice issued by the Secretary of State in 1973 as a standard for all local authority audits was based entirely on the objectives and methods of the District Audit Service at that time. We have continually refined our objectives and methods since then and these are very largely reflected in the Draft Standards for the Audit of Local Authorities and Other Public Bodies recently published by CIPFA."

4/11 The code of practice: "An auditor has a duty to report on matters which should be brought to the notice of the council and the public."

The hopes and anxieties of the Society regarding the future conduct and development of the audit of local authorities are worth recording. They are sufficiently set out in the final paragraph of the submission:

> "The Society is concerned to ensure that under the proposed Commission the existing high standard of specialised service for local authority audit shall continue and indeed be improved. In our view it is essential that:
>
> a. The cohesive audit effort which the District Audit Service now provides is maintained;
>
> b. The full and free exchange of information and ideas between auditors continues under the overall guidance of a professional head of service (a role at present performed by the Chief Inspector of Audit);
>
> c. The present independence of auditors in all professional matters is preserved;
>
> d. Resources commensurate with the needs of the work including the expanded value for money role are made available."

It is pleasing to record that the Audit Commission has made these concerns its own, and has made it possible for the Society to continue and expand its activities. The future of the Society is, as ever, in the hands of its members. There is no sign of any diminution of enthusiasm on their part, and one may look with confidence to a future in which the Society will flourish and make an increasing contribution to the effectiveness of the District Audit Service and the work of the Commission.

4/12 1970: Local
governemnt re-
organisation. The
Common Market – The
"Moulin Rouge"?

R U DAVIES

Largely responsible for compiling the first edition of *The Local Government Auditor*. Author of *Parish Council and Town Council Accounts*. Retired as District Auditor for 9AD in 1984, and now has time to enjoy his books, the theatre and his garden.

Officers of the District Auditors' Society

Meetings of the Society were held at least twice yearly until the outbreak of the First World War; thereafter, they were held annually.

Chairmen
(1846–1968)

T S Simkiss 1846 to 1851, 1853 to 1863, 1865 to 1868

F W Ellis 1852, 1855

W J Patterson 1856, 1862

G Barnes 1857, 1858, 1866, 1869, 1871, 1873, 1875

J Hunt 1857

W C Hotson 1858

T Hoskins 1859

W Rees 1860, 1864, 1866

J Segram 1868, 1869

G S White 1870, 1872, 1878, 1879, 1881 to 1883, 1891, 1894, 1895

F Merrifield 1874 to 1876, 1878, 1879, 1881

W Knott 1877

H Lloyd Roberts 1877, 1880, 1885 to 1892

E B Prest 1880

F D Boggis-Rolfe 1882, 1883, 1893

J Dolby 1884, 1892

Sir R D Green-Price 1895, 1897, 1898, 1900 to 1902

T K Howell Roberts 1896

A Carson Roberts 1896, 1905, 1906, 1928

A G Chamberlain 1897 to 1900, 1903

S D Jerrold 1899

L H Wraith 1901

F J Adams 1902

G L Gibson 1903

P J Hibbert 1904

Ward Oliver 1904

S D Jerrold 1905, 1906, 1908

H H Walrond 1907, 1908

H Lyon 1909 to 1911, 1920 to 1925

M W Dixon 1911, 1912

W Young 1912, 1913

A Q Twiss 1914, 1915, 1919

W D Easterby 1927

E H V Weigall 1930 to 1934

E S Mills 1935

J Orchard 1936

O E Brigden 1937

L P Walker 1938

E M Tuke 1946

C R H Hurle-Hobbs 1947

D F Belchamber 1948

W Maginn 1949

C A Hughes 1950

H L Stevens 1951

A D Hughes 1952

G Russell 1953

C R H Hurle-Hobbs 1954

A S Higlett 1955

A R Parr 1956

F J Laycock 1957

A R Dean 1958

O Barraclough 1959

A W Vale 1960

A R Parr 1961

M C C Sullivan 1962

F R Smith 1963

A Long 1964

E Fieth 1965

S A Hills 1966

R Jones 1967

R K Edwards 1968

*Presidents
(1969–1982)*

C D Lacey 1969

C H Chidgey 1970

B Northey 1971

E M Clarke 1972

J Speirs 1973

N S Middleton 1974

E S Sant 1975

J G Teesdale 1976

P F Kimmance 1977

H Harrison 1978

A J Kappler 1979

I M Pickwell 1980

E C Thomas 1981

J C Fuller 1982

*Honorary Secretaries
(1846–1982)*

J C Meymott 1846–1872

Geo M Arnold 1873–1878

H Lloyd Roberts 1878–1883

P D Boggis-Rolfe 1884–1890

L H Wraith 1891–1897

F Gaskell 1898–1904

W Young 1905–1909

S Wilkinson 1909–1915

W Young 1919

N M Griffiths 1920–1927

J N Richards 1928–1932

A R H Hobbs 1933–1952

W D Munrow 1953–1958

S V Collins CB 1959–1965

S T Evans 1965–1970

S A Hills 1970–1976

J C Nicholson 1977–1978

I M Pickwell 1979–1982

The Demise of James Hunt Esq, District Auditor, December 1857

B T Cousins

B T Cousins

5/1 James Hunt – a
fine figure of a man.

It is 128 years since the death of a former district auditor
was reverently commemorated by means of a large and
prominent tombstone in a churchyard at Warwick. This
tombstone records the sudden death of James Hunt on
22 December 1857, at the age of 63, and quotes a
pointed verse from St Paul's Epistle to the Romans:

> "For rulers are not a terror to good works, but to the evil.
> Wilt thou then not be afraid of the power? Do that which
> is good, and thou shalt have praise of the same." (Romans
> c13:v3)

The events which actually led up to his death are
connected with one of the largest frauds ever discovered
by district auditors, and for this and other reasons the
story is not without its interest.

James Hunt was born in Oxford in 1794. He was
successively chemist, accountant, a member of the Old
and New Corporations and sheriff. After serving for two
to three years as Chairman of the Board of Guardians, he
was appointed in 1850 to the position of district
auditor. His district covered Warwickshire and
Oxfordshire, and for ease of travelling he moved to
Chipping Norton.

He is described by a number of his contemporaries as fine, large, muscular, well-built, and generally healthy; of 18 to 20 stone; a remarkably fine man, in good health, active and temperate. It must be added whilst quoting these testimonials that in the first place they were all given after Hunt's death and that in the second place there is considerable evidence that temperance was not amongst his virtues.

There are several tributes to the efficiency with which he undertook his duties, and there seems no doubt that he was a popular man. The records, for example, of the Warwick Union, the Birmingham Board of Guardians and the Poor Law Board all contain appreciations of his zeal and expressions of regret at his passing. Considerable space was devoted in the 'Warwick Advertiser'.

In appearance he was excessively corpulent; the medical evidence relating to his post-mortem referred to 'an enormous deposition of fat under the skin covering the abdomen'. There were more serious disabilities too, but these were not apparent.

On the evening of Friday 18 December 1857 — in his eighth year as DA — he met a friend, the proprietor of the *Oxford Chronicle*, at Gracy's Hotel, Oxford, and walked with him to the station, saying he was going to Birmingham.

5/2 Clippings from Warwick Advertiser.

The train waited as usual at a small station outside Oxford, Handborough, while an express, from Euston Square and Bletchley, had additional coaches added and departed. Five minutes later at 7.30, the ordinary train, bearing Hunt, also left in the same direction. Hunt is reported to have complained bitterly of the delay.

The express had reached a point within a mile of Charlbury when its engine broke down. Although the guard ran back along the track with a red lamp and a detonator, 'the ordinary train came up at full speed and dashed into it with terrible violence. There were many persons injured'.

Hunt was travelling alone in a first-class compartment, and later said he was thrown across the carriage by the impact, and felt a great strain across the lower part of his body, with much pain. A farmer friend who was travelling on the same train, helped him out, and together with others assisted him in walking three-quarters of a mile along the track to the nearest cottage. This friend went on to Charlbury and sent back a fly from an inn there, the landlord of which knew Hunt well. He stayed overnight at this inn, but said later that he did not know how he had got there.

The following day he went on home to Chipping Norton, spending the afternoon in the company of two other gentlemen in one of the local inns.

On Sunday December 20, he hired a carriage to Banbury and went on from there to Warwick, arriving in time for dinner. His purpose in travelling again to Warwick was to attend a trial in which he was a witness. He said he was bound to come to Warwick, but a friend who met him said he was 'more fit to be in bed'. He was very worried about the loss of some papers in the accident and upon arrival was said to be 'very much excited about a case at Assizes at which he was a witness'. He was 'most talkative and excitable at dinner'; the landlord's evidence goes on to suggest that his appetite was unimpaired. During dinner he collapsed and was taken in great pain into another room, and thereafter attended continuously by the town surgeon.

The case with which Mr Hunt was concerned was the prosecution of two former officers of the Birmingham Board of Guardians for embezzlement. The fraud had been discovered at an audit he had held a month previously.

It was the duty of one Edward Griffin, senior clerk in the levy department, to carry out a weekly check of the records of Henry Gibbs, collector of the poor rate in two wards in the centre of the town, and see that the cash was paid in.

The system then in use continued with very little modification until 1929, so far as I can ascertain, and was based upon a three-part checkbook. The collector first tore off the first part, which comprised the demand note, and left it at the ratepayer's property. When he received payment he removed the second part and handed that to the ratepayer as a receipt, leaving in the book merely the stump or counterfoil. All items unpaid at any time thereafter had two slips left in the checkbook.

It was Griffin's duty to examine the books and report to the Guardians any item not recorded in the Collection and Deposit book. A similar fraud to this one had recently occurred in London, and Griffin had assured the Clerk at that time that the weekly check was taking place.

On many occasions Gibbs, the collector, had omitted to show items received in the proper way, and had retained the cash. Griffin on his weekly inspection had initialled the third copies as though all was in order. Gibbs records that at the previous six-monthly audit, 'as I was coming out of the room Griffin put a note in my hand: "Have you got through alright, if you have, let me have £2". At that time he owed me £140'.

On the morning of the November audit over 100

stumps were initialled by Griffin, who told Gibbs to post the amounts in the paid column without a date, and say they were paid after 29 September (the end of the half-year), assuring him 'the Auditor will not look at the deposit book after 29 September; he has nothing to do with it after that day'.

The amount of the deficiency, as stated at the trial, was £1,079. 18s. 19d, which in terms of value must now represent a most substantial figure. The subsequent certificate of surcharge was in the sum of £1,154.9s. 10d, made up as follows:

Collected and not accounted for	£1,072.9s.6d
Casting errors	£100.18s.0d
	£1,173.7s.6d
Less other errors	£18.17s.8d
	£1,154.9s.10d

This fraud illustrates principles of everyday audit work that are true whatever the period of history or whatever the amount involved.

The hearing of these charges was commenced on Tuesday 22 December before Mr Baron Channell at the Warwick Winter Assizes. Counsel for the prosecution, after rising to present his case, to quote from the contemporary report, 'mentioned, with an expression of personal sorrow, that information had just been communicated of the death of Mr Hunt'. He had in fact died 25 minutes before the hearing commenced.

Gibbs and Griffin were both found guilty and each sentenced to two years' hard labour.

An inquest on Hunt's death was held at the 'Globe' in Warwick on Christmas Eve before the Borough Coroner

and 15 jurymen. After medical and other evidence had been given, the Coroner adjourned the inquest in order that an inspector from the Board of Trade might provide further details of how the accident had occurred. A post-mortem had shown that the collision had caused an

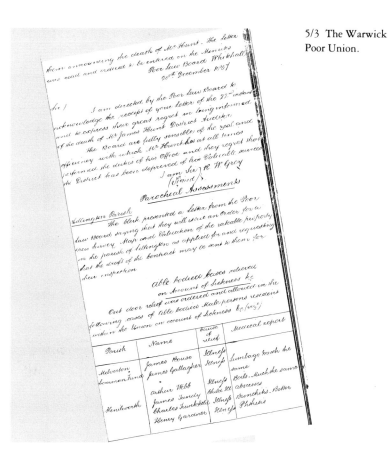

5/3 The Warwick Poor Union.

extremely large clot of blood (the size of a man's head) to burst. Death from this cause was said to have been inevitable, but was accelerated by the accident. The interment took place that afternoon.

The jury at the resumed inquest found that death had been precipitated by the accident, but that no blame attached to anyone. Two sisters of Mr Hunt took proceedings against the Oxford, Worcester and Wolverhampton Railway Company, and succeeded in obtaining £500 in damages and £600 in costs. This Railway, during its brief independent career, had a shocking reputation for unpunctuality, mishaps and breakdowns, and was indeed known familiarly as the 'Old Worse and Worse'.

Early in 1858, a public subscription was opened in Warwick for the purpose of erecting a suitable memorial in St Paul's Churchyard in his honour. A special committee was formed from prominent townsfolk in order to carry out this purpose. The subscription list was headed by an item of 10 guineas from the Earl of Warwick, and soon reached £50. There is no trace of a record of the full amount collected. The memorial was erected later in the year, and is the one we see there today.

5/4 James Hunt's tombstone.

B T COUSINS

Has spent 36 years in the District Audit
Service and is a Fellow of the Chartered
Institute of Secretaries. At one time engaged
on quality control audit inspections, he now,
for his sins, manages No 9AD as their DA.
Keenly interested in bridge, music and
travelling in foreign parts.

A Case of Fraud and Corruption in 1907

M D Propert

6/1 ". . . being too drunk to walk, a carriage and pair would be chartered to drive the councillors home."

The following is extracted from the proceedings of a meeting of the District Auditors' Society on 13 October 1911. The members evidently thought that this paper presented by Mr M D Propert on a particular case of fraud and corruption was of some interest as it is one of only a few reproduced in such detail in the minutes.

The circumstances in connection with the case, or rather series of cases, are so unusual, that it may be of interest if some of the salient features are touched upon during the long drawn out proceedings, covering a period of nearly three years, before the guilty parties were brought to justice.

The parish in question was a rural parish forming a portion of a Rural District Council, and it comprised and made up practically the area of the Rural District Council, there being one other parish only concerned.

The parish, owing to colliery developments, had become populous, at the date of audit there being about 30,000, with a rateable value of about £120,000.

The Parish Council consisted of 15 members.

The two Officers, John and Albert Jones (brothers), were no doubt the principal villains of the piece. John was Assistant Overseer and Clerk to the Parish Council, and Albert acted as Assistant Overseer, with collection of the rates, and 'Surveyor' to the Parish Council.

The accounts in which the bulk of the frauds occurred were those of the Parish Council for the year ended 31st March, 1907, but sundry frauds also occurred in the Overseer's Accounts, which finally developed into a bewildering number of charges and counts, covering 14 pages in the Assize Calendar, which will give some idea of the mass of detail involved.

1. The Audit. The Audit was opened in July, 1907, by my predecessor, but nothing much had been done, because the Accounts were not balanced, or properly vouched. In the preceding April election there had been a 'furore' in the Parish in consequence of the publication of the Union Parochial Balance Sheet, and the Union Abstract Book, from which it appeared that John and Albert had drawn huge sums, in addition to their salaries, eg John

£560.10s.0d.	Half-year ended March 1905
£400.0s.0d.	Half-year ended Michaelmas 1905
£960.10s.0d.	

and Albert

£605.1s.0d.	for period from 20 February 1905 to 31 March 1905
£575.0s.0d.	for period from 1 April 1905 to 30 September 1905
£1,180.1s.0d.	

in addition to salaries at the rate of £350 per annum, with other large allowances.

The total expenditure for the year amounted to £6,185. A cursory examination disclosed the fact that there were serious irregularities.

The previous year's expenditure was allowed at £3,796. The development, however, had been very rapid. In 1901, it was only £56; 1902, £412; 1905, £2,582.

The result of the Election in April 1911 had been that the Jones' faction was defeated, a great majority of new members coming on. They had endeavoured to investigate the accounts, but never realised the gross frauds and corruption that existed. The result was that in May or June following, the Parish Council declined to put up with John's methods, and terminated his appointment as Assistant Overseer, and his brother Albert took his place.

I took up the Audit in October 1907, and had endless trouble with the Accounts. They were hopelessly involved, and it was evident that there had been gross irregularities in the Parish Council, Overseers' and Special Expenses Rate Accounts.

No satisfactory account could be got from John Jones of his receipts and disbursements: a large number of cheques had been drawn in favour of J. Jones: many vouchers were missing, &c., and the Minute Book was useless. The 15 old Members appeared at the Audit, and also the 15 new Members, the Rural District Councillors, and numbers of Ratepayers.

After several 'field days' at the Audit, proceedings were taken against the Assistant Overseer, John, to compel the production of Cash Accounts, &c. Solicitors and Accountants came on the scene early, and by dint of pushing and threatening, I finally got the Cash Accounts signed and vouched, and they proved the undoing of the Clerk and his brother.

Similarly with the Main Accounts of the Parish Council, it was only after threats of proceedings that I was able to get the account recognised by the Parish Council, so that I could officially deal with the Accounts.

Having got the Accounts into form, the Audit was abandoned, and fresh Notices issued in January 1908, and it was not until 30th April 1908 that the Audit was closed.

Sixteen certificates of disallowance, including surcharges were necessary, the Reasons, &c., being very lengthy, covering over 100 brief sheets.

The principal amounts disallowed were:

Disallowance and Surcharge upon Parish Councillors	£1,263
Disallowed in Wages Cash Account of the Clerk	£ 396
Disallowed in General Account	£ 503
Overseers' Assistant Overseer (A E Jones)	£ 314
Overseers' Receipt and Payment Book (Poor Rate)	£3,174
Overseers' Receipt and Payment Book (Special Sanitary Rate)	£1,534

with sundry other smaller sums.

In addition some £700 was forced out of the Brothers Jones, prior to closing the Audit, being the balances admitted to have been in their hands.

Without going into details, there can be no doubt that the Brothers Jones had, for the preceding two or three years, been exploiting public funds, and helping themselves and their friends. The following will illustrate the extraordinary state of affairs existing in the Parish, and how the monies were purloined:

(i) Cheques were signed by the Overseers or Parish Councillors, anywhere, and at any time, and in blank very often. When John Jones wanted any money, he simply filled up a cheque, and got a Councillor or Overseer to sign. An inspection of his private banking account showed that when it was run down, he would simply pay in an Overseers' cheque, or a Parish Council's cheque, e.g. Parish Council cheque £70, and so on. A number of counts in the indictments dealt with these items.

(ii) The parish being a large one, about nine miles long, meetings would take place at some of the outlying parts. John, the Clerk, would attend. After the 'business' was over, the 'Rising Sun', a public-house, was a favourite spot, John and his boon companions would remain behind until 'stop tap', all then being too drunk to walk, a carriage and pair would be chartered to drive the Councillors home. The cost would be smuggled through and a voucher obtained, e.g. 'To carting 20 loads of ashes to footpath'. There must have been thousands of loads of ashes charged for.

(iii) A Cemetery scheme gave Albert Jones the opportunity of piling up charges to the extent of over £2,000, and enabled John Jones, ostensibly, to disburse hundreds of pounds in wages, most of which went into his own pocket, and those of his friends.

The Parish Council were looking about for a site, and Albert was supposed to prepare plans. He began drawing on account. £400 in 1905, and by March 1907, he had drawn £1,719 (of which I disallowed £1,294). He prepared three sets of plans, developing from £9,000 to £14,000, upon which he charged five per cent on each occasion on the estimates, with other preliminary charges for surveying &c.

Beyond digging a few trial holes, nothing was done, and there is no Cemetery today.

(iv) Wholesale swindling in the Parish Council and Overseers' Accounts.

Quantities of goods for the private use of Albert and John were paid from the cheques of Overseers and the Parish Council. Pudding basins, night lights, crockery, dog kennel, double barrelled gun, building material for houses, &c. were undoubtedly got by the Jones and paid for by the Authority, faked and bogus invoices being put forward.

(v) By the forged Minute of the 20th February 1905, John and Albert drew between them £2,000 – to which they had no right – to September 1905.

(vi) John and Albert Jones, with their Uncle and Nephews, received and drew during the year ended 31 March 1907, from the Overseers and the Parish Council, sums in the aggregate amounting to £4,900. During the preceding year, a brother of John Jones, named James, a contractor, drew approximately £2,000

for work said to be done on footpaths, cemetery, &c. The Brothers Jones drew inflated salaries, in addition to other large allowances, for which there was no legal warrant.

(vii) There was no trouble in getting funds. John, being Assistant Overseer, transferred whatever was required from the Overseers' Accounts to the Parish Council. He did not bother with precepts. In the year 1906 he transferred £3,000. In the year 1907 it jumped up to £5,500, whereas in 1901 it was only £50. Although in the demand note, the Parish Council expenses were put down at 2d. in the £, it worked out at 11d. in the £, or £2,483 in excess of the statutory limit. He did not seem to care what account the charges were drawn upon, using Overseers' cheques for Parish Council and vice versa.

(viii) The larceny of £300 by A E Jones in September 1906, as the Judge at the Assizes put it, was a very clever 'cover up'.

Three hundred pounds was drawn from the Overseers' bankers on 2nd June 1906, and paid into his private Banking Account. No entry or charge appeared in the Overseers' Receipt and Payment Book. Under date, however, of the 29th September 1906, there appeared a charge of £300 for 'Parish Council (Burial Account) Precept' in the Receipt and Payment Book, and, although a cheque was drawn in favour of the Parish Council, and placed to their credit, on the same date there was a contra entry in the Parish Council Banking Account, thereby cancelling the credit, and having the effect of refunding the said sum of £300 to the Overseers' Banking Account. Notwithstanding this, the £300 was allowed to stand as originally charged in the

Overseers' Receipt and Payment Book, with the result that the balance as shown in the Receipt and Payment Book as the 30th September 1906, was made to agree with the Bank Balance of that date.

The services of A E Jones were dispensed with by the Parish Council on the 31st March 1908, during the Audit.

2. Public Inquiry. In December 1909 the Inspector, Mr Willis, came down and held a Public Inquiry, and after sitting four days, he adjourned the proceedings *sine die*. The conclusions arrived at at the Audit were fully confirmed.

3. Police Court Proceedings. On 14th April 1910 John and Albert were arrested on warrants issued at the instance of the Board, and the first day's hearing took place a few days later, special days subsequently being fixed. The prosecution was undertaken by the Director of Public Prosecutions. Six Councillors were brought in and charged with a number of offences, conspiracy being the main charge, although in the cases of three ex-Members of the Parish Council, information was laid under the Public Bodies Corrupt Practices Act 1889 (52 & 53 Vict. Ch. 69) for corruption.

The convictions under this statute may form a useful precedent. The circumstances under which the information was laid were briefly: when in March 1907 it was found that the large sums of money drawn for salaries in 1905 by the Assistant Overseers had come to be generally known, the Parish Council on the 18th March 1907 appointed a Committee of six Members to report on the salaries paid to the Assistant Overseer and Collector for the half-years ended 31st March 1905, and 30th September 1905. This

Committee appears to have done nothing, but after the Election, and defeat of the friends of the Jones, there appeared, entered in the Minute Book, what purported to be the Minutes of a Special Meeting held 13th April 1907 (two days before the old Parish Council went out of office): 'That this Committee are satisfied that the Minute respecting the salaries paid to Mr John Jones and Mr A E Jones for the period ended the 31st March 1905 and 30th September 1905 was properly read out and passed at the meeting held on 20th February 1905, and duly signed by the Chairman, James Davies.'

Now of the Members who were originally appointed, only three received notice, who were friends of A E Jones, David Lewis (deceased), Rees Thomas and John Roberts. James Davies, who had not been appointed, attended. All these Members received a guinea for attending this Meeting, cheques being drawn and signed by themselves, and counter-signed by the Clerk. Thomas Thomas, another Member, also attended, but made no charge, and drew no money from the Treasurer. Absolutely no investigation was made and the resolution was accepted without any question. It was clearly intended to bolster up the Minute of 20th February 1905 and was spoken of at the Trial as the 'whitewashing resolution'.

There was no authority for its being in the Minute Book at all, but the friends of the Clerk were going out of Office on 15th April. The new Council, at their first meeting held the 15th April, wrote across this Minute 'Rejected.'

I disallowed each of the guineas charged.

Each of the Members who received the £1.1s.0d. were

charged under several counts at the Assizes, 'Being a Member of a certain Public Body, to wit, a Parish Council unlawfully and corruptly by himself did receive a certain gift and advantage for himself, to wit, a sum of money of £1.1s.0d. from A E Jones and John Jones, then being servants and officials of the said Public Body, as a reward for, and on account of himself, the said Rees Thomas, to being such Member of such Public Body, forbearing to do something in respect of certain proposed matters and transactions in which the said Public Body was concerned, to wit, forbearing to investigate, check and examine the Minute Book and Accounts of the said Public Body, and forbearing to ascertain the just and true amount of salary due and payable to the said A E Jones and J Jones, as such servants and officials for the year 1905, on or about the 13th April 1907.'

They were also jointly charged that they 'unlawfully did conspire, confederate and agree together with the Clerk and Assistant Overseer to unlawfully and corruptly receive to themselves as members of the said public body, diverse gifts, rewards, inducements and advantages &c.'

The prisoners were all committed on 15th June for trial at the then ensuing Assizes, commencing 16th July 1910.

4. Grand Jury. The indictments came before the Grand Jury on 18th July and some of them were of immense size, the indictment for conspiracy running to 500 folios with 85 counts. The indictment for falsification of books of account ran to 200 folios with 38 charges, and so on, and there were about 20 indictments. Fourteen pages were occupied in the Assize Calendar in setting out the various charges. True bills were found on all the indictments, and on all counts.

5. Assizes. Trial at Assizes. The prosecution opened with indictments of John Jones for forging and uttering receipts and when he was found guilty on three of these indictments, the brothers were jointly indicted for forgery under the Forgery Act 1861 (forging Minute Book), and they were found guilty. The main conspiracy indictment was next taken, and this covered the whole range, including charges for corruption &c. The Jury brought in a verdict of Guilty at 3.30pm on Saturday 29th July.

6. Sentences. The sentences upon the prisoners were:

John Jones. Five years' penal servitude for forgery of Minute Book, and for each of the charges of forging the workmen's receipts, three years, to run concurrently, and a fortnight's imprisonment for conspiracy.

A E Jones. Five years' penal servitude for forgery of Minute Book, and a fortnight's imprisonment for conspiracy, to run concurrently.

Rees Thomas (ex Chairman). Six months' imprisonment in the Second Division for conspiracy, two months for corrupt practices, to run concurrently, and a Declaration of inability to hold any public office for seven years.

Joseph Cooper. Four months in the Second Division for conspiracy.

James Davies. Two months' imprisonment for corrupt practices, and a Declaration of inability to hold any public office for seven years.

John Roberts. Three months in the Second Division for conspiracy, two months for corrupt practices, to run concurrently, and a Declaration of inability to hold any public office for seven years.

David Roberts. One month in the Second Division for conspiracy.

John Davies. Found guilty of gross negligence. (Discharged 'Not Guilty').

7. *Decision of Board.*

(a) In the case of John Jones, the Local Government Board have upheld all the disallowances, and declined to remit £919.

(b) In the case of Albert Jones, all the disallowances and surcharges have been upheld, and remission has been refused as regards £326.

(c) The appeals of the Councillors have not yet been decided. They will possibly be allowed to lapse.

8. *Monies Recovered.* In addition to the balances recovered, about £700, some £1,200 should be recovered upon the Bonds of Officers.

M D PROPERT

He was appointed an Assistant District Auditor on 22 April 1896 and became the District Auditor for Glamorganshire on 1 April 1901.

Carson Roberts — An Appreciation

B H Gilham

Carson Roberts retired as long ago as 1928 but continues to be remembered within and outside the District Audit Service. He is revered not only for what he achieved in his time but also for the legacy of knowledge and experience which he left.

In the realm of local government finance, Carson Roberts laid down some fundamental accountancy principles, perhaps now taken for granted, and established certain operational audit standards for local government. He clarified the law relating to local government audit, and as a result of the court cases he instigated, he established legal principles still regarded as authoritative today. Finally, his clarity of exposition and purpose, his relevance today, could well assist contemporary auditors with their current problems and complexities, if no more than by providing perspective and understanding to fundamental principles.

To appreciate the size of the strides made by Carson Roberts and where he fits in the scheme of things, some historical perspective is needed.

In the 19th century, local government consisted of many small, single-purpose authorities created by

Parliament to meet each need the legislators belatedly recognised. For example, the outbreaks of cholera on a large scale scared Parliament into the Public Health Act 1848; the Thames was an open sewer until Parliament was so overcome with the stench that it was compelled to legislate. Examples of such *ad hoc* authorities were the boards of guardians, dispensing poor relief locally, then a major local function; the local boards of health; the highway boards; school boards and so on, created as each need arose.

These needs arose out of the Industrial Revolution and its consequences – factories, overcrowding and squalor, the lack of sanitation and clean water, bad roads falling into disuse because of the developing railways, illiteracy and the lack of education (particularly among the working classes required by the new industries).

As each *ad hoc* authority was created so it was made subject to district audit but not the boroughs. These

7/2 "Accounts of local authorities" by Carson Roberts.

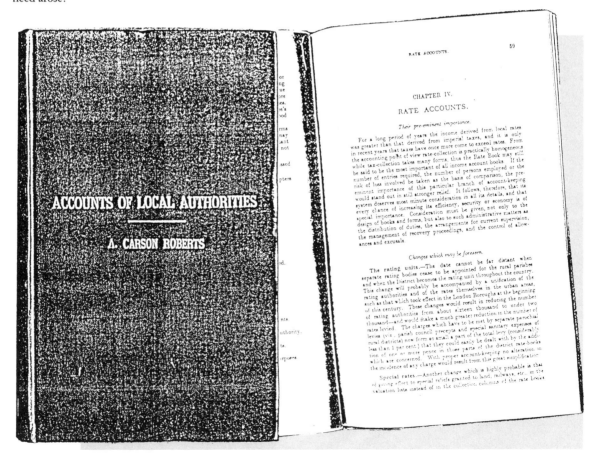

had been 'reformed' in 1835 (following the Royal Commission Report on municipal abuses) before the system of district audit was established in 1844.

These various authorities were amalgamated into general purpose district councils by the Local Government Act 1894, superseding the previous urban and rural sanitary authorities created by the Public Health Acts 1872–1875. The county councils were established to take over the administrative functions of the justices as a result of the Local Government Act 1888. All these authorities (except for the boroughs) were made subject to district audit, and under the 1894 Act, parishes also became subject to district audit despite opposition, some of it abusive and indignant.

The district councils continued to levy separate rates for different purposes until the Rating and Valuation Act 1925 which combined all these rates into the uniform general rating system we know today (argued for and forecast by Carson Roberts in chapter IV of his *Accounts of Local Authorities*).

The 19th century was therefore a turbulent period of expansion, of changes and problems for which local administration had to be developed and tailored to cater for the needs of the new communities.

Some idea of the general laxness in local administration over a considerable span of time can be gleaned from the Royal Commission report on borough abuses leading to the Municipal Corporations Act 1835 and to the fact mentioned in paragraph 1.24 of *Local Government Audit Law* that in 1893 'the 38 district auditors had between them made 3,500 disallowances'.

In the midst of so much chicanery, local ineptitude and downright muddle, district auditors were trying to impose not only standards of financial probity by proper accountability but also constraining local authority activities to those authorised by Parliament, then more restricted – hence the doctrine of *ultra vires*. This they did by frequent imposition of disallowances and surcharges for fraud or illegality - the twin abuses in those times. As a result, with the beginning of the 20th century, reverence for the district auditor (or rather for his powers) gradually gave way to acceptable standards of financial probity and respect for the law.

It was at this stage that A Carson Roberts started to make his mark. He entered the Audit Service in 1891 and introduced accounting and audit standards by giving them wide currency in his text books published between 1919 and 1930.

Whereas today's entrants depend on CIPFA's professional accountancy training, or have a commercial accountancy background, former students took the departmental professional examinations and were weaned on Carson Roberts and his text books.

To the students in the late 1940s, such text books may have seemed out of date but not to the experienced. When Carson Roberts retired in 1928, the minutes of the District Auditors' Society recording the event contain a similar but chastened view expressed by one of its then members:

> "Mr Wallis Grain . . . vividly remembered that when he entered the audit work, his feelings were rather outraged by the suggestion which was made to him that if he wished to sail in smooth waters he should make all speed to digest a 'Carson Roberts' text book. With the arrogance of youth,

he secretly decided he would not, as he thought, be shackled in a conventional groove in this way but he very soon discovered that, to put it bluntly, he could not do without the essential aid to the beginner afforded by this expert knowledge. Now, as then, old and new members were alike under immense obligations for the instructive and stimulating ideas . . . diffused to them by Mr Carson Roberts".

Carson Roberts became as well known outside the Audit Service as within it. Such was the value and demand for his book on *Accounts of Local Authorities* that the Local Government Board made arrangements with HMSO for its general publication.

Although double entry book-keeping had long been known, it was seldom utilised in local government because most local government activities were then on a small scale, administered by small local bodies. Many of their officers were unqualified or untrained and local finance was simply geared to funding payments out of the yearly or half-yearly rates. For example, L M Helmore in his book *The District Auditor* mentions that as late as 1927 there were 12,000 unpaid overseers collecting the rates until they were replaced by the 1,500 rating authorities following the Rating and Valuation Act 1925.

So local authority accounts were kept simple, deliberately so, on a cash basis (receipts and payments), as parish council accounts are today. The shortcomings of such a limited method of accounting were not important for these small authorities, rating merely for what they spent. The larger and growing general purpose authorities created under the 1888–1894 Acts, however, began to need something better.

Some standardisation was prescribed by the Local Government Board, and in 1907 a Departmental Committee, appointed by the President of the Local Government Board, recognised the increasing importance of fuller accounting for these growing local authorities. Its Report recommended the double entry system of income and expenditure accounts leading up to a balance sheet; but the Committee Report was advisory only.

In 1919, Carson Roberts was made Technical Adviser to the Ministry of Health so his influence on local authority accounting and audit promulgations after that date was significant and evident.

Double entry was first prescribed by the Housing Accounts Order 1920 (SRO 1920/487) but this related to housing accounts only. Subsequently, a double entry and standardised system was prescribed for rating accounts by the Rate Accounts Orders 1926 and then for all the accounts of boroughs by the Accounts (Boroughs and Metropolitan Boroughs) Regulations 1930.

Although these Orders and Regulations were mandatory only for the accounts to which they related, they set the standard. Carson Roberts played an influential role not only as Technical Adviser but also as a propagandist through his text books.

Although the Institute of Municipal Treasurers and Accountants (later CIPFA) was founded in 1885, its influence was bound to be limited because many of the finance officers to district councils were not professionally qualified or members of the Institute. It therefore fell to district auditors to inculcate better accounting standards. Following the 1926 Orders and the Borough Accounts Regulations 1930, the income and expenditure basis and better accounting standards became the 'norm' for all district councils. For this, Carson Roberts and district audit can claim some considerable credit.

Carson Roberts not only grasped the basic fundamentals but explained them simply and clearly. His expositions of them can be as readily assimilated by today's students as they were by yesterday's.

In his book, *Local Administration – Finance and Accounts*, Carson Roberts uses the Accounts Regulations 1930 as a basis for his explanations, modestly omitting any reference to his key role as Technical Adviser. These Regulations had been discussed and agreed with the Local Authority Associations including the IMTA and therefore they enjoyed wide support. Such a basis was adopted by district audit in their efforts to encourage better standards in local government.

Briefly, Carson Roberts recognised only two classes of accounts, personal and impersonal, which had to be clearly described and identified at the outset. The debits on the personal accounts (showing what those persons had received by way of services, supplies or cash) and the entries on the impersonal accounts (debits recording expenditure, and credits recording income) can then be readily understood. The balance sheet becomes a natural consequence, showing the assets and liabilities on the personal accounts (e.g. debtors, stores, investments, cash and creditors) and the deficits and surpluses on the impersonal or final fund accounts.

Carson Roberts swept away the confusions engendered by such unnecessary classifications as nominal and real accounts, still, alas, confusing students today (such

confusions he described as 'absurd and very misleading'). This approach by Carson Roberts to the underlying theory is so 'illuminating' that it is still being quoted today by CIPFA in their current Financial Information Service (volume 2.II.2 appendix A chapter IV).

It is suggested that this simplicity tends to be overlooked or even misunderstood in the welter of today's complex systems and computerised accounts.

In chapter XXXI of his book *Local Administration: Finance and Accounts*, Carson Roberts 'deals with the defects which prevail in many of the small and some of the large accounts'. Unfortunately, some of these may not be irrelevant today e.g. incomplete or omitted personal accounts, incorrect headings or ambiguity in the title to accounts, improper merging of accounts, insufficient description of special entries, abuse of the journal system, suspense accounts, gaps in the control accounts system.

In case it should be thought that Carson Roberts is now quite outmoded, it might be worth referring to some of the subjects he mentioned that may well be receiving some consideration even today. For example, in *Local Administration: Finance and Accounts* he addresses such problems as:

– the recording of real property and capital assets,

– the distinctions between capital assets and deferred charges;

– differences between the commercial and municipal systems;

– accrued charges and bad debts reserve;

– the spread of insurance risks;

– direct labour and 'market rates' for recharging client departments;

– comparative cost statistics and their value.

On capital financing, Carson Roberts was equally lucid. He explained the methods and accounting involved, clarifying the difference between loan and capital outlay.

Backed by the Borough Accounts Order 1930 (issued as regulations), he swept away the complications of earmarked sinking funds which he eliminated in favour of 'that beautifully clear and simple plan' of loans pooling which became adopted by even the smaller district councils well before the 1974 reorganisation. If Carson Roberts preached the message, it was mainly district auditors who saw to it that the precept was put into practice. As recently as 1960, the IMTA published a research study on *The Pooling of Local Authority Loans* in which the pioneering work of Carson Roberts was acknowledged.

Amongst other accounting expositions, he explained the division of the balance sheet into two sections, one relating to loan and capital and the other to revenue, known as the Double Account System. In this way, one could demonstrate not only the difference between capital assets, deferred charges and revenue assets but also the extent to which they had been funded by loan and revenue.

The narrative form of balance sheet now prevalent may need the source and application of funds statement, but

is it too fanciful to suggest that the double account system was the forerunner of such a statement?

These are only some of the accounting principles introduced, developed and explained by Carson Roberts for application in local government. Although *Local Administration – Finance and Accounts* and his other text books were written for the circumstances of the time, they contain fundamentals which are relevant and helpful to the present.

Carson Roberts did pioneering work in formulating operational audit standards. As long ago as 1908, the minutes of the District Auditors' Society record the proposal by Mr A Carson Roberts to compile 'a comprehensive list of audit processes . . . of codifying them and of setting them out'. The Society agreed and appointed a committee with six sub-committees (with powers to co-opt!) well before anything like the audit standards and the CCAB of today!

In 1909, the Local Government Board issued instructions laying down the main principles governing the conduct of local government audits, and in 1919 Carson Roberts published his text book *Audit Law and Audit Work*. This was undertaken at the request of the District Auditors' Society in 1913, and that part on audit law was a revision of a book produced in or about 1894.

This more comprehensive book of 1919 was a significant step forward in making generally available a much needed guide to the audit of local authorities, all the more impressive because no such publication had appeared before. Although clearly intended for the practitioners of the time, the book should not be dismissed as irrelevant today.

Indeed, some of the audit principles and standards propounded then not only have their relevance today, but seem to be echoed in some of the guidance being issued currently. Of course, it can be argued that fundamentals always remain the same, but they need to be developed and applied for the changing circumstances and needs of the time.

Some of these fundamentals referred to by Carson Roberts might be mentioned if only to illustrate the extent and depth of audit perceptions then and their relevance to today's differing circumstances:

Efficient accounting systems and internal controls

Carson Roberts refers to 'gaps in the control account system' and to the need for 'the organisation of efficient accounting systems'. Nowadays, these matters tend to be fully described as 'internal control systems' and 'accounting controls' on which the accuracy and reliability of the accounts depend.

Significant failures here can strike at the roots of reliability in accounting and recording, hence the current emphasis on systems-based audit. It is interesting to note the contention by Carson Roberts, rather bold then, that a sound accounting system and efficient current supervisory check will preclude 'any form of single-handed fraud'.

Separation of duties

The Memorandum to the Borough Accounts Regulations 1930 stresses the importance of the separation of duties of 'providing information . . . and recording . . . from the duty of collecting or disbursing' which Carson Roberts describes as the 'mainspring of security'. 'In the allotment of duties . . . it should rank in front of any other consideration.'

It is suggested that even today, the details of complex systems can obscure a failure to comply with so fundamental a principle. How strongly Carson Roberts felt is indicated in his reference that 'where the authority neglects . . . to use its opportunities for distributing the duties of its staff . . . report is the Auditor's first duty'.

Current supervision and internal audit

The need for current checking, efficient supervision and internal audit is pointed out by Carson Roberts in his *Audit Law and Audit Work* and in his *Local Administration – Finance and Accounts*. He emphasises that 'it is of the greatest importance that district audit and internal supervision (by internal audit) should work together harmoniously'. This was written before 1919 but it was not until 1974 that principal authorities were deemed big enough for mandatory internal audit.

However, even for the smaller pre-1974 authorities, current supervision and check by the Chief Financial Officer were regarded as essential. Today's large authorities with their own internal audit departments demand a high level of audit planning, sophisticated documentation, and close liaison between internal and external audit. It might be claimed that these more sophisticated arrangements are elegant extensions of the concept already postulated many years ago by Carson Roberts.

Systems and compliance testing

'Walk through tests', 'compliance tests' and 'substantive

testing' are not terms used by Carson Roberts, but it seems in his *Audit Law and Audit Work* that these are the sort of considerations he had in mind when he referred to 'the principles which govern partial audit work'. For example, 'the rule where dipping discloses anything wrong' the test should be carried further. The efficiency of internal supervision and checks 'are matters of considerable importance to the auditor when deciding how far he should go'.

The desirability for 'discriminating tests' is emphasised by Carson Roberts who quotes with approval the 1909 memorandum from the Local Government Board on this issue.

This approach has long been well known to district auditors who early on rejected the idea of 'ticking and turning'. The terms mentioned above and this approach were fully explained in the Manual issued in the 1970s to students studying District Audit Law and Procedure and were no more than an adaptation from Carson Roberts' teachings. It has been developed further in the Audit Commission manual.

Balance sheet audits

'The verification of balances is a specially important part of the work which audit can never afford to omit.' 'Of all the tasks of audit there is probably none that calls for the auditor's personal attention more insistently that the examination of the balance sheet.' Current complexities may call for more sophisticated procedures for the final accounts audit, such as lead-in schedules and systematically presented working papers, but the fundamental importance of balance sheet audits was recognised by Carson Roberts back in 1919.

Materiality

Carson Roberts does not use this term but such a consideration seems to be in his mind when he says 'audit processes should always be exhaustive when they relate to large matters of account for . . . with these large transactions the risk is too great for any chances to be taken'.

Of course, the concept of materiality has had to be developed for the large complex organisations of today and more particularly in recent years but the concept, admittedly intended for the smaller audits, was not overlooked by Carson Roberts in 1919.

The bank slip test

Surprisingly, this test does not seem to be as well known in commerce. This lack of awareness elsewhere was commented on by Carson Roberts in *Audit Law and Audit Work*. 'It may be said that it does not yet form a recognised and regular part of any other audit system although many reports of district auditors showing how it has led to the exposure of falsifications have been made public.' Indeed, in the *Accountant* of the 2 November 1957 reference is made to it as 'a custom which is gathering favour with auditors'.

The bank slip test was explained in great detail in the minutes of the District Auditors' Society back in 1905! The efficacy of this test led to the Accounts (Payments into Bank) Order 1922. The test is fully explained by Carson Roberts and again in the *Local Government Auditor*; and is especially geared to the needs of small audits. It is perhaps a pointer to the high standards of auditing maintained by district auditors in past years.

Audit time

Audit planning requirements, current pressures, large scale complications and time-based fees have all necessitated better documentation and tighter time targets but it is interesting to note that in his book *Audit Law and Audit Work* Carson Roberts devotes a whole chapter to 'the allotment of audit time'.

Perhaps nothing is new but changes in circumstances and developments make it seem so! The circumstances and pressures are, of course, different now, but it is worth remembering that in the introduction to *Audit Law and Audit Work* there is listed the large number of local authorities subject to district audit in 1915. These amounted to nearly 25,000 (including about 7,000 parishes with accounts and 14,500 poor law overseers'

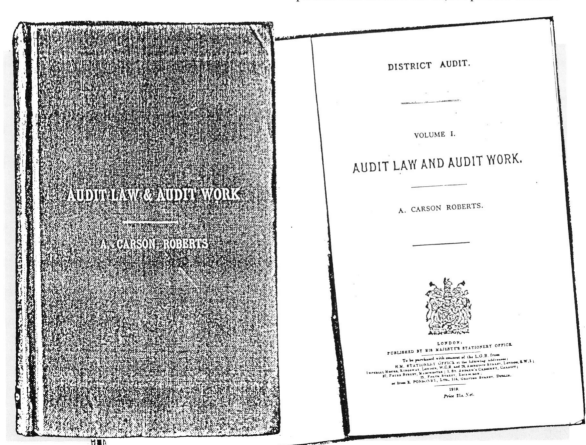

7/3 "Audit Law and Audit Work" by Carson Roberts.

accounts). Such authorities were not only numerous but variable and lacking in trained supervision.

The scale of the problem may be different now but perhaps more is now demanded of the auditor in increasingly complex situations, all of which have tended to introduce their own pressures on the contemporary auditor. Carson Roberts does not mention some of today's audit concerns such as 'value for money' or 'economy, efficiency and effectiveness'. He was dealing with the problems of authorities which were much smaller, where expenditure was closely confined and where management, dealing with small-scale activities, could be much closer to the action.

The above illustrations do not purport to be comprehensive but are intended to show the kind of audit standards preached by Carson Roberts and operated by his contemporaries and successors many years ago. Such operational audit standards were efficient for the circumstances of the age and embody fundamental principles that have relevance to today's differing needs and circumstances.

Audit Law and Audit Work was published in 1919. Volume I contained a digest of audit cases going back to 1839 and it was also a treatise on audit law. In fact, this volume was 'an extended and revised edition' originally issued some 25 years previously. The need for a work of this kind was recognised by the Local Government Board who published it by arrangement with HMSO. This book became the standard textbook on audit law and the forerunner of such classics as *The Law Relating to District Audit* by C R H Hurle-Hobbs and *Local Government Audit Law* by R Jones, the second edition of which was published in 1985.

These are the classic reference books on local government audit law. To underline this point, the author remembers an appeal case when the Lord Chief Justice took advantage of the lunch recess to refresh his memory by referring to *Hurle-Hobbs*, much to the relief of some well-versed members of the Society attending the Court!

The duties and responsibilities of auditors in practice and in commerce are well documented in text books on audit and in the body of general case law, but the special duties placed on the local government auditor by Acts and Statutory Instruments have created a separate branch of audit law special to local government. It was Carson Roberts who first clarified the law relating to local government audit by his text book on the law then applying. This served as a foundation for his successors to follow as legislative changes and developments in case law made further exposition necessary.

Carson Roberts was not just a legal theorist. He was actively engaged in various High Court cases which established important legal principles. Some of these principles may, perhaps, be taken for granted today.

The cases involving Carson Roberts are, of course, fully explained in the latest edition of *Local Government Audit Law* and are also helpfully outlined in the *Local Government Auditor*. For example:

Digest 18 *R v Roberts (Carson) ex parte Lawrence* 1907 – acceptance of tenders other than the lowest;

Digest 19 *R v Roberts* 1908 – contains guidance on 'any person accounting', 'policy and administration', and 'the auditor's report';

Digest 23 *Roberts v Hopwood 1925* – a local authority in

fixing wages must exercise its discretion responsibly;

Digest 24 *Roberts v Cunningham* 1925 – *Roberts v Hopwood* followed;

Digest 25 *Woolwich Corporation v Roberts* 1927 – *Roberts v Hopwood* followed.

Undoubtedly the most important was the celebrated case of *Roberts v Hopwood*. The case went on appeal to the House of Lords who decided in favour of the district auditor.

The minutes of the District Auditors' Society of 15 May 1925 record that 'the Chairman congratulated Mr Carson Roberts on his action in connection with the Poplar surcharge. His courage in carrying the case to the House of Lords had saved audit from a very serious situation'. It may well be that the consequences were of greater significance than perhaps the Chairman envisaged in 1925.

Briefly, the facts were these. Poplar Metropolitan Borough Council paid its lowest grade of employees, men and women, a minimum wage of £4 a week, unrelated to prevailing wage rates which had fallen with sharp reductions in the cost of living. The wages so paid (and even more so for women who were usually paid substantially less) were regarded as excessive by the district auditor and therefore contrary to law.

After allowing a tolerance margin of £1 for the exercise of the council's discretion, the district auditor surcharged the excess as contrary to law. (Ill-informed critics sometimes ignore the discretionary margin). The House of Lords upheld the auditor's decision and held that a local authority in fixing wages must exercise its

discretion reasonably.

Although there followed other cases relating to the power of a council to pay wages or to make other similar payments, the principle in the *Roberts v Hopwood* case stood mainly unchallenged until it was subject to reconsideration in *Pickwell v Camden LBC* in 1983. The legal issues are explained in Digest 81 of The Local Government Auditor and fully considered in chapter 6 of *Local Government Audit Law* (2nd edition).

The political issues at Poplar in the 1920s and those arising from the audit action are described in Noreen Branson's book *Poplarism 1919–1925*. She also explains some of the social circumstances that induced Poplar Council to take the action it did, as well as the political issues involved. Poverty then was very real. It is interesting to note the parallels that might be drawn to more recent political dissensions, such as those over the district auditor's surcharge on the Clay Cross councillors in the 1970s for their failure to increase rents in accordance with statute, or the current problems over rate-capping and the audit action arising from delays in the fixing of a legal rate.

However, there were other consequences arising out of the Poplar surcharge beside the well-known legal principle of paying reasonable wages. The political disturbances arising from audit intervention at Poplar and elsewhere provoked Mr Neville Chamberlain, then Minister of Health, to say in 1927 'They are not my auditors. They are entirely independent of me. I have never attempted to give a district auditor instructions . . . it would never have been of any use if I had.'

Equally, as a result of the Clay Cross intervention,

Mr Crosland, Secretary of State for the Environment, said in 1975 'I have no power to interfere with the work of the district auditor. In no circumstances would I dream of doing so.'

The independence of the district auditor was upheld long ago by the Court in 1894. It was reaffirmed in 1927 and in the 1970s despite political and other pressures. Such independence is being maintained today, reinforced by the independence of the Audit Commission.

Another consequence of the action by Carson Roberts at Poplar and at the other metropolitan boroughs was to reveal the ineffectiveness of the district auditor's surcharge powers on those without the means to reimburse the large-scale losses involved.

Carson Roberts surcharged the councillors at Poplar with £5,000 for excess wages paid in 1920–21. Appeals followed through to the House of Lords in 1925. In the meantime, the Council adhered to their policy of paying wages as before, so Carson Roberts surcharged them further for £11,500 in 1922–1923, £22,000 in 1923–1924, £24,600 in 1924–1925 and £23,000 in 1925–1926, surcharging from year to year despite the mounting storms. Carson Roberts also went to Woolwich and Bethnal Green with similar results.

To the summonses to enforce a recovery of the original £5,000 surcharge, George Landsbury, then a Councillor, suggested a 'whip round'. This amused his fellow councillors who did not have the means to meet such a demand. Also the hiatus was causing political embarrassment for Mr Neville Chamberlain, no friend of theirs!

Since the Poor Law Audit Act 1848, the Poor Law Commissioners, their successors the Local Government Board and the Ministry of Health had had the power to remit a surcharge, irrespective of the legalities involved, purely 'on the merits of the case'. To this Mr Chamberlain resorted, issuing an order to cancel all these embarrassing surcharges (which the Councillors could not pay), including the original surcharge of £5,000 which had been upheld in the Court.

For various reasons, the opposition on Poplar was incensed by all this and so they challenged the order in the Court who cancelled it on the grounds that once there had been a Court decision remission could not be granted. Back to square one!

All this continued to cause political eruptions and dissensions. Another answer was sought and found in the introduction of the Audit (Local Authorities) Act 1927, which relieved of personal liability all those who had been surcharged but automatically disqualified all those surcharged for more than £500 from holding office for five years. This disqualification provision continued and is enshrined in the Local Government Finance Act 1982 but now for amounts exceeding £2,000 (in certain circumstances the Court can waive the disqualification).

The action taken by Carson Roberts at Poplar in the face of so much tribulation resulted in reasserting the independence of the district auditor and revealing the limitations in the recovery of amounts surcharged and the limits on the Minister's powers to remit, and led to the disqualification provisions still applicable today. Such disqualification provisions were invoked at Clay Cross (and elsewhere) and may perhaps be relevant to the present problems over rate-capping and rate levies.

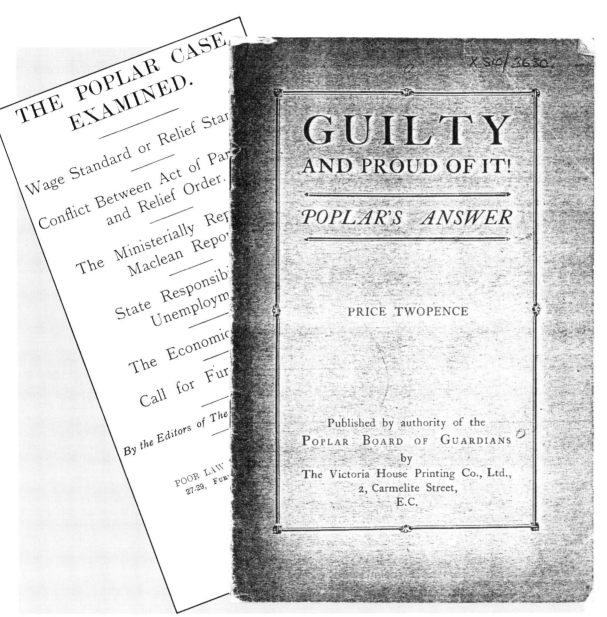

THE POPLAR CASE EXAMINED.

Wage Standard or Relief Stan

Conflict Between Act of Par
and Relief Order.

The Ministerially Rep
Maclean Repor

State Responsib
Unemploym

The Economic

Call for Fur

By the Editors of The

POOR LAW
27-29, FUR

GUILTY
AND PROUD OF IT!

POPLAR'S ANSWER

PRICE TWOPENCE

Published by authority of the
POPLAR BOARD OF GUARDIANS
by
The Victoria House Printing Co., Ltd.,
2, Carmelite Street,
E.C.

7/4 Poplar case examined. 7/5 Guilty and proud of it.

However, whether the audit provisions are appropriate to political confrontations and to the large-scale losses that might be involved is perhaps arguable.

Carson Roberts was appointed to the district audit service on 8 May 1891, and became district auditor for the London Boroughs on 28 March 1894. It should be explained that, at that time, appointments of auditor were made by the President of the Local Government Board, generally from lawyers, accountants or from those associated with past or present district auditors. Subordinate staff were mostly clerks personal to the district auditor.

In those days, there were many more district auditors (often one to a county) and some of these might be appointed first as assistant auditors and then to district auditors when they had acquired experience and expertise. As a consequence, Carson Roberts was admitted to the District Auditors' Society in 1892 as an assistant auditor before being elevated to district auditor in 1894.

Paragraphs 1.29 and 1.31 of *Local Government Audit Law* provide a fascinating account of the 'patronage' method of appointments and of the 'father and son' tradition. Particular reference is made, by way of example, to the Roberts dynasty. Carson Roberts was the third generation of a family of district auditors; his brother Douglas was also a district auditor and became one of the four Inspectors of Audit.

Carson Roberts was appointed Technical Advisor to the Ministry of Health on audit and local government finance in 1919. He retired in 1928 and died in 1942.

These seem to be the only personal details known of Carson Roberts today but perhaps much can be deduced from his many achievements.

The Society's minutes of 1925 record 'his courage' in persevering all the way to the House of Lords in the Poplar case and this was certainly true. His surcharge had been reversed in the Divisional Court and the Court of Appeal and he had been told by the Ministry of Health, who, under the arrangements prior to the Local Government Act 1933, had to approve the incurring of costs by a district auditor before they could be charged on a local authority's funds, that they would find difficulty in giving him his costs if he went to the House of Lords. He replied to the effect that they should wait until they were asked.

He went to the Lords and won, and costs followed the event. He took a very considerable risk as there was, at that time, a convention that Government departments, if they lost in the Court of Appeal did not go to the Lords. But that was Carson Roberts – brilliant, courageous and sometimes quite intolerable.

As Technical Advisor to the Ministry of Health he was influential in the preparation of the Accounting Orders and Regulations of the time, a writer of textbooks and also prolific in ideas on accounting principles, loans pools, operational audit standards and principles of audit law. From all this, one can deduce not only a very busy and distinguished district auditor but also an innovator with both courage and perseverance. From his writings, one gets the impression of a sharp and perceptive intellect combined with a realistic understanding of the problems of lesser mortals, but whether his tolerance matched his brilliance only his

contemporaries could say. His long-lasting
achievements suggest a man of vision who would not be
out of place today.

B H GILHAM

Joined district audit in 1939 and returned in
1946 after service overseas in the RAF. Had
two spells as a training officer at Audit HQ,
one in 1956 and another 20 years later; also
engaged on quality control inspections.
Retired as DDA at Bristol in 1981.

The Defalcations of Jesse Varley

R U Davies

The following account is based on the published report of Sir Harry E Haward (Comptroller of the London County Council) who was commissioned by the President of the Local Government Board in August 1917 to investigate the affair and on a memorandum sent to district auditors by the Local Government Board in July 1918.

In mid-January 1917, the Chief Clerk of the Education Accounts Department of Wolverhampton Borough Council fell in front of a train at Wednesbury Station and was killed. This tragic event, possibly suicide, tormented a young junior assistant in the Department for several weeks, until finally he had to confide in a friend of the family, a clergyman. After hearing his confidences, the reverend gentleman, who was also a member of the Education Committee, immediately took the unhappy young man to see the Town Clerk. As a result, one of the largest frauds in the history of local government, which had lasted for eleven years, was brought to light, and on 19 February 1917, Jesse Varley, Accountant Clerk to the Local Education Authority of Wolverhampton, was under arrest on charges of larceny, falsification of accounts and forgery.

In order to keep his manipulations secret during the years in which he carried on his fraudulent activities,

8/1 ". . . and kept three motor cars".

Varley would only allow himself or his Chief Clerk, who met his end so tragically and who was in collusion with him, to attend upon the district auditor. He gave strict instructions to all his staff to keep away from the audit room, and to refer any audit requests or queries to him. Varley remained each night in the audit room until the auditors had gone and locked the door, taking the key home with him. The caretaker even had to apply to him for the key next morning, before a fire could be lit.

One year, the district auditor applied for the use of an office boy to perform menial and routine tasks. Varley sent along his newest recruit, the young junior assistant. Among the tasks set him by the district auditor was to call out all the salary receipts for the year. As the years went by, the young man became increasingly suspicious about the genuineness of some of the bundles of receipts. The sudden and questionable death of the Chief Accountant finally propelled him to voice his suspicions and seek advice.

Over a period of eleven years, from 1905–1906 to February 1917, Varley defrauded the Borough Council of £84,335.4s.7d. This was an enormous sum for those days. Varley's salary at the time of his arrest was £325 per annum – a good salary, for he was getting £50 a year more than his nominal chief, the Secretary to the Education Committee.

In the first year, 1905–1906, his misappropriations totalled £2,530 and increased year by year, with a break in 1908–1909 when none was misappropriated, until in each of the last two complete years he defrauded the Council of over £14,000. This was the equivalent in each of those years of a rate increase of 8.5p in the pound, or an addition of 17 per cent to the expenditure on education.

Apart from the amount and the long period over which the fraud extended, the other remarkable feature is the ingenious and daring manner in which the fraud was perpetrated.

The sums misappropriated by Varley were derived from monies drawn from time to time ostensibly to pay teachers' salaries and various scholarship grants.

The manner pursued by Varley, stated shortly, was to obtain, by inflating the monthly requisitions for the teachers' salaries, possession of larger sums of cash than were required for the payment of such salaries. He appropriated for his own use the excess, and accounted to the district auditor for the money so embezzled by means of false entries in the salaries books, supported by false printed minutes purporting to authorise the payments to individual teachers and others, and by the production of forged receipts for such payments.

Each month, Varley requisitioned from the Borough Accountant a cheque for the total salaries, etc. for the month which he cashed, and he and his Chief Clerk made up the individual pay package for each teacher in accordance with the Salaries Book. Payment was made to each teacher upon presentation of receipts for sums due. These receipts were prepared by Varley from the Salaries Book kept by him, and were sent to the head teachers of the schools, who after appending their certificates as to the amounts being properly payable, handed the receipts to the teachers for presentation at the Town Hall.

As the cheques for the cash advances for the payment of salaries were drawn in the name of the Borough Accountant, it was necessary for Varley to keep a spurious Salaries Cash Book. This was debited month by month with the amount of the cheques received, and credited with amounts which purported to have been paid. This was submitted month by month to the Borough Accountant, who ticked and initialled the *debits*. This spurious book was kept under lock and key by Varley, and only discovered after his arrest.

Apart from the spurious Cash Book, no false entries whatever were made until the close of the financial year. The Salaries Book contained nothing but genuine matter throughout the whole of the year. Thus, if at any time the Borough Accountant had extracted the payments from the Salaries Book and compared them with the figures in the Salaries Cash Book which was submitted to him monthly, the fraud would have presumably been discovered.

At the end of the financial year, the names of the teaching staff were copied into a new Salaries Book for the new financial year, and the old one was then appropriated by Varley and his Chief Clerk in order to prepare the final accounts. It was never possible to obtain the old Salaries Book again until after audit.

The Salaries Books generally contained about 80 folios, and of these between 50 and 60 were used. So, to cover up his misappropriations during the year and be ready for the annual audit, Varley would turn to the first blank page, and would proceed to enter fictitious payments of salary to visiting teachers at the School of Art and Technical School and to other supply and reserve teachers. He would also insert maintenance allowances for all scholarship holders, although, in fact, Wolverhampton Education Committee was not in the habit of granting such allowances. Nevertheless, all the entries had a ring of truth about them. All the teachers

whose names were falsely used were part-time or peripatetic, and all the names of the scholarship holders were genuine.

Having entered fictitious payments sufficient to cover his embezzlements, Varley had to be able to produce authorising committee resolutions and signed receipts.

Each month three copies of the printed minutes of the Education Committee were certified by the Chairman and Secretary, and at the end of the year a complete set was bound into one volume and formed the official record. A few days before the commencement of each annual audit, Varley applied to the Secretary for the official volume. He then broke the binding, extracted various pages, and inserted others authorising the employment of his spurious teachers. The false printed matter was introduced in such a manner as not to interfere with the consecutive numbering of the pages. Varley then sent the broken volume to the Council's printers with an order for its rebinding, and had it returned to him ready for handing to the district auditor.

The preparation of false receipts was a comparatively simple operation. Varley himself forged the signature of the supposed recipients on each spurious receipt, and used facsimile signature stamps, of which he had quite a collection, to complete the confirmatory certificates of the Heads of the Technical School and School of Art, and of the Secretary of the Education Committee as appropriate. Each salary receipt had to bear the signature of the Head of School to a certificate already printed on it reading 'I hereby certify that the person named herein is entitled to salary for the period stated . . .'.

Varley was now able to provide the auditor with seemingly genuine entries in the Salaries Books, and receipts and minutes supporting all the spurious payments.

On the completion of the audit, the bound volume of minutes was again broken, the false minutes extracted, the original printed pages replaced, and the book rebound and returned to the Secretary of the Education Committee.

Similarly, the binding of the Salaries Book was broken, the pages on which the false entries had been made were extracted, and blank pages which were printed when the book was ordered were inserted in their place and the book rebound. Varley took care to remove the bundles of false receipts from the audit room himself immediately the audit was over, and locked them away in his private office. These, with the other false evidence, the spurious salary sheets and minutes, he regularly destroyed after the completion of each subsequent year's audit.

Varley had to keep the spurious salary sheets for a full year so that he was prepared to meet the possible request from the auditor for the previous Salaries Book in order to check forward the names and annual salaries. For example, there were records of the 1916 Salaries Book having been rebound after taking out false entries and replacing the blank sheets after the 1916 audit, then rebound again after taking out blank sheets and replacing false entries prior to the 1917 audit, and finally rebound once more after removing the false sheets and replacing the blank sheets after the completion of the 1917 audit.

It seems curious that the Council's printers never once in all the 11 years queried any of the requests to bind and rebind the various salaries books and volumes of minutes. The Council's printers were, however, not bookbinders, and accordingly any bookbinding orders were sent away to a sub-contractor. The firm stated to the inquiry that, on receiving a book-binding order, the parcel was frequently not even unpacked, and moreover, they had an official order signed by the Chief Officer of the Department.

These were the days when local authorities customarily sent out, attached to each official order form, a proforma invoice for the tradesmen or suppliers to return. Varley always took great care that the orders and proforma invoices for the rebinding of salaries books and minutes referred only to 'rebinding books' or 'rebinding volumes of reports'.

The scale of Varley's defalcations relative to the Education Committee's total expenditure meant that he had to manipulate the figures in the Committee's estimates and annual accounts in order to conceal his operations.

Varley each year inflated the estimates of the expenditure as far as he dared, and in order to keep the rate levy within acceptable bounds also inflated the expected income. At budget time, the yearly approximate/actual figures which he reported to committee bore no relation to fact, or, of course, to the much higher figures which appeared in the actual accounts presented for audit. It appears that no one ever compared the final accounts figures for any year with the estimates or the reported approximate/actual figures for that year.

It was the Committee's continuing policy to maintain a working balance of £10,000 on the Education account, and the annual estimates approved by Committee each year so provided; but Varley's increasing greed quickly exhausted this balance and in the last five years of his defalcations, the Education Committee's bank account became increasingly overdrawn, until at 31 March 1917 the account was £20,160 in the red.

The Borough Accountant and the Education Committee could not, of course, fail to note the overdrawn balances on the Committee's monthly bank statements; but the principle explanation offered by Varley for the overdraft and its increases were delays in the payments of government grants. This explanation was supported by paragraphs in the district auditor's Statutory Report for 1914–1915: 'the elementary education account was overdrawn to the extent of £5,543.12s.1d, due, I found to the non-receipts of certain grants during the period of the financial year'. The auditor's report, however, was based on information derived from the same tainted source as the Committee's, and not on his own investigation, for the grants outstanding on 31 March 1915 were only £557.0s.0d.

Varley also used the device of spurious outstanding balances of government grants in order to square up the annual balance sheets. The figure of outstanding government grants counterbalanced the large decreases in the cash balances, with the result that the annual balance sheet showed that the surplus of assets over liabilities remained about the same, thus giving the impression that the financial position, notwithstanding the overdraft, was satisfactory – that the accounts continued to show a working balance of £10,000.

Oddly, no charge for interest on the overdrawn bank balances ever appeared in the Education Accounts. These charges were debited to the General Rate Fund (not subject to district audit). Varley had persuaded the Borough Accountant that 'such interest could not be legally paid out of the Education rate, and that if it had been paid the auditor would have surcharged'.

For many years, Varley lived in a style altogether beyond that which could have been supported on his salary. He and his wife and family of five lived in a large house with 13 acres of grounds, and kept three motorcars. He let it be known that his wife was possessed of money. It is reported that Varley had the effrontery to remark on numerous occasions that he was losing money by continuing in office.

Varley was tried in July 1917 at Stafford Assizes where he pleaded guilty to the charges proffered against him and was sentenced to five years' penal servitude. At the same time a receiving order was made against him, and he was adjudicated bankrupt. At the public examination, his statement of affairs, without admitting any liability to the Council, showed a surplus of £19,516.11s.5d. The Council submitted proof of a claim for £72,740.0s.0d. Varley was also covered under the Council's fidelity guarantee policy for £1,000.

Varley succeeded in his defalcations for such a long period of time because he was not subject to any supervision or check by the Borough Accountant or by the Secretary to the Education Committee, and was allowed to establish complete personal control over all the accountancy and financial work in the Education Department, including the cashing of cheques for the payment of salaries. Varley was a dominant character.

He prepared all the financial reports and advice to the Education Committee, even the annual estimates and accounts, and would brook no interference in these matters, or allow any advice to be offered to the Committee other than through himself. Although he signed jointly with Varley the Education Committee's annual estimates and accounts, the Borough Accountant admitted that he and his department took no hand in their preparation, or responsibility for them.

The district auditor failed to ascertain that there was in fact no check or supervision exercised by the Education Committee or the Borough Accountant over Varley. Even worse, the district auditor unwittingly allowed himself to be caged in by Varley. Varley or his deputy was continually in attendance in the audit room, always ready and willing to find the answers to any and all queries raised. The auditor failed to act independently, to search out facts for himself, or to seek corroborative evidence. Things were taken at their face value, and explanations provided by Varley accepted without question.

The fraud shocked the District Audit Service. It was notorious in its day, in the same way as the Grays Building Society fraud which came to light in 1978. In that case, the Secretary of the Building Society stole in excess of £2 million from the Society's funds over a period of 40 years. There is a marked similarity between the two cases. Both succeeded because of the same sort of failings – lack of supervision, no separation of duties, weak internal check, and an auditor who failed to carry out his duties in a fully independent manner.

The report of the inspectors appointed by the Chief Registrar of Friendly Societies on the Grays Building

8/2 The Express and Star Wolverhampton, 1924, reporting Varley's crimes.

Society fraud sums up these matters in a telling manner:

For biographical note on author see page 51

"Mr Jaggard (the Chairman and Secretary of the Society) managed to dominate the scene at Grays. It is that very dominance which provided the foundations for his fraud. It is a striking aspect of business at the Grays that the staff never discussed their work with the directors; and the auditors never talked business with the directors or the staff. All communications ran through Mr Jaggard who was thus able to prevent the directors and auditors from discovering what was afoot and the staff from recognising the evidence that lay before their untutored eyes."

Memories of the Period 1917–1939

A W Vale OBE

I have no doubt that until the outbreak of the first Great War district audit was a very agreeable occupation which did not interfere too much with one's private life; but I have no experience of those days. When I joined the service they had come to an end under the pressures of war. Nevertheless, that is the impression I received.

In fact, those very pressures brought about my accession to the staff. The local district auditor, H F Buckland, had in the summer of 1917 lost all his staff. He asked the headmaster of my old school, Brentwood School (Essex), if any senior boys would give him a month or two before call-up, until other help arrived. Two of us did so, in the same spirit as students nowadays take up holiday employment. They were H E Stevens, who died a few years ago as district auditor in Chester, and myself.

I suppose until our arrival the DA had thought that war time conditions were difficult; thereafter he knew that war was hell. We expected in those bloody days to be dead or maimed within six months of call-up, and saw no reason why audit problems should cloud our brief lives. With surprise and interest, therefore, but with no sense of personal responsibility, we watched the DA

deteriorate into a glum, taciturn man, chainsmoking to keep his nerves under control. I will only add that time has revenged him, and I have since realised on more than one occasion exactly how he felt.

I have referred to the local district auditor. There were three grades of auditor in those days – metropolitan, county, who took only county council and related audits, and others who were each in charge of something like the present SADA's area.
There was one Inspector of Audit, a Mr Burd. I never met him. It would be misleading to say that we did not know what he did, for it never occurred to us that one so august that he might be presumed to commune direct with the deity would do anything – in such a case just being seemed enough.

Assistant district auditors and district auditors in those days held patronage appointments. Their offices were in the personal gift of the President of the Local Government Board. Selected applicants worked for six months as volunteers, that is to say for expenses only, and if favourably reported upon were appointed at the end of that period – not, as nowadays, by the issue of a few cyclostyled papers, but in most seemly fashion, by appearing before the President in top hat and frockcoat, and shaking hands as a token of commission.

What passed on these occasions is naturally not recorded, but it is reasonable to suppose that the President would seek to send his auditor forth with some few kindly words of encouragement and advice; and this is confirmed by the story that John Burns, when President, dismissed an appointee with the words 'My advice to you is to keep an eye on the workhouse master who wears spats.' I am glad to be able to pass on this tip.

The original selection of candidates seems to have been somewhat a matter of chance. Ernest Hicks, one of my early DAs, told me he was yachting with an assistant secretary when the latter suddenly asked him if he would like to be an auditor. He said 'yes' and in due course so he was.

The rank and file of the audit staff were appointed by DAs subject to the concurrence of the Department. The man of power here was an officer of the Department – a personality of no title but great influence and honoured name – a Mr A C Hobbs. He it was who ran a sort of employment bureau for the benefit of DAs and their staffs, arranging appointments and transfers. Of course, this ended in 1922 when the auditors' staffs became established civil servants.

Although rates of pay for staff were fixed by the Department, salaries were paid monthly by the DA, who had a cash account on an imprest basis from which he also paid his own and the staff's travelling and subsistence expenses. I well remember that the day allowance for the staff was 3/6, a magnificent sum out of all proportion to our salaries. Yet there were older members of the staff, on earlier scales, who could claim no less than 10/-. You must remember that in the provinces one could get excellent lodgings – bedroom, sitting room and full board – for £2.2s.0d a week, and landladies were eager to have their names on the audit lists.

This was one of the charms of the Eastern Counties Audit District to which I moved after the end of the war. The centre was London, but all the work lay in the county towns of the home counties. Consequently, one lived happily on the subsistence allowances which one drew every day of the year, and only spendthrifts touched their salaries except for luxuries. The abolition of these districts in 1921 seemed at the time a most ill-advised step.

Life on the county audits was far removed from the hustle and bustle of the parish audits which filled half the programme of the other districts. The county audit caravan moved in stately fashion from town to town, like a medieval judge on assize. True, the trumpeters were not called out to herald our appearance, but at some audits – the Isle of Ely was one – one or two constables were posted at the door of the audit room. I never really knew why; not to keep out mobs or suppress riots, still less to control objectors. Presumably it was to mark the importance of the auditor and his proceedings, and if so it seems very proper. Sometimes, out of pity for the boredom of these poor fellows, we gave them some vouchers to stamp.

The close of the audit brought me, as a junior, special responsibilities, for I had to marshall a procession of county-hall caretakers with trucks and barrows, supervise the loading of trunks of law books and bags of files and papers, and oversee their progress to the station and the despatch of the luggage to the next audit. At this sight, the citizens knew that the audit was as good as over for another year. Only the audit report – which in those days could run to some length – remained to be received.

I will digress a little to say that in my early days there was no unseemly rushing from audit to audit. If the work ran out on a Thursday night we adjourned, more often than not, to the following Monday. This reluctance to start a new audit on a Friday may have been due to superstition, but I like to think it is attributable to a courteous reluctance to embarrass the next authority by a too early arrival.

I must refer here with regard and admiration to my ADA of those days, Clement Gibson and with gratitude

too, for I learnt much from him. I was his clerk and we were described as peripatetic. Perhaps as a solatium for this, and certainly for being liable to be moved about the country wherever help was needed, we received special allowances. Having heard that, you will not be surprised to hear that after a few years these appointments were abolished. Seriously, however, I have always regarded this as a mistake. A small number of good and keen ADAs each with a good clerk, available to bring instant aid to hard-pressed DAs in times of special stress, gave much strength to the audit service, but, more than this, it gave these selected men invaluable experience of persons, places, situations and methods. I have always hoped that the practice would be resumed.

I have mentioned the preoccupation of the DAs of non-

9/1 A 1920's Lagonda.

9/2 "Keep an eye on the workhouse master who wears spats".

county districts with parish audits. Apart from a sprinkling of boroughs and urban districts and the odd county borough, their time was spent in half-yearly audits of the accounts of boards of guardians and overseers, and yearly audits of rural district councils and parish councils.

The overseers, you will remember, were appointed compulsorily to oversee the collection of rates. This they did usually by appointing a paid assistant overseer – some of these worthies still survive as clerks to parish councils – after which they returned to their private affairs with a sense of duty done, until a notice of audit reminded them that the day of judgement had arrived.

Obviously the opportunities for error and fraud in these circumstances were considerable, and though individual amounts of rates, or items of expenditure, might be small by our standards, the possibility of large losses in the aggregate was great. Internal checking was generally non-existent, and the audit staff working rapidly through a large number of small accounts had to be expert and vigilant not to miss anything. There was a standard time allowance of 20 minutes a rate, on which the day's schedule for the run of parishes was based. Any considerable hold-up that was not dealt with in masterly fashion could result in chaos, and a room seething with a growing crowd of disgruntled overseers and their assistants.

Although overseers' audits were a busy time, like the parish council audits we know today, they were of interest because of the different types of country folk one met. Most of my contemporaries had a favourite story of some incident at this type of audit. Mine concerns O E Brigden, who while vouching a receipt and payment account turned to the assistant overseer and said 'What are all these faggots – firewood?' 'No sir' said the man, 'Them's fergots' – the balancing entry, in fact.

One unfortunate result of the frequent handling of these small accounts, I think, was the temptation to exact too high a degree of precision, and a consequent tendency to take formal action in petty cases which is still sometimes used as a reproach to us. But let us recognise, before we feel too superior to these ancients, that they did their duty as they saw it, without fear or favour, and with no regard to expediency; and that they were men of their times, not of ours. Our times are different, but their good qualities are still in demand.

This somewhat rigid attitude was in step with that of the Local Government Board who probably inherited it from the Poor Law Board. It must be remembered that the earlier history of local government was not calculated to inspire confidence in the honest handling of public funds. However this may be, boards of guardians were held in a firm grip by pincers consisting of the poor law inspectors on the one hand and the district auditors on the other – somewhat as (in milder form) is now the case with the police. Everything and everybody was subject to detailed report to the Department – our Saturday mornings were spent in completing numerous forms setting out the condition of each of the many prescribed books kept by each officer of the guardians. (At this time many DAs provided an office at their homes for which they received an allowance.)

Of course, this control was more apparent than real, for there were serious defects in some of the prescribed systems. It would be tedious to review these now, but it is not surprising that frequent and considerable frauds occurred in this field until the guardians were abolished.

Once the hurly-burly of the parishes was done, the poorlaw audits, at any rate outside the densely populated areas, were not unpleasant in the absence of widespread unemployment and heavy out-relief; and as one would expect from the close regulation of the guardians' affairs the accounts were somewhat stereotyped. As an example, the ledger of the large West Bromwich Union to the end was built up from a stock of loose sheets with the narrations printed in.

The number of audits held at residential institutions in remote places made the audit lunch something more than a casual snack. Mental hospitals – we called them asylums then – generally put up a very liberal meal from their own farm produce, often with a quart jug of milk to make good any nutritional deficiencies; but workhouse meals could also have their features. When I was in Bedford I had an anxious time each spring. It was vital to stave off the DA's demands for a draft programme until the weekly reports on the asparagus crop at Ampthill enabled a date to be fixed which would give the fullest satisfaction.

One of the happiest features of audit life has always been the co-operation of different grades of staff in small working groups. In fact, I regard this close contact as responsible not only for the high efficiency of audit sections, but also for their freedom from disciplinary and other establishment difficulties. These communal audit lunches fostered this relationship. No doubt it was inevitable that, from time to time, a junior member of staff would become overpresumptuous and take liberties; but the only serious example I can call to mind was one which was traditional in the South Essex district. There the DA and his clerk, speeding from the station to the Orsett workhouse in a horse-drawn cab, were overturned on a corner into a pond. Only the clerk

survived. It was widely believed that he had kept his head above water by standing on his chief.

In my early days, train and cab were the usual modes of transport, and there was a degree of staying away which would send present-day wives marching on the Audit Commission. Buses outside the towns were few and unreliable, and in large towns, of course, the tram reigned. A number of DAs rode to audit on horseback, but not always to the joy of their clerks. An ADA told me how fervently he used to pray for fine weather when he was an audit clerk. He himself always cycled to audit; the DA rode his horse. However, if it turned wet, the clerk cycled home again in the rain – but this time leading the DA's horse, while the owner returned by train.

The first man I worked with who used a car for audit travel was O E Brigden. It was my good fortune to have several spells of service with him, and I cannot fail to declare my indebtedness to a man who was an outstanding auditor with a profound comprehension of accountancy in all its aspects, and of income tax in particular. I first worked with him at the time when I was preparing to take my ADA's examination. There was no official tuition, still less time off for study, but the apprenticeship system, which I have already praised, more than made up for this.

Among the pioneer audit motorists, I particularly recall Mackenzie with his passion for open Lagondas, and a surprising trip from Chester to London with Goddard. The journey took 24 hours, and nearly everything vital dropped off and had to be replaced, after long walks by one village blacksmith after another.

Train journeys are not usually very eventful but one

which I made from Ledbury to Birmingham was so educational that I will tell you about it. Three of us had had a long week on a fraud. At the last minute on Friday we ran to the station and tumbled into the train gasping. Then the quick-witted man among us saw a parcel left on the rack. He was just in time to hand it to a porter as we moved off. We sat back with a warm glow of satisfaction; about then, the man who owned the parcel came back along the corridor. Such incidents give full practice to the tact and diplomacy we so much prize.

As I have said, 1921 was the end of an epoch which I suppose had continued without much alteration since the district auditors had become civil servants in 1868. The Inspector of Audit was Sutherland Wilkinson, but there had arrived a Technical Adviser on Audit Matters – Carson Roberts, who was also a Metropolitan Auditor. (There were then two other metropolitan auditors, with 13 senior auditors and 37 other auditors.)

In 1923 four Inspectors of Audit were appointed, and Mr Wilkinson became Chief Inspector. The original and only holders of the title of Inspector of Audit (until it was revived in the 1970s) were E S Mills, John Orchard, Nugent Simner and Douglas Roberts. The distinguishing mark of the Inspectorate was an eye-glass on a cord, and I can assure you that in those days the high table at our meetings presented a glittering spectacle.

The year 1924 saw great changes in the staff. A Deputy Chief Inspector was appointed, the number of DAs was reduced to 18, there were 23 senior ADAs and, in a blood transfusion from the Department, 29 junior ADAs were appointed. The list of these contains many

distinguished names – Beal, Bridgwater, E F Davies, Goddard, Higlett, Hurle-Hobbs, C A Hughes, Maginn, Parmiter, Russell, H L Stevens, E Thomas, G Thompson, E M Tuke and Alan Wilson.

The year 1927 was remarkable for an historic event, namely the appointment of the first woman to the Audit Service, Miss Warren. In 1932 three of the Inspectors were reabsorbed into the body of the DAs and the survivor disappeared in the following year; but although they vanished, the Inspectors, like the Cheshire Cat, left a souvenir behind them in the shape of the word 'Chief' in the Chief Inspector's title. Another experiment was made in 1933 with the appointment of 24 Audit Officers and the next year saw the rank of JADA grade II introduced.

Post-war events had a profound effect on our duties. The removal from local government of the gas, electricity and hospital services took away much of interest in audit work. Hospitals were particularly prone to

9/3 Southall Gasworks, August 1931.

mismanagement and rewarded careful auditing. I have always regarded our exclusion from the hospitals as a regrettable adherence to constitutional principles. On the other hand, the abolition of public assistance or, at any rate, the outdoor relief side of it was, to my mind, a release from a great burden of unprofitable work.

I have referred to the appointment of Carson Roberts as technical advisor to the department and this was part of the fresh thinking about local government which followed the first war. In 1919, with *Audit Law and Audit Work*, Carson Roberts had laid the foundation for organised training of ADAs and, less obtrusively, provided DAs themselves with some basic thoughts on their functions. His second volume of the same year, *Accounts of Local Authorities*, stimulated and at the same time gave evidence of new interest in this subject. To

my mind, however, the event which really brought home to the working local government accountant the need for change, was the requirement of the Housing Accounts Order of 1920 that housing accounts should be kept on income and expenditure lines. Until that time, all but the largest authorities had kept their accounts on receipt and payment principles.

Carson Roberts followed up the attack with the reformation by regulation of rating accounts after the 1925 Act, and again with his book *Local Administration: Finance and Accounts*. In short, he was the herald of a new view of local government accountancy; and I assert that district audit has played an honourable, yet largely unrecognised, part in making the accounting systems of local authorities equal to their obligations.

A W VALE, OBE

Joined as a junior clerk in 1917 and returned after active service in World War I. In 1953 he was appointed District Auditor for the Kent and Sussex authorities. Retired in 1965, but continued to work part-time as an audit examiner at the GLC audit until he was 77 years old.

Foundations of the Modern Service (1918–1945)

E J Burdon

In 1918, the District Audit Service consisted of one Inspector of Audit, E P Burd (salary £900–£1,000), and 49 district auditors, of whom two were metropolitan (£750–£850), five were described as 'county council districts' (£700–£850) and 42 as 'provincial' (£500–£850). There were also 22 assistant auditors (£300–£450).

The appointment of district auditors and, it would appear, of assistant auditors was the personal prerogative of the President of the Local Government Board in office when a vacancy occurred. The assistant auditor grade was, apparently, a probationary grade from which promotion to district auditor was almost automatic.

Two years later, in 1920, the Inspector of Audits was W S Wilkinson, and there were 57 district auditors – three metropolitan, six for county council districts and 48 'provincial', with 24 assistant auditors, including C R H Hurle-Hobbs who was, it is believed, the last of the 'patronage' appointments. Although the officers discussed were listed as part of the establishment of the Local Government Board, they were not civil servants, though paid from central funds, but when the Ministry of Health was created by a statute of 1919, they were

brought under its aegis.

Nowadays, the idea of appointment of such officers by patronage would be rejected, but it sustained the district audit service for three-quarters of a century and produced a body of incorruptible, effective, and fiercely independent auditors. Selection of candidates for appointment must have been carried out with discernment. They seem generally to have been men of some substance – in Victorian or Edwardian terms, minor gentry. In 1900, for example, the list of district auditors shows a baronet, Sir R D Green-Price, and the Inspector of Audits was Hugh Lloyd Roberts, one of a dynasty which left an indelible mark on the service. The auditors came of a class which would ordinarily have private means, personal connections, or professional standing sufficient to ensure emphatic resignation if any attempt at improper pressure occurred. This was, no doubt, true of many senior Crown servants before the First World War and for a while after it.

The function of the Inspector of Audits was to ensure that efficiency was maintained, that law was applied consistently in all areas – though here the meetings of the Society of District Auditors, founded in 1846 and

10/1 Group picture c. 1920.

the oldest association of auditors in the world, must have been influential – and to provide discreet liaison with the central departments.

The Inspectorship can have been no sinecure. How seriously the auditors took their independence and indeed their position can be judged from the fact that when the new Audit Service was set up as part of the Ministry of Health in the early 1920s, the first Chief Inspector of Audit was W Sutherland Wilkinson, the existing Inspector, and not the obvious candidate, the brilliant and forceful A Carson Roberts. In 1920, the latter was shown as Metropolitan District Auditor and Technical Adviser to the Ministry on audit matters at a higher salary rate than the Inspector of Audit; he had already done much to bring local authority finance and accounting into the 20th century. But the district auditors of the day submitted a memorandum to the Permanent Secretary of the Local Government Board to say that they were not prepared to work under Carson Roberts and W S Wilkinson became the first Chief Inspector.

It is, of course, possible that other factors operated. In 1925, Carson Roberts took the Poplar case to the House of Lords after losing in the Divisional Court and Court of Appeal. It is known that he did so against the wishes of the Department, which went so far as to threaten to refuse him a certificate for costs; though, as he won, the matter was academic. Just possibly, it had occurred to the Department that he might have proved an embarrassingly strong colleague as Chief Inspector of Audit.

It will be clear enough from this incident that the district auditors were intractable material for incorporation into the machinery of the newly created Ministry. Indeed there is known to have been some dissension between the auditors and the Department about the mode of recruitment of future members of the directing grades. That battle the auditors lost; the Ministry of Health circulated to all departments a letter inviting suitable candidates, not necessarily professionally qualified, to apply for appointment as assistant district auditors, and in about 1924 the service was radically reorganised.

It is important to realise that local government up to this point was very different from what we have seen since 1930. There were far more local authorities, most of them much smaller than those within the experience of staff now serving – within the writer's service, Scammonden (population 297) and Shap (population 304) were still urban district councils, and many others were not much larger. This meant that most of them could not afford properly qualified full-time staff. Moreover, the authorities had far fewer powers, and Whitehall was far less active in local government matters. Consequently, the district auditor was the only contact with central government which most of them ever had. He appeared as predictably as Halley's Comet, but more often and much more alarmingly. If he felt that he was an officer of some importance, few at that time would have disagreed with him; and the possibility of appeal to the High Court against his decisions prevented him from seriously abusing his position.

Of course, the district auditors of the day had their faults – without citing examples, those of us who worked in our early days with the last of them, and have talked to staff transferred from the old organisation, know well that they could be holy terrors. But they built a tradition, and built it well.

After the assimilation of the audit service into the Ministry of Health, the number of district auditors was much reduced. England and Wales were divided into six areas, each under an Inspector of Audit, and each subdivided into four districts, except the metropolitan area which had three, one for poor law accounts, one for the London County Council, and one for the metropolitan boroughs. In each area, the Inspector was also a district auditor for one of his districts, except in the southeastern area, where W Sutherland Wilkinson, now appointed to the new post of Chief Inspector of Audit, was a district auditor with N M Griffiths – later to become Deputy Chief Inspector – as Inspector for the area.

There were, in 1925, 22 audit districts in the six areas, including the metropolitan and 16 district auditors from the old organisation now acting as senior assistant district auditors, retaining however the title of district auditor until either promoted or retired. Assistant auditors from the old organisation became either senior or junior assistant district auditors. Appointments under the new arrangements had brought up the number of junior assistants to 39, and there were 26 senior assistants.

10/2 Doncaster 1925.

Personal employees of the old district auditors who had come over into the new Service entered in the clerical officer grade, to which many ex-servicemen were also appointed, and after the institution in 1927 of open examinations for the general clerical officer grade, recruits in their late teens also came on to the staff in this grade.

Clerical officers of experience became higher clerical officers, and were given supervisory duties. In 1931 they were converted into audit officers with the same maximum salary – £500 per annum – as junior assistant district auditors, and we find 24 of them in the Audit Service. They were given powers of allowance of accounts, but when the Local Government Act 1933 came into force in 1934, it ceased to be possible for allowance to be delegated to other than district auditors or assistant district auditors. The audit officers were therefore converted to junior assistant district auditors, grade II.

Also soon after 1930, recruitment to the audit staff began from the open executive examination. It was possible to offer salaries and prospects better than in most departments, so that the cream of the pass list came to district audit. These entrants were appointed as audit assistants, who underwent approximately three years' training before sitting an examination which qualified them for appointment as junior assistant district auditors grade I after the institution of the grade II post. This examination was set and marked by a panel of three district auditors, and included high marks for satisfactory performance at an oral session which was much feared by most candidates, since there were almost no limits recognised by the panel on the questions asked.

Surrey and part of West Sussex came to be used as a training area, which was staffed almost entirely by audit assistants under one senior and one junior assistant district auditor. Selected clerical officers from audit sections up and down the country were also promoted to audit assistant and transferred thither for training and preparation for the examination.

In 1936–1937, Sutherland Wilkinson retired from the Chief Inspectorship and Clement W O Gibson succeeded to the office. He envisaged a district audit staff of which every member, save clerical officers, would be qualified or in training, but in which the time between qualification and promotion to assistant district auditor would be a good deal longer than had heretofore been the practice.

However, war broke out in 1939; the training area was wound up; and no more audit assistants were appointed, though those with two or three years training were allowed a final chance in December 1939 to sit the examination. Three of 14 candidates passed.

Soon afterwards, most of the younger trainees went into the forces or other war work, and the audit staff became heavily involved in the verification of local authority claims for grant on expenditure on emergency services – civil defence, auxiliary fire service, evacuation of civil population, war damage, and many others.

Nevertheless, essential audit work on normal services was continued throughout the war. But the emergency workload was considerable, and its effect might have been a serious reduction of the independence from central control of the district auditors, had not Clement Gibson stoutly resisted such encroachment.

10/3 County Hall Warwick, 1926.

Indeed, at the very end of his career as Chief Inspector, when comments made to the Public Accounts Committee deprecating the value of district audit work on the emergency services claims during the war led to a resolution of criticism, he submitted a memorandum setting out the achievements of the Service in that field which led to formal withdrawal of the criticisms. It also led to the elevation of the Chief Inspectorship to Undersecretarial status, enabling appearance in person before the Public Accounts Committee and raising the Chief Inspector from 19th to 6th in the hierarchy of the Ministry of Health. This gave future incumbents of the office much enhanced influence in the councils of the Department.

The audit service is again where it ought to be – outside the civil service, but still in the service of the Crown and of the law. The modern district auditor, though much less an autonomous legal tribunal than the giants of the past, still exercises judicial powers and must therefore be guaranteed independence. The Audit Commission has the necessary powers and long may it exercise them.

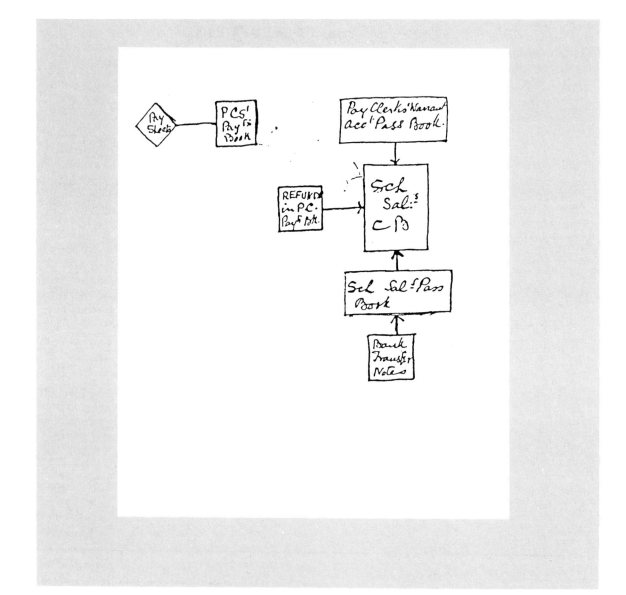

10/4 1920's flow chart.

Audit in the 1930s

Tom Peel

When I joined the District Audit Service in 1936, the staff, apart from directing officers, was predominantly composed of clerical officers of the general clerical class of the civil service. Even higher clerical officers were few and far between and numbered only two or three per district. The normal avenue of recruitment at that time was from the Civil Service Commission's annual clerical examination, but many of the existing staff had been taken on following the First World War after a period of non-established service. There were a few entrants each year from the Civil Service Commission's annual executive examination, but they became audit assistants and went directly to the newly formed Surrey School.

Not all the section heads were qualified assistant district auditors. There were a number of junior assistant district auditors (grade II) who had not taken the ADAs, qualifying examination and were not normally eligible for a further promotion. Thus, professionally qualified personnel were very thin on the ground. Despite this, the Service occupied a highly respected position in local government circles, and, thanks to their unique expertise in local government matters, managed to do a pretty effective job.

11/1 The added excitement of a stay away audit.

There was no organised training for new clerical officers, or audit clerks, as they later became known. One avenue for promotion was by way of the Open Executive examination for which existing staff enjoyed a two-year age allowance, though most of us, who joined audit at that time, were absorbed by H M Forces before we were able to take full advantage of that concession and had to await the post-war Reconstruction Examination.

There was another rare avenue of promotion available to the ambitious clerical officer. This was by special selection as a potential 'high-flyer' and being sent to join the Surrey School as an audit assistant. I remember being advised by an ageing ADA (grade II) that I might try 'accidentally' dropping a volume of 'Lumley' on the DA's toe as a method of 'getting noticed'.

For the less adventurous young clerical officer training was a matter of 'picking it up' as one went along in the audit room. At the start it was pretty dull stuff, progressing from 'cast this' or 'compare this with that' to 'doing the wages', 'having a look at the stores' or 'getting in the schools' stock and stores books and inventories'. But the potential boredom of this 'tick and turn' approach was relieved to a considerable extent by the variety afforded by the work, the change of scene, change of authority, change in mode of transport – bus, train, car.

Much more important than audit work was the immediate meticulous training in how to apply for an imprest for expenses, complete our 'diary', and claim the two shillings and sixpence nine-hour day allowance, always paying due regard to the restrictions imposed by the five-mile radius patrolled by the 'audit crow', inside which the allowances were not payable.

Most impressive, however, was the rapid absorption into the audit family – working and travelling together in small close-knit groups, lunching together and partaking in lunchtime games in the local park or in the audit room if wet. Then the added excitement of the first 'stay-away audit' when one actually took one's tennis racket and/or bathing trunks to work (golf clubs came many years later!), booking in at the 'best value for money' guest house. It was especially at these stay-away audits that one came to make the lasting audit friendships which spanned a lifetime.

The bonds within the local families were, however, more tenuous than one supposed. The exigencies of the Service were paramount. Young clerical officers were not then immune from summary uprooting for transplant to another district at a few weeks' notice. I well remember as a callow youth of 19 being dispatched from Preston almost overnight to join E R M Castle's team at Worcester. But once the initial shock of the suddenness of the upheaval and the indignity of being once again partially dependent on financial backing from my father was over, it was comforting to find that the same family spirit prevailed.

One stroke of luck I had at that time was finding myself sharing digs with a Tattersall's Ring bookmaker and being given 'information' prior to the 1939 Ascot July meeting which enabled me to achieve a rapid popularity in Mr Castle's eyes as a gifted picker of winners. He had a keen interest in racing and rewarded me with a free day at a point-to-point meeting.

One soon settled down in the new environment with new friends and new interests. It was probably all good training for the much more traumatic transfer to H M Forces which was soon to follow.

The accounts presented for audit in the thirties were much less sophisticated that those we encountered in the rapidly changing post-war years. Records were almost universally produced by clerks, wielding pen and ink, filling large bound ledgers in neat manuscript; but they nevertheless recorded the efficiency or otherwise of local authorities in providing many of the same services as their present-day counterparts, and some which they no longer tackle such as gas, electricity and water undertakings, the running of hospitals and the administration of the Poor Law. Thus, in some respects, the scope of district audit investigations covered an even wider area than they have since local authorities lost some of their functions.

These areas of activity provided a source of some of the more colourful reminiscences of audit 'old boys' in later years when swapping yarns during late night sessions at annual meetings of the Society. The lavish hospitality of the masters and matrons of the Poor Law Institutions, and particularly of the medical superintendents and senior nursing staff at the mental hospitals, earned an enviable reputation. The modest charges they were persuaded to levy on visiting audit staff, if only for

11/2 1930: Halcyon days – afternoon tea at the workhouse audit.

appearance's sake, made the subsistence allowances achieve heights never imagined by the Treasury officials when they fixed the rates.

It might be suggested by the cynical that the considerable deference afforded to the 'auditors' by 'the audited' was prompted by a wish to temper the zeal with which the former carried out their investigations. I think it owed more to the courtesy and impartiality of the section leaders and the conduct they demanded of their staff. Audit abounded with characters at that time but all had a common quality of integrity which commanded respect.

One district auditor of that period was known to propound in later years a well-reasoned and near convincing pet theory that had she been favoured with the benefits of a district audit system, France would not have fallen in 1940 and history would have been changed. Who knows?

In the absence of readily available computer print-outs of relevant statistics and abnormalities in the accounts, as enjoyed by today's audit staff, information had of necessity to be dug out from sometimes voluminous prime records. The meticulous records kept at residential institutions were models of costing and portion-control, recording detailed weighings-out of portions on a meal-by-meal, day-by-day, week-by-week basis to tie up miraculously with immense manual stock records and balanced to fractions of an ounce.

11/3 Stay away audit, Bognor 1934.

Too miraculous? Well, one must assume an element of working back from the desired result and 'Oliver Twists' must have been conspicuous by their absence. But these painstakingly compiled records had to be maintained and they achieved their objectives of economy and balanced budgets. From an auditor's viewpoint, these records demanded equally painstaking examination and, strangely, there seemed to be time to do it.

There were many more authorities in those days, some of them very small indeed, which could only be spared a small slice of the audit manday cake. Many were too small to allow an adequate separation of duties and internal audit was usually completely absent. Thus, the district auditor was the main, and often the only, safeguard against fraud and corruption. 'Value for money' and 'efficiency' exercises did not figure largely in the audit plan.

It will be appreciated that under the circumstances of the period regularity auditing dominated our audit efforts. The old provisions of disallowance and consequent surcharge did not disappear until the 1972 Act and a virtually impossible duty 'to disallow every item of the account which is contrary to law' was even then revealing itself as an unobtainable dream. Despite the rigidity of the audit provisions of the Local Government Act 1933, the eminently practical district auditors of that era earned a reputation for being fair-minded, and for having a helpful, commonsense approach and a common aim of furthering the honesty and well-being of local government.

Many of the senior directing staff who tackled the post-war problems so ably learned their trade and their understanding, yet firm, approach as clerical officers in those immediate pre-war years.

TOM PEEL

Joined district audit as a Clerical Officer in 1936. Survived 6½ years war service in the Royal Engineers and retired in 1977 as Deputy District Auditor in London. A keen participant in audit cricket and golf.

The Surrey Training School

Arthur Long

My time in the Surrey Training School was limited to the first 21 months of its existence, and before writing about it, it is best for me to offer some background information – both general and personal.

I entered the Civil Service, via an open Clerical Class examination, in August 1929, and was sent to district audit in Doncaster as a clerical officer. My best opportunity for early advancement at that time lay in taking the open Executive Class examination, although there was then no opening on district audit for executive officers and success would have necessitated a transfer.

A change in my prospects occurred in 1931. Up to then, the most senior posts on district audit had been open only to those who secured an appointment as JADA grade I. (There was also a post of JADA grade II, which was essentially a senior clerical grade and has no part in this narrative.) JADAs grade I were recruited in two ways: firstly by appointment from those (mainly, if not exclusively, graduates) who passed the 'Inspector of Taxes' exam, and secondly by promotion from a clerical grade.

Such recruits were given the rank of JADA, and were given responsibilities forthwith. Their retention in the district audit service as JADA grade I was, however, conditional on their passing the 'Qualifying Examination as JADA grade I'. That examination, which henceforth I will refer to as the 'QE', was conducted by the Deputy Chief Inspector of Audit and a panel of two or three district auditors.

The change in 1931 was as follows. Those selected as potential JADAs grade I were no longer to have the title and responsibility of JADA, but were to be called 'audit assistants'. Clerical officers were eligible for promotion to audit assistant. Public open examination entrants were to come from the Executive Class examination, which was taken at age between 18 years 6 months and 19 years 6 months, with an extra two years' grace for serving civil servants. Audit assistants were to work under JADAs or SADAs. They were to be promoted to JADA grade I only if they passed the same QE as already existed, and if, after that, they served a further six months in charge of an audit section to the satisfaction of their district auditor.

In the summer of 1932, helped by a correspondence college, I passed the open Executive Class examination, and was very pleased to be assigned to district audit as an audit assistant. My new centre was to be Cambridge.

I recall now that when I took my leave of my DA in the West Riding he said that the Cambridge section 'needed strengthening' and that he thought this was one reason for my posting there. Throughout my service as a clerical officer I had served, in succession, under three first-class superiors, each of whom had been instrumental in forwarding my education. I soon found on arrival in Cambridge that in this respect my luck had at last run out.

I was told that I would be expected to take the QE in 1935. Literature, presumably similar to that supplied to the old style JADA entrant, arrived from the Chief Inspector's office. This consisted of old examination papers (an examination syllabus was surely provided, though memory of this is now dim), a number of King's Printers' copies of statutes, a heap of departmental circulars and a range of audit instructions, such as the periodical 'Audit Notes' of the time.

The most useful items provided for my use were two books, both written by a former district auditor, Carson Roberts. First there was *Audit Law and Audit Work*, a publication restricted to district audit use, covering audit procedure and audit law reports. Then came his *Local Authority Administration – Finance and Accounts*, a very large book which anyone could buy and which was much appreciated by IMTA students, for example. These two were classics of their kind, and went a long way towards equipping any reader for the QE, which consisted of two papers on 'Accounts and Audit' and two papers on 'Audit Law and Local Government', followed by an interview with the examiners.

Other reading matter came my way. The bulkiest of these was an ancient copy of Glen's *Public Health* (a forerunner of Lumley) for which a friendly clerk to a council had no further use, he having acquired something more up to date.

I picked up a fair amount of knowledge of local government practice, especially on the accounting side, from experience in the council offices where we carried out audits. With the rest of the Cambridge section, I

12/1 At the Surrey Training School 1939.

12/2 Students v Graylingwell Mental Hospital 1936.

went up to London about once a month at the Department's expense to meetings of Clement Gibson's Metropolitan Audit District Students' Society. I studied as best I could, in my own time. And that was just about that.

The shortcomings of these training procedures were raised by the staff association (the District Auditors' Association) and through their efforts and those of Clement Gibson (later to become Chief Inspector of Audit) the proposal was formulated to establish a training school in E H V Weigall's district in Surrey. So after about twelve months in Cambridge I was summoned to CIA's office, along with three other audit assistants, Roberts, Eagle and Brain.

There we were told that we four were to be posted to Surbiton, in Surrey, to form a training section under an SADA, A R H Hobbs. We all arrived in Surbiton on 1 September 1933. All of us had previous audit experience, though Tom Roberts, fifteen years older than the rest of us, had by far the longest.

A R H Hobbs was a relative of Carson Roberts, and cousin to C R H Hurle-Hobbs. My chief recollections of him (apart from the name 'Reggie') are of geniality and imperturbability. Under him we carried out audits in Surrey and in West Sussex. Those in West Sussex were 'stay away', which added to our enjoyment and helped to bring us closer together.

Reggie told us from the start that we must not look to him for book knowledge. We could get that from books. Only if we ran into problems that really baffled us were we to come to him, and even then his role would rather be that of an arbitrator than of a fount of information.

He made no such disclaimer, however, of responsibility for our more general development. He believed that there was more to becoming a JADA than the ability to pass examinations, and did concern himself with how we dressed, how we spoke, and with our attitudes towards others, particularly towards local authority officers.

Reggie had an office in Surbiton, where we were supposed to go on Saturday mornings. Part of the attraction of the office was that Reggie had a small library there to which we had access. Here, however, we struck a snag in the person of the office secretary, one Brickly Hindmarsh.

Brickly, who had lost his arm in the First World War, had served under Weigall in times past and was a privileged person. He was good at cutting the young down to size, but the language that he used horrified Reggie, who never quite reconciled himself to the threat to all his standards of behaviour that this posed.

From the start, the school was much more than an ordinary audit section, even though we did audits on the same lines as operated elsewhere. The difference, to us, was fundamental – we were no longer each on his own.

12/3 Surrey School 1938; Surrey v Kent.

We acquired a reputation among local government officers of being happier talking than going through account books, but in the long run this probably did us no harm. In and out of the audit room, our talk inevitably turned to the work, and 'shop talk' went far beyond the requirements of the QE.

In the spring of 1934, Tom Roberts passed his QE and departed, but our numbers began to increase. Other audit assistants, some who had already begun their training elsewhere, some straight from the Executive Class examination, and some from promotion boards, arrived in Surbiton. At the same time Reggie was joined by a young JADA grade I, J B B Kendrick, who showed signs of wanting to bring order into our technical training.

I do not remember having any prescribed course of reading. One read all of Carson Roberts, and committed to memory a good deal of the wording of the audit provisions of the Public Health Act 1875 and the Local Government Act 1933. We had access to the local government periodicals, and we must have tried our hands at drafting audit reports, although I cannot now recall any details of this.

Apart from this, we read as widely as we could – anything that seemed likely to crop up in examination questions. As the spring of 1935 approached, I myself, off my own bat, took the accounts paper of Alban and Lamb's IMTA correspondence course, to obtain practice with accounting exercises.

As our numbers grew, most of us shared lodgings with another trainee, or had lodgings in the same area. I was particularly lucky in that Frank Smith, who was a contemporary of mine but arrived in Surbiton in 1934, settled in digs a hundred yards or so down the road from mine. The pattern of our studies (we still had to do our studying in our own time) was to read (or write) most weekday evenings until after 9 pm, and then to meet and go for long walks to clear away the cobwebs. Others had their own variants on the same routine.

Frank and I both passed the QE in March 1935, and left the school a few weeks later, and I cannot do full justice to the eventual success of John Kendrick's efforts to rationalise training and to enhance a corporate spirit among the trainees. Looking back on it now, my recollections of the Surrey School are all happy ones. We had, in a phrase then unheard-of, 'job satisfaction'. The fact that we had to direct our own studies to such a great extent gave us freedom to pick and choose, with a concurrent acceptance of responsibility for the consequences of omissions of our own choosing.

The school continued to flourish right up to the early years of the war. Laurence Tovell has referred nostalgically to his own experience. He joined the School in 1938 in company with Neil Middleton, Cyril Gay, Ernie Southgate, Jock Price and Bill Bird. At that time, A D Hughes was the SADA in charge and Bill Munrow the JADA.

Laurence referred to the stimulation of working with the unique combination of young men, who were the cream of the pre-war executive entry to the Civil Service, and older men such as Ernie Southgate who, by virtue of their past performance on audit and their future potential, had been selected to attend the school.

He recalls that local government in Surrey in those days was well-managed. Local government finance was not bedevilled by the kind of complex legislation which characterised the post-war period; there was no inflation and the pace of life was leisurely and conducive to study.

But it was the leisure time activities which he remembers most. He recalls the summer of 1939 when he, and half a dozen others, rented a bungalow at Bognor for five weeks during the West Sussex County Council audit. He spent his evenings and weekends swimming, playing football on the beach with Bill Munrow and anyone else he could persuade to abandon their studies, and playing cricket for the audit team. Matches were arranged against the West Sussex Police and Graylingwell Mental Hospital. It was, as he relates, the end of an era because two days after his return to Surbiton war was declared.

The school had advantages which may not have been in the minds of its founders. By the time that I left, more than a dozen audit assistants were stationed there. We all knew each other very well indeed, and after we each departed there were gatherings of one sort and another (often purely social) which enabled us to renew existing contacts and form new ones. So by the time we came to carry responsibilities ourselves, we were surrounded in the Service by colleagues who were friends of long standing. And when John Kendrick came to be Deputy Chief Inspector and then Chief Inspector of Audit, he had serving under him DAs, DDAs and SADAs, many if not most of whom had been his pupils in Surbiton.

The influence of the school stayed with us for over forty years. What better testimonial could anyone ask for?

12/4 ". . . the pace of life was leisurely and conducive to study".

ARTHUR LONG

As District Auditor in Newcastle in 1960s tried hard to pursue rumours about Poulson and others, but the necessary evidence was not available. Proud of having attempted in a disallowance in 1973 to scotch the introduction of "creative accounting" and of, in retirement, having twice won the Hurle-Hobbs trophy.

The Second World War

Members of the District Audit Service played their full part, both in the armed services and on the home front, in the war years, 1939 to 45.

A recent search of the Society's archives brought to light a memorandum written in March 1947 by the then Chief Inspector of Audit, Clement Gibson, in which he briefly recounted the part played by members of the Service in the armed forces:

"In all, one hundred and sixty-nine members of the permanent staff – very nearly a third of its total strength – enlisted in the three combatant services or in the wartime equivalents available to women. Twenty-two of them found their way into the Royal Navy, and the remainder were more or less equally divided between the Army and the Royal Air Force. Details of the number who volunteered for service in advance of the due date of their call-up are not now available, though the percentage, as I can personally vouch, was a high one; while, at the outbreak of war and owing to their peacetime associations with the Reserve organisations of the three Services, no less than twenty-four, many of whom would otherwise have been exempt from military service, were called to the Colours. Audit's contribution can confidently challenge comparison with that of any other analogous service.

A marked feature, however, lies not in numbers alone but in achievement and, although the scope of review in this regard is limited by the traditional reticence of Servicemen in speaking of their war experiences, ample proof of the resource and determination displayed in the 'art of war' is furnished by the details set out below.

Just over four-fifths of the total number enlisted in the Forces are known to have attained either commissioned, warrant or non-commissioned rank, the precise numbers being 65, 4 and 68 respectively.

One member of the staff was accorded Membership of the Order of the British Empire (Military Division), another won the Military Cross while others gained between them three Distinguished Flying Crosses (one coupled with the Air Crew (Europe) Medal and Clasp) and one Distinguished Flying Medal, to say nothing of yet another three who were mentioned in despatches. This total of ten awards of official recognition of exceptional service, when expressed as a percentage of Audit personnel and in relation to that of the Armed Forces as a whole is, of course, an almost incredibly high one.

A heavy reckoning, however, was paid for the foregoing bright record of achievement and one in every eight of those of our colleagues who went will never return to us. Twenty-one made the supreme sacrifice and the following is our proud Roll of Honour.

13/1 German flying bomb.

13/2 Churchill inspecting air raid damage September 1940.

T Bell
K G Bellingham
K Burrenston
G T Canterbury
R T Clark
J Cunliffe
J D Drew
J Dugdale
A H Eades
R B Fennell
T R Furness
J Hanley
F A Hemsley
G Lindley
T M Nicholls
H W Ostergaard
J R Payne
A E Roberts
D E A Seager
A J Trenerry
H J Waterman"

A flavour of the conditions on the home front during the last war is graphically conveyed in some notes contributed by J B B Kendrick.

These jottings are confined to experience in the London Audit District.

Working conditions were bad. Audit staff were reduced in numbers through men joining the Forces; likewise the staff of the metropolitan boroughs and the London County Council. All were in physical danger through bombs, incendiaries and the resulting damage to buildings and railways. Audit staff suffered no harm, though several had their houses damaged.

My own most vivid recollection is of a Saturday afternoon when I was living temporarily at Blackheath. The German bombers were in strength and carved a way up the centre of Lewisham borough on their way to the Surrey and London docks. The bombing continued throughout the night and subsequent nights.

My extra-official activity was as a Warden in the Air Raid Precautions Service.

During this period there was no particular number of the ordinary run of audit cases (eg failure to account for money collected); but there was, however, all the work for several years lying behind the two cases *Re Hurle-Hobbs ex parte Surridge* (1944) and *Re Hurle-Hobbs ex parte Riley and another* (1944). Both cases involved a great deal of research.

In the *Surridge* case, several London boroughs had, to use the modern word, 'privatised' the refuse collection and disposal work during a number of years. I confess I cannot remember out of which of the borough audits the case arose, but I do remember that many thousands were recovered from the contractor, that the business of examining his records was laborious once produced, and that it and the formal hearings were held in daylight accompanied by no bombing, though perhaps a 'doodle-bug', ie flying bomb, may have passed overhead.

Not so in the *ex parte Riley* case. The hearings were held on a number of nights in the Finsbury Town Hall when bombs fell nearby on several occasions. We lost no glass, but few of us did not start or instinctively 'duck' when a bomb exploded or shrieked as it fell. At times it was hard to suppress a chuckle at the sight of us after such happenings".

Professional Training Post-War

A Pyke

14/1 'Surrey School'.

In the six years preceding the 1939–45 War there were the first signs in the District Audit Service of some form of professional training. The students were grouped together in Surrey with the senior officer responsible for their training, but I understand that there was no prescribed course of study; the whole field of local government accounts and audit was open to the examiners and each student was left to cope as best he could – with the help of his fellow students.

In 1939 all examinations for recruitment to civil service posts were suspended, and it was some seven years before they were recommenced. By then there were large numbers of posts to be filled in many departments – including the District Audit Service. In addition to the normal entrance examinations, a special series of reconstruction examinations was held to give candidates who would normally have joined the civil service during the war years an opportunity to do so when they returned from the Forces; it is also likely that the large numbers of recruits required to bring the civil service up to establishment could not have been found from 'normal age' entrants (16–19) without lowering the entrance standards. This policy meant that the District Audit Service took in about 60 of these reconstruction entrants, aged 22 to 27 and a further 50 younger students through the normal entry examinations over a period of two years.

The writer was one of the reconstruction entrants in September 1948 – aged 25. I started work at the Sheffield audit in No 11 AD with Harold Watkinson, Cliff Whiteside, Phil Court and Ron Dunkerley – all due to commence studying within a year of entry.

To cope with the large numbers involved, a more formalised training programme was required. The new entrants were to be found in every district: there could be no question of a resumption of professional training on the lines of the 'Surrey School'.

In 1947, a correspondence course was started for students – this was provided by a Training Section in the Chief Inspector's office under a DDA (Training). Students were given a firm timetable and were required to complete written work at the end of each stage of the course (about three weeks at each stage).

My recollection is that the only text books we had were *The Law Relating to District Audit* by Hurle-Hobbs and Carson Roberts, two books from the early 1930s, but we were expected to read large chunks of Lumley's *Public Health* – available in District offices. The *Brown Book* (later it became the *Black Book*) was to be closely studied together with important statutes – the Local Government Act 1933, and the Local Government Superannuation Act 1937.

The *Brown Book* was considered to be so important that one of the candidates at the oral examination was asked 'what do you consider to be the *vade mecum* of your study course?' Students of the time will have little difficulty in identifying the examiner concerned!

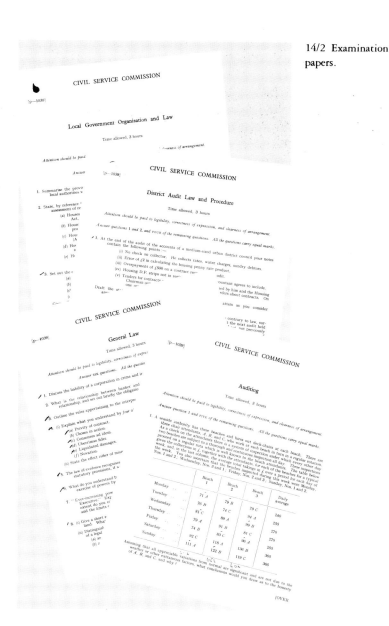

14/2 Examination papers.

14/3 Formidable oral test.

FORMIDABLE ORAL TEST

Students took 12 months to prepare for the preliminary examination with papers in:

– Book-keeping and accounts;

– Accounts of local authorities;

– Auditing;

– Local government organisation and law.

There was a further two years to prepare for the final examinations with six papers – the four subjects of the preliminary examination to a higher level, plus two further subjects:

– District audit law and practice; and

– General law.

The examinations at both levels included a formidable oral test. For some candidates this was held the day after the written part was completed. Some regarded the completion of the written part, quite understandably, as meriting some relaxation and an occasion to be suitably celebrated. This sometimes left the participants below their best when they attended the oral the next day.

To give some idea of the numbers undergoing training at that time – there were 56 taking the preliminary examination in June 1950 of whom 25 passed, nine were referred (failed in one subject) and 22 failed. The study course was arduous – nearly all to be done in the evenings and at weekends. Officially half a day per week was allowed for study in the audit room (if the work permitted).

Most of us persevered but after five or six years in the Armed Forces it was not surprising that some students found it difficult to settle down to the amount of work needed to pass – particularly with a correspondence course. There was a rigid policy of two attempts only at either stage of the examination and those who did not make it were transferred to posts in the Department – in those days it was the Ministry of Health.

In the early years after the War the Service was very short of ADAs, so that officers successful in the final examination usually found themselves promoted very quickly. Indeed, in 1949–50 some officers were promoted to ADA on a temporary basis before they had taken their final examination.

The in-house correspondence course method of training had the advantage that it produced qualified officers who had a specialist knowledge of audit work in local authorities, but it also had a number of disadvantages. The qualification was not recognised outside the District Audit Service; though the course was arduous and comprehensive, it was not easy to convince people outside the Service of that. Specialist knowledge was acquired but a good case could have been made for a broader-based syllabus which would have improved our relationship with our clients.

The examinations of the Institute of Municipal Treasurers and Accountants were an obvious alternative, and in 1958 the old system of internal examinations came to an end. Our students took the examinations of the IMTA (as it then was), though some staff, outside the main stream of professional training, studied for ACCA examinations and eventually this qualification also came to be recognised. The IMTA syllabus was supplemented by a special paper for district audit students in District Audit Law and Practice which was set and marked by a district auditor.

Correspondence courses continued to be the recognised method of training though now they were provided by one of the specialist firms in this field; the Chief Inspector of Audit's role was limited to monitoring the progress of the students. Towards the end of the 1970s there were further changes.

The format of the examination was changed by CIPFA in line with a policy of graduate recruitment for students; and to provide the wider perspectives needed by present-day financial managers and advisers, the execution of an original project and report thereon was introduced in the final year of the course. Block release or day release for study at polytechnic colleges became the accepted method, so that the old die-hards could, with some justification, grumble that things were different in their day!

A PYKE

Joined audit after war-time service in the artillery. Appointed DA at Newcastle in 1979, and in 1982 became Chief Inspector of Audit with the difficult task of guiding the Service through the opening years of the Audit Commission. Since retirement in 1985, devotes himself to his interests in cricket, golf, rugby, bridge and music.

C R H Hurle-Hobbs

R Jones

Mr C R H Hurle-Hobbs (commonly known as 'H-H') was district auditor for London from 1938 until his retirement in 1954. During that period he was a dominant figure in the district audit world. As stated in his obituary in *The Times* of 21 January 1976, 'he was an authority on the law of district audit and the author of the standard reference book on the subject'. His influence on audit law was, and continues to be, outstanding, both as auditor, in the initiation of action resulting in important case law, and as author, in clarifying the law and imparting knowledge and understanding of it to practitioners and students.

He was also a great character. His most overtly notable attributes were perhaps his profound veneration of the law in general and the district audit system in particular, and the formal dignity which he brought to the exercise of his public duties.

Of thickset build and medium height, with heavy jowl and dome-shaped, bald head, he had an impressive appearance, a stately gait, an awe-inspiring manner on public occasions, and a formidable reputation. Dame Evelyn (later Baroness) Sharp, when Permanent Secretary of the Ministry of Housing and Local Government, once confided to the District Auditors' Society that whenever she heard the name of Hurle-Hobbs she thought of Jehovah! But it must be added that his dignity was invariably coupled with the utmost courtesy and that he was also possessed of an innate kindliness, and of a quirky sense of humour, sometimes displayed on public occasions but more often in private. These characteristics ensured that he was regarded by the audit staff of his district with great affection, as well as respect.

It is a privilege to be invited to write this potted biography and appreciation of the great man. Unfortunately, in the absence of official records, available material about his early life and career is scanty, but I am grateful for assistance received from John Kendrick, who worked closely with him, first as senior assistant and then as deputy, from 1938 to 1953, and from the Librarian and Keeper of the Records of the Middle Temple. This account is also enlivened by personal recollections volunteered by Ted Thomas, who was assigned to the London Audit District on entering the audit service from a post-war reconstruction examination, and by Bernard Gilham, who served in that district as a JADA from 1952 to 1956.

Charles Rienzi Hurle Hurle-Hobbs was born in 1889, the son of Thomas Henry Hurle Hobbs, a pharmacist of Upper Edmonton, Middlesex. (The second, hyphenated Hurle was added to his name by deed poll in 1936.) A relation, Mr A O Hobbs, was a staff clerk in the Audit Department of the Local Government Board, where his duties apparently included the running of a sort of employment agency procuring staff for district auditors, who until 1920 or thereabouts appointed their own clerks. So it was by this route presumably that the young Charles Hobbs joined the audit service on 1 April 1909. (His cousin, Arthur Reginald Hurle Hobbs, also joined the service in that year. He, too, became a district auditor, latterly of No 9 District, and was Honorary Secretary of the District Auditors' Society from 1933 to 1952.)

The Office List of the Local Government Board at 1 April 1912 records C R H Hobbs as one of the two clerks of H V C Roe, district auditor for the Cambridgeshire Provincial Audit District. The auditor's salary scale was £500 by annual increments of £20 to a maximum of £675, the clerk's £100 by £7.10s.0d to a maximum of £150. A little later, on 31 May 1913, he was admitted as a student to the Middle Temple, when he was recorded as living at Turrett House, Upper Edmonton. He wasted little time in getting through his Bar exams, since he was called on 5 July 1916. It is believed that he served in the Royal Artillery during the remainder of World War I.

At some time during these early years he is reported as on audit in Surrey where his fellow clerk was Mr Frank Mobbs, a delightful character who in the 1940s was general factotum in the office of the London Audit District. He was wont to enthuse about the athletic prowess of his former comrade and present chief, as shown in particular in a heroic sprint for the train at Reigate carrying two fully loaded audit bags – a story evoking some scepticism in the light of the then somewhat corpulent profile of the subject.

He is next heard of as an assistant district auditor in South Wales, for a period not precisely known, but at least from 1927 to 1931. Of this period Bernard Gilham writes:

"The fame and reputation of Hurle-Hobbs was still remembered in southwest Wales forty years after he had left the area. I know because I was there! For example, the locals recounted with awe how he used to dress formally for dinner every night – even in remote places like Fishguard. Clerks to councils remember how it was a signal honour to be invited to play tennis with Mr Hurle-Hobbs – but they always ensured that they never won.

At an audit of parish council accounts one of the parish clerks proudly boasted that he had been attending the audit every year for 50 years. With typical audit caution, we checked his receipts and payments book before admitting the claim. We then congratulated him, much to his delight. In the afternoon, we were visited by another parish clerk who boasted with equal pride that he had been attending the audit every year for nearly 40 years. To his evident dismay, we had to tell him of the 50-year claim. For a few moments he seemed rather despondent and then he suddenly brightened up and exclaimed 'Ah, but I was once surcharged by Mr Hurle-Hobbs!' We agreed that for that he deserved a special accolade."

It was at this time that Mr Hobbs, as he then was, first took up residence in chambers in the Middle Temple. The Law Lists from 1927 to 1941 show his address as 5 Essex Court, those from 1942 to 1973 as 2 Garden Court. During the earliest part of this era he may presumably have treated the Temple as his permanent base and travelled weekly to Wales for his audit duties.

15/1 Middle Temple, where Hurle-Hobbs was in chambers.

Subsequently, he spent his weekdays in the Temple, travelling at weekends to his family home in East Preston, Littlehampton.

He was a regular attendant in Middle Temple Hall for dinner, but on occasion a chosen few were privileged to enjoy personal hospitality in his chambers, a memorable experience establishing that his talents extended beyond law and auditing to the more fundamental field of cookery. There is no doubt that he greatly treasured his life in chambers and the life style of the Temple.

At some time between 1931 and 1935 he was transferred from Wales to the London District where he established a high reputation as senior assistant to Clement Gibson, the then District Auditor, who later doubled this post with that of Deputy Chief Inspector of Audit. In 1938, when Gibson became Chief Inspector, Hurle-Hobbs succeeded him as District Auditor for London.

During the war years he was assisted by a powerful team including two future Chief Inspectors, John Kendrick and Bill Munrow, and a future distinguished district auditor, Alex Dean. Some brilliant audit work in those years resulted in the great series of cases which established the name of Hurle-Hobbs securely in the annals of local government audit law.

In 1944 came the Finsbury case (*Re Hurle-Hobbs, ex parte Riley*), in which the court upheld a surcharge on the town clerk and the leader of the council for negligence and misconduct in concealing from the council material information concerning an abortive scheme for deep air-raid shelters; and the Lambeth case (*Re Hurle-Hobbs*) where the court reversed a disallowance of *ex gratia*

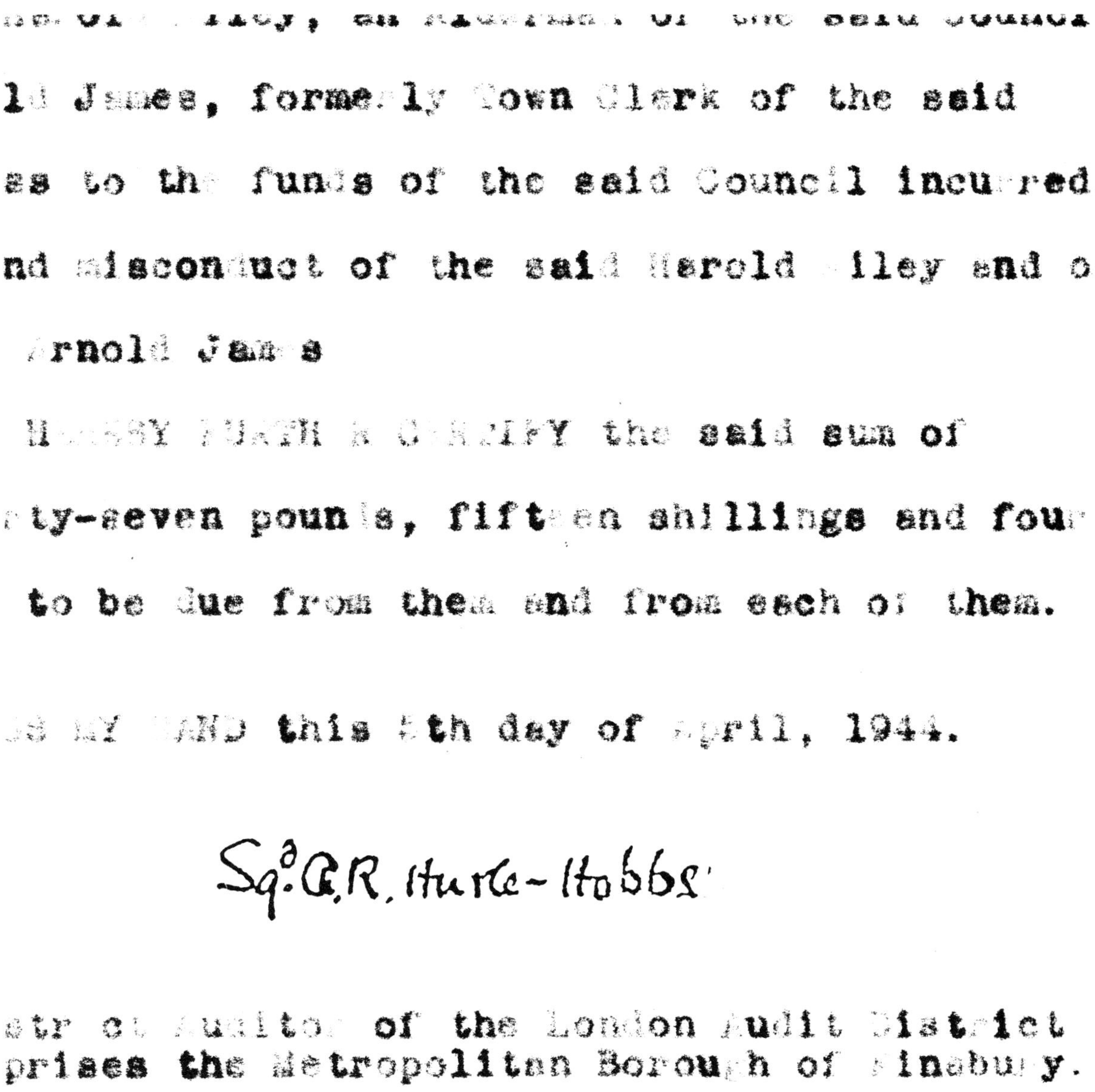

ne. of ...ley, an Alderman of the said Council
ld James, formerly Town Clerk of the said
as to the funds of the said Council incurred
nd misconduct of the said Harold iley and o
Arnold James
HEREBY FURTHER CERTIFY the said sum of
nty-seven pounds, fifteen shillings and four
to be due from them and from each of them.

ER MY HAND this 5th day of April, 1944.

Sgd. G.R. Hurle-Hobbs

str ct Auditor of the London Audit District
prises the Metropolitan Borough of Finsbury.

15/2 An extract from Finsbury's extraordinary audit showing Hurle-Hobbs signature.

payments to a refuse contractor in respect of increased costs due to the war.

This is not the place for legal commentary on the cases, but it is noteworthy that in the Lambeth case H-H, being dissatisfied with his counsel's performance in the Divisional Court, conducted his own case in the Court of Appeal and was said by du Parcq LJ 'to have presented powerfully as well as temperately arguments which had to be considered very seriously'.

There followed two cases arising from a large fraud perpetrated on the London County Council by one Dickson, the managing director and effective controller of Hortensia Garages Ltd, which had a cost-plus contract with the council for repairing vehicles. The fraud was discovered by district audit, but the investigation ran into difficulties because the company's accountant refused to produce documents which he held. The statutory penalty of a £2 fine having proved ineffective, the district auditor applied for a subpoena to compel production of the documents, but in *R v Hurle-Hobbs, ex parte Simmons*, 1945, it was held that the provision for a statutory penalty precluded the court from issuing a subpoena. However, the case was important in establishing clearly that the auditor's powers as to production of documents extended to documents belonging to and held by persons external to a local authority.

Despite this setback the fraud was established and Dickson was in due course convicted, and his appeal to the Court of Criminal Appeal dismissed. A surcharge of £20,000 followed, but this was reversed on appeal, the Divisional Court holding that the auditor's duty, under the Local Government Act 1933, to surcharge 'any

person' causing loss by negligence or misconduct did not extend beyond members and employees of the local authority (*Dickson v Hurle-Hobbs*, 1947).

The judgement was delivered by Mr Justice Atkinson, who went out of his way to be offensive. The auditor, he said, 'would be well advised if he stuck to his auditing' and ceased 'usurping the functions of the court'. H-H was exceedingly put out, as well he might be, the case having arisen directly out of fraud discovered at audit and being based on a reasonable interpretation of his duties under a statutory provision not previously considered by the courts. In the London Audit District the name of Atkinson was mud, and so it remains today among loyal survivors of that era. The case was taken to the Court of Appeal, who upheld the decision of the Divisional Court, but without peevish rebuke and in terms implicitly recognising that the auditor, faced with a problem of construction and an absence of authority, had not acted improperly or unreasonably in making the surcharge. Honour was satisfied.

The last of the line of Hurle-Hobbs cases, *Pentecost v London District Auditor*, 1951, is of little relevance nowadays, but caused quite a stir at the time in upsetting previous judicial authority to the effect that 'negligence', in audit statutes, meant gross negligence, or negligence involving moral culpability. Hurle-Hobbs had followed this authority in dismissing an objection by local government electors alleging loss due to negligence by council officers. The court felt that he was wrong in applying the test of 'gross negligence', because 'negligence' in the audit provisions meant simply negligence in its ordinary sense. However, they also held that his findings of fact did not disclose any negligence in its ordinary sense and therefore dismissed

Health Act 1875. This was all changed by a series of statutes between 1927 and 1933, culminating in the Local Government Act 1933.

The poor law code was abolished and substantial changes made in the remaining audit provisions. The result was naturally to limit severely the utility of Carson Roberts as a reference book for auditors and others concerned with audit law; while for students endeavouring to grasp a new and recondite subject, the task of wrestling with its largely obsolete pronouncements was something of a nightmare.

The appearance of the new book 16 years after the passing of the 1933 Act therefore met a long-felt want. A second edition in 1955 dealt with the revisions required by the *Pentecost* case and introduced some further matter in order to make the work more comprehensive. It survived as a most valuable aid to all concerned until the changes made by the Local Government Act 1972 necessitated a further fresh approach, for which it provided a solid foundation.

the objectors' appeal. The long-term result of this case was that district auditors generally, and others concerned, became convinced that the auditor's negligence jurisdiction should be dropped, as eventually it was with the enactment of the Local Government Act 1972.

A further most important contribution by Hurle-Hobbs to the subject of audit law came with the publication in 1949 of his book *The Law Relating to District Audit*. The only previous book on the subject, Carson Roberts on *Audit Law and Audit Work*, was published in 1919, when there were two separate codes, poor law audits being still basically governed by the Poor Law Amendment Act 1844 and other audits by the Public

15/4 From the same match; Hurle-Hobbs is on the right.

The annals of the District Auditors' Society show a substantial contribution by Hurle-Hobbs to its deliberations, again largely reflecting his particular interest in the legal side of the audit function. His first learned paper, on *The liability of members of local authorities and architects in respect of overpayments on works contracts*, appeared in 1925. After other contributions in 1927, 1933 and 1935, an occasion should perhaps be recorded when, in the light of subsequent developments, it must be recognised that 'Homer nodded'.

In 1936 he delivered a paper on *The attributes of district audit which preclude its being conducted as a concurrent audit*, in which he concluded that 'such an application is not only impossible from a practical point of view, but, if possible, would render District Audit almost completely ineffective'. It is also recorded that the Chairman thought there would be an almost general acceptance of the speaker's views and suggested that the meeting might wish to incorporate this in a resolution; but that after discussion it was decided that no formal resolution should be recorded. However, the opposition to current auditing remained strong for a long time. As late as 1961 the Society minutes record that a proposition in favour of current audit did not meet with general acceptance of members and it was not until 1965 that the pendulum began to swing the other way, when a proposal to undertake an experiment in current auditing by agreement at the new London boroughs in No 10 District elicited the backing of the Chief Inspector and a wholly favourable reaction from a conference of district auditors.

Hurle-Hobbs was elected Chairman of the District Auditors' Society in 1947 and again in 1954, though he was already retired by the time of the 1954 meeting and a special resolution had to be passed that he should remain a full member until the close of the meeting 'notwithstanding anything which may appear to the contrary in the Rules or previous Resolutions of the Society'. In between his two years in the chair he had delivered two more weighty papers to the Society, a disquisition on the effects of the *Pentecost* case in 1951 and a masterly survey in 1953 of the auditor's position in relation to 'policy', which is impressively consistent with subsequent case law and still merits close study today.

At the close of the 1954 meeting he generously presented to the Society, for competition at the annual golf meeting, a George III flagon by Francis Crump, London, 1773, now known as the Hurle-Hobbs Trophy – a piece so handsome that a distant prospect of housing it for a year might almost have tempted one to take up the wretched game seriously.

H-H was keenly interested in all sporting activities connected with district audit, and displayed a strong preference for everything to be won by the London District or members thereof. But he was not himself a great enthusiast for golf; displaying impeccable judgement as always, his game was cricket. Rumour had it that he was still playing village cricket in Sussex in his seventies. Certainly right up to the time of his retirement he was opening the batting for the London District in audit matches, and memory recalls him scurrying between the wickets at a fair speed, especially when his own runs were in question. It must have been a great grief to him that in those palmy days of audit cricket the London team always took a pasting from the superior talents of No 8 District.

The respect and affection in which H-H was universally held by his staff are typified by the following reminiscences, which also illustrate his enthusiasm for the law and for the procurement, as he saw it, of a due respect for the position of the auditor by the prescription of a dignified formality.

Ted Thomas writes:

"Everyone who knew him held him in high regard. He was a colourful person with a commanding presence and yet he was by no means forbidding or lacking in warmth. As with all newcomers, he interviewed me on arrival at some length and while he showed a distinct interest in the fact that I had served in the Lord Chancellor's Department, he showed none at all in my service with the Ministry of National Insurance (as it was then called). Not until much later did I appreciate that this reflected the emphasis which he placed on the law and the auditor's statutory functions. Audit programmes always made substantial provision for a search for illegality and most district conferences included learned papers on legal subjects.

Anxious to ensure that students in his district did well in the examination paper on audit law, H-H held a number of tutorials in his room at which he passed on a wealth of knowledge and experience of this subject. We were certainly privileged to be briefed in this way, but unfortunately this did not manifest itself in the examination results.

The opening of audits in London was a rather formal, if not solemn affair. H-H was a meticulous timekeeper and could always be relied upon to enter the town hall on the stroke of eleven o'clock. Some thought this could have been achieved only by pacing the perimeter of the building until the appointed hour arrived. Already assembled in the council chamber were the chief officers on the one side and senior audit staff on the other, together with students who

had not previously witnessed such a ceremony.

The town clerk would be invited to identify the minutes and the treasurer the accounts, after which the officers generally were asked if they had any matter to bring to the auditor's attention. Hurle-Hobbs would then announce that the audit would proceed from day to day. It was his practice to use a monocle on such occasions as this, more, one suspects, for effect than for reasons of optical necessity."

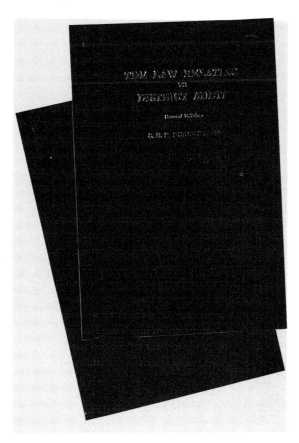

15/5 Hurle-Hobbs' text books.

Bernard Gilham also remembers, with awe, the formalities of opening the audit and his recollections supplement the account:

"On the entry of the DA, the assembled officers and members (and any others present) would stand up spontaneously to mark their respect until graciously invited by the DA to sit down. Hurle-Hobbs always appeared to me to be pleasantly and modestly surprised at this show of respect but, I was sure, would have been offended at its absence – but this never happened!

On one memorable occasion, the tram (yes, the tram), programmed carefully to arrive at the Metropolitan Water Board offices just before eleven, was marginally late to the ill-disguised fury of H-H, so that he entered the assembly at two or three minutes past eleven. However, he had recovered his composure by this time and, snatching the initiative, remarked on his arrival, 'Ah, gentlemen, I see your clock is two or three minutes fast'. They not only agreed, but promised to put it right.

Of the formal questions to the officers – they rarely admitted to anything; perhaps there was a feeling that to do so at this rather formal stage might be regarded as lèse-majesté. The DA would then allow some relaxation in the formality of the occasion by making some sort of informal remark in a pleasant but royal manner, at which those assembled felt able to shift their sitting position or even offer one or two remarks themselves (but only the bravest and most senior seemed to do this).

Even in those days, I never ceased to be surprised (and always impressed) by the style of the occasion and even more surprised at the respectful acceptance by the important officers and members attending. Such pomp and circumstance seemed to me to be more akin to the opening of the Assizes but without the trumpets! But then I should not have been so surprised because Mr Hurle-Hobbs carried it off with so much natural dignity and courtesy that acceptance was assured. Only he could have done it."

My own service with Hurle-Hobbs was limited to a mere 18 months in 1946–47, but it was a period not without influence on the rest of my life on audit; in particular, it was long enough to allow him to exercise upon me his talents as a persuasive recruiting sergeant for the Bar. So, in due course, I found myself attending Middle Temple Hall to eat the dinners deemed a requisite part of the Bar student's training – and thereby hangs another Hurle-Hobbs tale.

The seating arrangements in Hall include, below the High Table occupied by the Benchers (the governing body of the Inn of Court), a small table known as the Ancients' Table, which is occupied by the most senior barristers (other than the Benchers) in Hall on any given night. One evening early in my dinner-eating career I noticed that Hurle-Hobbs, evidently the only barrister in Hall, was seated alone at the Ancients' Table and looking not very happy about it. Shortly afterwards I found that he was conducting me across the Hall, in rather a dazed state, to take my place as a temporary Ancient, the cynosure of all eyes or so it seemed to me. I certainly had the eye upon me of an august official holding the title of Butler, and no sooner was I seated than he was bearing down in full sail and conducting an inquiry into the startling departure from protocol of a student's gown appearing at the Ancients' Table. I foresaw myself being evicted with ignominy, but my sponsor was unperturbed.

The matter was referred to higher authority and eventually we were informed that despite the absence of precedent, the Benchers had in all the circumstances authorised me to remain *in situ*. Moreover, when they subsequently entered in procession, two by two, High Court judges and eminent counsel, they each in their turn, in accordance with custom, bowed graciously to the occupants of the Ancients' Table, and Hurle-Hobbs and I stood up and gravely bowed back to each couple as they passed. Altogether, it was a highly memorable experience for me, and Hurle-Hobbs was as pleased as Punch because, as he often reminded me subsequently, We had established some case law!

After he retired from the audit service, Hurle-Hobbs fulfilled what must have been a long-held ambition when he entered into practice at the Bar. From 1955 to 1965 his entry in the Law List records his working chambers at 3 Temple Gardens, in addition to his residence at 2 Garden Court.

It was rumoured that he suffered a little ribbing from his learned friends about the whiteness of his wig, and it is not known whether he collected many briefs. He did appear as counsel in one audit case, however, *Dean v DA for Ashton-in-Makerfield*, 1960, in which he argued that a person surcharged under the 1933 Act by direction of the Minister had no access to the court, either to appeal or to apply for relief.

Mr Hurle-Hobbs continued to take an interest in audit affairs for many years after his retirement. The minutes of the District Auditors' Society show him as in regular attendance at meetings until his last appearance in 1971. He died on 26 December 1975 at the age of 86.

Little is known of his private and family life save that he had a married daughter, Audrey, and a son, Basil, who served as a pilot in World War II. His working life was devoted to the District Audit Service and he took the utmost pride in his role and standing as the District Auditor for London; it is understood that for this reason,

15/6 The flagon presented by Hurle-Hobbs for the annual DA's Society Golf Meetings.

in the 1940s he declined the offer of the post of Deputy Chief Inspector of Audit and hence the prospect of succession as Chief Inspector.

He could be said with truth to be an auditor of the old school, his service spanning the era of poor law audits and patronage appointments, an era almost unimaginable in the present day. As this account has shown, the emphasis of his mind was primarily on the legal aspects of the Service but he also took a keen interest in practical auditing and his mind was open to new ideas; after his retirement he showed himself in conversation to be receptive to the increasing emphasis then under way on questions of value for money. I believe he would be content with, and proud of, the Service as it is today.

REG JONES

After gaining his BSc at Manchester University he joined district audit and was sent to the Surrey Training School. Called to the Bar in 1953; appointed DA in 1961 and Inspector of Audit in 1975. After retirement in 1978, wrote *Local Government Audit Law*, became financial editor of *Encyclopedia of Local Government Audit Law* and finds time for the Citizens' Advice Bureau, cricket and choral singing.

Developments in the mid-twentieth century

John Speirs CBE

The period from 1950 to 1980 was one of great change in local government. The development of new welfare services and the expansion of existing services, such as housing and education, led to a vast increase in expenditure. This was accompanied by the development of new management techniques and, of course, by the introduction of the computer.

These changes were mirrored in the District Audit Service. Efficiency aspects of accounts under examination had always been of interest to district auditors. But up to this time, this had, in the main, been incidental to their regularity objectives.

By the late 1950s, the great majority of local authorities were reasonably responsible and well-managed in their financial administration. Legality of expenditure and discouragement of misconduct remained audit objectives; indeed, on occasions, the statutory powers still had to be used. But these instances invariably related to very public political differences between local and central government. They hit the headlines well before the district auditor became involved. These cases apart, there was little mileage for the auditor in spending a lot of time searching the accounts for illegal items of expenditure.

16/1 The overall review.

Almost the same could be said of the second main regularity objective – the prevention or detection of fraud. True, fraud was never going to disappear. But there was not a lot of it about; the majority of cases were trivial in amount; and in total it was a mere drop in the ocean when set against the overall volume of local government expenditure. Finally, there was not the same need in governmental accounts as in commercial accounts for extensive testing to ensure that the published accounts properly reflected the financial state of the business.

All in all, therefore, regularity auditing had become a less than fully satisfying business for the auditor. The over-riding purpose of the audit, however, was to protect the interests of the ratepayers, and it was clear that there was plenty of scope for his time and expertise in the value for money (VFM) field.

Much of the creative thinking in the Service and Society at this period was therefore concerned with shifting the emphasis of the audit from regularity to VFM without increasing the cost of the audit or the risk that serious fraud would go undetected.

At the same time, we were having to cope with the new risks and opportunities presented by the computer.

As I have already said, district auditors had always taken an interest in the value for money (VFM) aspect of accounts or services under audit; indeed, the project approach to VFM work was not unknown in the early post-war years. Direct labour organisations and central stores are two examples which come to mind.

Generally, however, I think it is fair to say that most suggestions made by auditors arose incidentally out of their examination of the accounts for regularity purposes; accordingly, they related more often to financial systems than to operational services. For example, the use of surplus cash, competitive tendering, debt recovery, and budgetary control would be the sort of areas most likely to feature in audit suggestions in the years immediately after I joined the service in 1947, as compared with the efficiency of bonus systems, the organisation of housing maintenance work, or fuel efficiency, to name a few of the items which were common subjects of VFM projects by the time I departed in 1979.

The fact that the Service had much to offer in this wider field was well demonstrated at Bradford between 1958 and 1961. The City Treasurer arranged for the secondment of three SADAs from No 3 AD to join internal O & M teams undertaking reviews of, first, his own accountancy section, then his revenue section, and finally the welfare services department. This was a part-audited county borough, and the fact that we were asked to do the job in the first place indicated that our work in the VFM field must have made some impact, even at that relatively early date. Also, since we were invited to undertake the successive later reviews, it was obvious that our contributions must have been appreciated.

Early in 1963 I was asked to do an article on District Audit for *Telescope*, the IMTA students' journal. This contained clear references to VFM as an audit concern – summed up, as I recollect, in terms such as 'local government is big business' and 'there are at least as many savings to be made by the auditor in the VFM field as in the regularity field'.

For all these brave words, however, the preponderance of audit time was still being devoted to regularity work.

The Service was tied in theory to 'the discriminating test audit', and the detection of fraud was still a paramount objective.

A number of district auditors were very conscious of this limitation and I recall discussions in the early 1960s about the need to bring about a change in emphasis. A review of the Society minutes reveals a number of significant contributions which signposted the dramatic change in audit methods which occurred over the second half of that decade in response to this perceived need for change of emphasis.

I would start as early as 1962 with a paper given by Mr Peart about an investigation into a health department's systems. Mr Peart made a number of points which, in retrospect, can be seen to have had considerable importance:

– The need to back up systems recording with tests to establish that the systems were being carried out in practice;

– The possibility of programming system reviews over a period of years;

– The need to consider the part which internal audit might play in the review of systems.

Unfortunately, the Society itself was not, it seems, ready for these ideas – 'the meeting was generally inclined to the view that (this) type of investigation was best limited to selected fields rather than for universal application'.

I picked up the cudgels myself the next year. In a paper on *Objectives, standards and methods of district audit today*, given with the blessing and encouragement of the Chief Inspector of Audit (Mr B B Kendrick) and the Deputy Chief Inspector (Mr W D Munrow CBE), I argued for the introduction of a system-based approach to regularity auditing with a view to limiting the time spent on detailed checking, and freeing it for use in more productive directions. I suggested that unless audit standards more in tune with the present day were formally adopted, 'DAs would go on attempting to give too high a protection against the risk of fraud and leave themselves far too little time for more useful work designed to … detect major sources of waste and extravagance'.

I suggested that the onus for maintaining defences against fraud lay with the authorities themselves, and their internal auditors in particular; and that the main role of the external auditor was to ensure that they fulfilled these obligations – not to act as a long stop if they failed to do so. In what was undoubtedly a tactical error, I drew attention to current developments on these lines in the commercial audit field.

My recollection is that this paper took off rather like a lead balloon. First thing on Friday afternoon was never a propitious time, and it seemed to me that the only people who had stayed awake were those opposed to any suggestion that we might relax our standards to any degree on the regularity front, or to whom the idea that we might have anything to learn from the commercial auditor was anathema.

On reading again the summary of the discussion at the meeting it seems that this impression may not be wholly correct. Some support was recorded for the idea of revising our audit objectives, for recognition of the importance of efficiency audit, and even for placing greater reliance on internal audit.

What is certain is that over the next few years a great deal of thought was being given to the subject in a number of audit districts with the full encouragement of the Chief Inspector. Two important papers were presented to the Society on the subject – *Experiments in management auditing* by Mr J M G Ward in September 1965 and *The audit of management* by Mr P F Kimmance in September 1967.

How all this was brought together in No 2 AD's *Reappraisal* and the Society's *Audit review panel report*, and emerged in the *Structured Audit*, is dealt with elsewhere in this book.

What impresses me most is the speed with which this change of direction was implemented. As an example, when I joined Pete Chater, as his Deputy, in Exeter late in 1965, I was given a specific brief to experiment with the introduction of new methods on the lines we had discussed from time to time at DAs' meetings over the previous two years. By the time I left to go to No 1 AD in 1970, the new approach was well beyond the experimental stage. All the ingredients were there, and had been tested, for a planned audit approach designed to reduce as far as possible the time needed to satisfy

16/2 Essential tasks 1.

regularity requirements and release resources for the VFM objective shortly to be given formal recognition in 1973 in the new Audit Code of Practice.

I think it fair to say that it took time for many of the senior audit staff to adapt to the new approach. Examination of records aimed merely at checking that a system was operating correctly, as opposed to checking directly the propriety of the transactions, never seemed to be 'proper auditing'. There was also opposition to what was seen as over-formalisation of procedures and excessive record-keeping. Nevertheless, based on my subsequent experience in No 1 AD, I feel sure that we could never have coped with the continued expansion of local government in the 1970s, plus the extra work presented by local government reorganisation, and still found time for significant district-wide VFM projects, had this major change in audit methods not taken place.

The Society minutes themselves perhaps provide the most convincing evidence of the change in emphasis which occurred. Analysis of papers presented over the five years 1950 to 54 shows only two out of 35 related to management topics; 1956 to 60 produces four out of 44; while the 1970 to 74 figure is 14 out of 38 – a dramatic increase. The change begins in the early 1960s when management subjects (organisation and method, work study, bonus schemes etc) begin to appear with increasing frequency and to replace the old stalwart of academic discussion of various aspects of the district auditor's jurisdiction and statutory powers.

So far I have concentrated on those developments which led to changes of audit practice in the VFM field. There were, of course, many other significant changes during the period.

Notable, among them, was the work on computers. In conjunction with Mr A J Thomas CIPFA of Kingston College of Technology, we developed early in the 1960s a course for auditors designed to produce enough expertise for them to be able to check the security of computer systems, and to make suggestions for in-built checks, both to improve security and to improve effectiveness as an aid to management. These courses

16/3 Essential tasks 2.

were subsequently adopted by a number of other public audit services, including Exchequer and Audit and some overseas services.

To supplement these general courses, a number of auditors were given specialist training as either programmers or systems analysts. These officers did much to enhance the reputation of the Service in this field.

Links with the then IMTA Computer Committee were established and we made a substantial contribution to their first publication on computer systems and security.

The production of updated 'accounts and audit regulations' and, for the first time, of a public code of audit practice were also significant steps towards the improvement of standards in the field of accounts and audit.

Lastly, one might mention the production of an annual report on the Service. Initially this was an internal management tool, but in our evidence to the Layfield Committee its wider potential was noted. This has since materialised.

I think we can feel proud of the progress we made in bringing VFM work into the forefront of local government audit objectives. At about the time this was happening, a book was published by Mr E L Normanton which contained a review of practice in public audit services across the western world. It was encouraging to see that we were well up with the leaders in our appreciation of the importance of this aspect of our work. And if, at that time, we fell a bit short of the achievements of the General Accounting Office in America, this was more a matter of lack of resources than lack of will or awareness. Much has happened recently, with the advent of the Audit Commission, to correct this.

However, I feel that we must admit that these developments took place rather in isolation – a matter of a common reaction within individual public audit services to similarly perceived needs, rather than a co-ordinated approach to the updating of objectives and methods.

Even more significant than this specific development, I feel, was the extent to which over this period the District Audit Service 'came in from the cold' and began to play its full part with other institutions in the development of audit practice.

Prior to 1960, reference in the Society minutes to wider perspectives are few and far between – the only one I can find is a paper by Stanley Hills in 1960 placing the district audit system into an international context. Speakers from outside the Service were a rarity.

After 1960 all this changed. Speakers from outside became commonplace, discussing a wide variety of topics including management, computers and internal audit. The Report on the Service, once a confidential 'in-house' document, became a public document with relevance for local authorities generally.

I have already mentioned participation in the former IMTA Computer Committee. This was later extended to wider co-operation with LAMSAC on computers and a range of other matters, such as bonus schemes and fuel efficiency. The adoption of the IMTA (now CIPFA) qualification in 1958 was the key to much wider participation by district audit representatives in professional studies and working parties undertaken by the Institute.

Most dramatic of all, perhaps, has been the sea of change in our relationship with the auditing profession in general. In my 1963 paper I injudiciously suggested that we might have something to learn from current commercial practice. Four years later the District Audit Review Panel grudgingly endorsed this – 'District audit has a single lesson to learn from professional audit – the keeping of efficient records of audits'.

Since then, we have seen a team of district auditors lecturing to a course of chartered accountants in 1973 on the subject of management auditing, as an introduction to the broadening of their objectives, post-reorganisation, under the Code of Practice. We have seen chartered acccountants participating in routine DA meetings twice a year. And I recall personally the large number of pleasant and rewarding discussions which I had with Mr S A Middleton FCA of Coopers & Lybrand, then Chairman of the ICA's Local Government Committee, on the subject of audit management in general and management auditing in particular.

On one of the last of these meetings, I floated the idea of developing questionnaires for operational services on the lines of those already in use for functional systems. To my surprise, he told me that this idea had already been the subject of development work by their American partnership and a lengthy book published on the suject; surely an elegant testimony to the value of wider professional co-operation.

One final comment on the subject of VFM auditing. The CIPFA Report for 1984–85 dropped through the letter-box just as I was completing this paper. It contained the following paragraphs on the *Role of External Audit*:

> "External audit has also shown in the last year the contribution which it can make to VFM in the public sector. The National Audit Office ... has made an important contribution with its wide-ranging VFM reports prepared under the new section of the National Audit Act 1983. Thirty-five reports have been published to date including an examination of waste arising from the operation of the rate support grant system.

16/4 Cyclical projects.

The Audit Commission ... has issued seven reports on reducing costs in local government services .... In addition the Commission has published two reports on the impact of government policies on local government's efficiency ....

In the National Health Service, the emphasis on improving efficiency has been through a restructuring of the management processes. No external agency, whether audit or central government, can substitute for good management and therefore the emphasis given to management within the Health Service shows a right sense of priority.

The issue which remains is how will improved management performance be measured and made public in a dispassionate manner?"

It is interesting to see how the wheel is turning full circle again. The thinking on the respective roles of authority and auditor which developed twenty years ago in relation to regularity is now being repeated in relation to management. CIPFA is surely correct in implying that in this latter field also it is for the organisation to provide sound systems and for the auditor to evaluate and report on them.

It is equally interesting to note that some of the Audit Commission's reports have referred to the impact of government policies on local government efficiency. In our evidence to the Layfield Committee (already referred to) we suggested that central government would be at least as likely to be exposed to criticism as local government if the external auditor were to be given a thorough VFM brief in the local government field. This view was based, partly at least, on our experience of the adverse effects on building costs of government policies related to improvment grants in the early 1970s. One cannot help but feel some satisfaction that, after so many years in which central government has concentrated on the mote in local government's eye and ignored the beam in its own, something is at last being done to adjust the balance.

JOHN SPEIRS CBE

Joined the Service in 1947 and retired as District Auditor of No 1AD in 1979. He was seconded to the Ministry in 1961 to work on local government reorganisation; in charge of audit training from 1962–65; served on the Audit Panel of the IMTA Computer Committee in the 1960s and on the Departmental Committee on DLOs in the late 1970s.

Reappraisal — A New Audit Philosophy

P F Kimmance CB

Many auditors can make justifiable claims to have contributed to the development of audit as we know it today. But undoubtedly it was Eric Keys who established a viable philosophical basis for its development and it was his drive and persistence which ensured its practical implementation.

Eric Keys was appointed district auditor of Number 2 Audit District (Preston) in 1960 and remained there for over a decade until his retirement. This period saw a very rapid development of local government services matched by somewhat inadequate attempts to improve district audit staffing. Eric Keys was very clear that there would be a serious failure in auditing unless its practical application was improved.

This led to an intensive study by the senior staff of Number 2 Audit District – Dick Edwards, the deputy (later succeeded by William Bird), Phil Court (at Ormskirk), Peter Kimmance (Bolton), Joe Lewis (Preston) and a little later, but at a vital junction, Eric Burdon (Preston). The result was an audit structure based on three interrelated stages – the overall review, essential tasks and cyclic programme.

In 1964 at a district conference in Preston, Stuart Collins (then Deputy Chief Inspector) suggested that the 'Reappraisal' exercise should be written up in the form of a report to the District Auditors' Conference. This was published in 1966, but by this time the ideas contained in the exercise were subject to wide debate, and the work was carried forward by an Audit Review Panel appointed by the District Auditors' Society.

The effect of all this activity was to lead to a much more systematic and analytical approach to auditing with an emphasis on management control and performance, rather than, as earlier, on the detection of fraud. This trend was recognised in the 1963–64 report of the Chief Inspector of Audit (Bill Munrow):

> "It is well recognised that the scope of auditing nowadays has expanded beyond detection of fraud which was one of its original main purposes. It has gone beyond the review of systems in the interest of security. Both remain important objectives for the auditor; but ever increasing importance is being attached to the service he can provide in his review of management control generally in the interests of efficiency and economy of administration."

Any present day auditor on reading the report on 'Reappraisal' (and Eric Keys' 1970 report on development) or the report of the District Auditors'

17/1

Society's Audit Review Panel will have no difficulty recognising the origins of current practice. The philosophy of the reports is reflected in the 1973 Local Government Code of Practice, and the Code issued by the Audit Commission a decade later.

It may be of interest to look at the background to these developments. Reappraisal laid emphasis on the proper use of 'comparisons of activities of authorities known to be similar in size and social background'. This led to the commissioning of a consultant to group authorities with social-economic similarities. Much effort was devoted to improving information. Staff from the Government Statistical Service were seconded to the Audit Inspectorate. The District Auditors' Society appointed a statistical panel which provided a valuable element of field experience to central processing. At the same time a useful dialogue with CIPFA was developed.

The linkman in all these activities was Jack Sprigg, who started his audit career in No 2 Audit District. He spent some time on secondment to the Civil Service Department working on 'performance measurement'. On his return he carried out (with Kash Pandya) an exercise which became known as the 'Epping Forest Study'. This was an attempt to produce a series of measures to be built in to the budgeting and accounting system.

The report on this work was widely criticised by the purists, since it contained a mixture of input and output measures. But the approach it advocated was successfully developed at Epping and other authorities. The Chief Executive who inspired the work was Peter Brokenshire, who finally came to rest at the Audit Commission, with a development of this technique ('authority profiles') as one of his responsibilities.

Although it would be satisfying to say that the profiles developed naturally from earlier work, it must be admitted that it arose from a presentational requirement when District Audit was competing for audits, prior to the establishment of the Audit Commission.

Another of the aims of Reappraisal was to limit the amount of time spent on regularity auditing. The original idea was to devote two-thirds of the audit time to keep auditing on a cyclic basis, including carrying out projects indicated by the overall review of external experience. Deep or project auditing was not new, but for the first time there was pressure on the auditor to devote a large proportion of his time to such studies.

As will be gleaned from the proceedings of the District Auditors' Society, 'audit of management' was part of these developments and it was the cause of heated debate among auditors. However, the work was strongly supported by the Chief Inspector (Bill Munrow) and the term 'value for money' began its remorseless progress.

Computers were not overlooked by reappraisal which advocated the development of specialists. Alan Edmonds and Bob Hutchings were the first to carry out this role on a service wide-basis and district specialists were slowly and painfully acquired.

P F KIMMANCE CB

His career on district audit was broken by a period of secondment as Finance Officer to the British Council which took him on many enviable jaunts around the world. As Chief Inspector of Audit from 1979–1982 he was deeply involved in the proposals for setting up the Audit Commission, and after his retirement he was appointed a member of the Commission. He served on the Council of CIPFA from 1979–83. Loves sailing small boats.

The Decade 1958–1968

Laurence Tovell

When Alan Wilson retired in June 1958 he was succeeded as Chief Inspector by Roy Bates who had been Deputy Chief Inspector for some nine years. John Kendrick, District Auditor No 14 AD was promoted to Deputy Chief Inspector. Some four months later the whole service was shocked and saddened by Roy's quite unexpected death during a visit of inspection of No 1 AD. John Kendrick was then appointed Chief Inspector and Bill Munrow, District Auditor Met AD, was promoted to Deputy Chief Inspector. When John Kendrick retired in 1965, Bill Munrow was appointed Chief Inspector until his retirement in 1968 when Stuart Collins took over.

Up to 1958, all members of staff recruited through the civil service executive grade competition were required to become professionally qualified. This qualification was issued by the Civil Service Commissioners following an examination which included local government finance and accounts, auditing, general law, and district law and procedure.

In 1958, however, it was decided to adopt the qualification of the then Institute of Municipal Treasurers and Accountants (IMTA) as the professional

qualification for district audit staff. The IMTA, which subsequently became the Chartered Institute of Public Finance and Accountancy (CIPFA), is the professional body whose qualification is specially designed to fit people to undertake the duties of accountants and financial managers in local government and other parts of the public sector. The decision to adopt the IMTA qualification undoubtedly enhanced the credibility of the district audit service and paved the way for considerable technical co-operation between the service and the IMTA which had important advantages for both parties.

At first, contact between the parties did not extend beyond the attendance of trainees at meetings of students' societies. Senior members of district audit were frequently invited to lecture on auditing and kindred matters at such meetings. If progress was slow at first, it was probably because it was felt that nothing must be done which might seem to compromise the independence of the auditor. By the end of the decade, any such misgivings had clearly disappeared and technical co-operation extended in a number of directions. The culmination of this process occurred in 1977 when the writer, at that time Chief Inspector, was co-opted a member of the CIPFA council.

Hindsight has undoubtedly demonstrated the wisdom of the decision to adopt the IMTA qualification. But one of the consequences, not unforeseen at the time, was to present a troublesome staffing problem for John

Kendrick and his successors. From 1959 onwards when the first IMTA trainees obtained the intermediate part of the professional qualification, there was a steady drain of staff to fill posts in local government for which the whole or part of the IMTA qualification was a prerequisite.

18/1 "Not quite what we had in mind".

There were three main reasons for this drain. The first was that remuneration in local government for qualified and part-qualified professional staff was undoubtedly higher than that paid to district audit staff, who were tied to civil service pay scales. Second was that because of the changing social and economic climate in the country as a whole, there was a growing resistance to the district audit practice of moving staff at times and to locations which did not accord with the individual's choice. Such a practice was almost unavoidable in managing a countrywide audit service. Staff began to realise that once in local government, they need not move again unless they chose to do so. A third reason was that in contrast to work in local government, district audit provided little scope for a change away from audit work.

Continuous efforts were made by the Chief Inspector to meet these objections. Pay incentives were introduced for staff at various stages of qualification, but these incentives were not good enough and the question of relative remuneration was still an unresolved problem by the end of the decade. Efforts were made to arrange secondments of staff to work in the finance and local government divisions of the Ministry of Housing and Local Government. But there were considerable practical difficulties involved, and not more than two or three members of the staff at any one time were able to take advantage of such secondment. A much more flexible and sympathetic attitude was adopted towards transfers. But not enough could be done in this direction to allay completely the misgivings of the staff.

By 1967 it was obvious that the concept of a wholly professional service was unattainable and probably unnecessary. Following the report of a working party set up to study the problem, the complement was divided into two streams – professional and non-professional – in almost equal numbers. Most of the professional staff were concentrated in the more senior grades who were in charge of the conduct of audits. This change at least recognised the facts of the situation, reduced to some extent the scale of the training programme, improved the promotion prospects for professional staff and introduced some stability into the complement. But the fundamental problem still remained.

The fact was that district audit was the equivalent of a large audit practice operating throughout England and Wales. The service was required to balance its budget by fees charged to local authorities. It was in competition with local government for staff and, to a limited extent, with firms of private accountants for work. The service needed flexibility in the recruitment, remuneration, promotion and management of staff which could not be provided by the rules of the civil service.

The situation became worse after local government reorganisation in 1972, when choice of audit was opened up to all authorities and many of the larger firms from the private sector became competitors of district audit. This problem was not solved until 1982 when, on the formation of the Audit Commission, the district audit service was hived off from the civil service.

From the operational point of view, this decade saw the beginnings of a shift of emphasis in the concept of the role of the public service audit. In the early sixties, many auditors felt that there should be more emphasis on the substance, rather than the form, of spending. The expression 'substance of spending' was synonymous with the expression 'value for money', which a decade later became an accepted objective of public service audits throughout the western world. Moreover, local government expenditure and the range of its activities were increasing rapidly all the time and yet the number of audit staff to deal with the situation remained static. It was felt that there was a need to develop an audit approach which made more efficient use of existing resources and had objectives more in keeping with the climate of opinion of the day.

To this end, in the mid 1960s, No 2 AD produced a document described as 'Reappraisal' which recommended far-reaching changes in the audit approach. It recommended a structured approach to the audit aimed at identifying and concentrating resources on the important issues, including the substance of spending. There is no doubt that this document had a tremendous influence on audit developments in the following decade.

Implementation of the recommendations was not without its problems. Perhaps the most difficult was the fear, articulated in many circles in local government,

that the auditor should stick to his last, not interfere in management. It was not until the end of the following decade, when the whole climate of opinion towards public spending had changed, that it was recognised that in many respects both auditors and management had the same objective, namely to ensure the efficient use of resources.

At the same time, many auditors felt that there were objections to the requirement imposed upon the auditor by statute to disallow every item of account contrary to law; and that the duty to impose a surcharge for losses due to negligence imposed an intolerable burden on the auditor and exposed officers and members in local government to risks which were not found in other parts of the public and private sectors. The ideas on how the auditors' powers might be amended, which were developed during the decade 1958 to 1968, were largely reflected in the changes to the audit code brought about by the Local Government Act 1972.

LAURENCE TOVELL

Joined the Service in 1938 and returned after war service in the Royal Navy. Appointed District Auditor in Birmingham in 1962, Deputy Chief Inspector of Audit in 1968, and Chief Inspector of Audit in 1976. After retiring in 1979, he chaired the joint CIPFA/DAS Society working party on Standards for the External Audit of Local Authorities.

The Audit Round prior to the Reorganisation of Local Government in 1972

A R Harris

The scope and style of auditing changed dramatically with the reorganisation of local government in 1972. Any consideration of the audit round prior to the 1972 reorganisation needs a starting point and, with so many conflicting claims, perhaps the most easily identifiable break with the past occurred in the immediate post-war period.

During the war years 1939 to 1945 both the audit service and local government had functioned remarkably well despite seriously depleted staff numbers; but it was inevitable that some work was very much in arrears. From 1946 onwards, the staff situation gradually improved, at least as far as numbers were concerned. Slowly audit sections returned to a reasonable size but there was unfortunately a dearth of experience. Those who had carried the burden during the war years now proved invaluable in the situation where the junior staff were almost wholly without experience of either local government or auditing. Directing officers were made up of those who, because of age or other circumstances, had not been in the forces and those returning from the war who had had some pre-war audit service and who were quickly retrained and promoted.

The strain on the directing staff was considerable. Not only were they under great pressure attempting to cope with their newly acquired responsibilities, but they also had to control, manage, direct and desk train a mixed bag of sometimes boisterous ex-servicemen to whom the proprieties of the audit room did not necessarily come naturally.

Local authorities were also in a similar situation, with large numbers of staff returning after an absence of several years. Work was substantially in arrears with, in many cases, the accounts for two or more years awaiting to be balanced and closed down. This state of affairs had repercussions on the audit service and it was not uncommon for the audits of two to three years to be undertaken simultaneously at some even large authorities. The certification of claims was particularly onerous, especially those relating to war damage.

Despite the strenuous efforts of all concerned, there was no magic formula for ensuring a swift return to normality and it was not until 1948–49 that, generally speaking, it was possible to conceive an audit programme relating to one year's closed accounts.

In 1947, training began for the new audit examiners recruited through the civil service reconstruction examinations for ex-servicemen. This training took the form of a correspondence course arranged and supervised by a training section at audit headquarters. The training period was three years with examinations at the end of the first and third years.

Armed with ever-increasing knowledge and confidence gained from a combination of the correspondence course notes, the *Brown Book* (a handbook compiled by senior staff of audit techniques and summaries of the law), practical experience and guidance from the directing officers, the new recruits soon developed into an efficient force. This rapid transformation was helped by the fact that most of them were mature students in their late twenties, determined to acquire professional qualifications and positions of responsibility as soon as possible. For some, success came sooner than could have been expected.

The Service was seriously short of directing staff, notably in the assistant district auditor grade. There appeared to be two options. One was to keep the Service going in its depleted form and to wait for suitable, qualified, directing officers to emerge after the final examinations, the first of which was programmed to announce results in the autumn of 1950. The second

19/1 The opening.

option was to select from the high achievers in the preliminary examinations – in 1948 and 1949 – and to promote them to the grade of assistant district auditor on the understanding that failure in the final examination would result in reversion to the audit examiner grade.

The latter course was adopted and a new breed of partially qualified ADAs was created, many of whom were eventually to become district auditors. The majority of these ADAs were required to move to new districts where they were put in charge of small sections with their own audit programmes. Although each had a SADA to look to for advice and support, the transition was quite dramatic and stressful. Few of the new ADAs had much, if any, experience of ledger or claims work, and very often found themselves having to direct long-serving audit examiners not only much older but vastly more experienced than themselves. That the system worked as well as it did is a tribute to the tact and understanding displayed by all.

Although it cannot be denied that the newly-appointed ADAs were seriously lacking in work experience and had had little opportunity to obtain or practice management skills, the types of local authority that usually made up an ADA's programme greatly facilitated the repair of those deficiencies. Apart from assisting the SADA at the major audit – the county council or county borough council – an ADA would normally have had his own programme, consisting of smaller urban district councils, rural district councils and their parish councils and a few joint committees or boards. This was also the time when rating valuation work was undertaken by assessment committees, whose accounts were subject to district audit. These committees were abolished when valuation work was

transferred to the Inland Revenue.

There was a lot of variety in the types of authorities and little similarity between authorities in their systems and records. Some of the smaller authorities audits could be completed within a week so that, in the space of one year's audit programme, a considerable number of audit tasks could be undertaken and repeated. This made possible the speedy acquisition of expertise and the ability to compare and assess the value of different records and methods of dealing with similar functions. Local authority staff in general were familiar only with their own authority's systems and it was soon evident that the district audit staff had much to offer by sharing their experience. Best practices were made available throughout the districts and many recommendations were made for improving individual systems on the grounds of greater efficiency and security. It was extremely satisfying for a trainee audit examiner to be able to discover a weakness, make recommendations and then see his proposals put into effect.

The geographical areas of audit districts vary considerably, then as now, and not all local authority offices were conveniently near to an audit centre. Daily travel was sometimes lengthy and tedious. Few of the staff had cars in the early post-war period and to acquire a new one meant being on a car dealer's waiting list for several years. Most travel, therefore, was undertaken by bus or train.

Daily journeys were often long and uncomfortable necessitating many hours away from home each day. Another consequence was that some audits which could have been reached daily by car became stay – away audits by public transport. Hotel accommodation was not then so plentiful so stay-away audits were arranged outside the busy periods. During the winter/spring of 1947–48 the author spent 20 weeks out of 26 staying away from home Mondays to Fridays at deserted seaside resorts in Kent and Sussex.

In later years, stay-away audits became fewer as car travel became more available. In fact in some districts the almost complete elimination of stay-away audits sometimes made the few that remained quite attractive, depending on their location, and the subject of some competition. It could be a welcome break to have a few weeks in late April or May at some pleasant spot after a winter of continuous urban audits.

On these occasions, more often than not, a section would all stay at the same hotel or boarding house; and in the evenings there would be outings to local beauty spots, visits to the cinema, or possibly theatre, and often late night sessions playing cards. By these means it was possible to get to know one's colleagues really well; but this closeness did not necessarily apply across a district and members of different sections could be complete strangers. The only opportunity to meet one's colleagues on other sections occurred at staff conferences and any

19/2 The auditor's opinion.

district social functions. Such opportunities usually occurred only once a year and both usually took place on the same day, the annual staff conference being followed by the annual staff dinner.

During the 1950s the directing staff posts were all filled and the staff structure became stabilised. Thereafter few vacancies occurred and many officers waited until the late 1960s for promotion. The effect of this seemingly endless wait was to produce a frustrated group of young qualified audit examiners. An intelligent review of the

19/3 System questionnaires.

seniority list, combined with an elementary knowledge of the nature of probability, gave gloomy results. It was fortunate for this group that the powers-that-be decided to phase out the in-house training scheme and substitute the IMTA examinations.

So it was that from 1960–61 the audit service began to produce audit examiners with the IMTA qualification, something that was much more marketable than its predecessor. Not everybody in the Service was – or is – convinced that the change was for the better, or that the new training was as appropriate to the work of an auditor. However, this is not the place to debate that point. To those with the IMTA qualification a new world of opportunities was opened, and over the next few years a large number of young qualified staff left the Service for posts in local government. The departure of these young officers meant that there was a constant need for new recruits who, in their turn, were liable to be seduced by the rewards offered by local government.

For a time the strain on the audit service was considerable, with sometimes half a section made up of students at various stages of training, many of whom would either not complete their studies or would not remain after qualification. There was, therefore, a constantly changing stratum of young audit examiners in whom there was a large investment by the Service and from whom the Service did not fully derive the benefits expected. At grass roots level, this meant that directing officers were deprived to a significant degree of the qualified assistance they were entitled to expect.

The Service became ever more conscious of the fact that its limited resources needed to be deployed with the greatest economy in order to achieve satisfactory standards of auditing. To improve control over the audits and to direct attention to where it was most needed, a reappraisal of the planning, reviewing and record-keeping procedures was carried out and recommendations were made which, with some local adjustments, were adopted throughout the Service. The reappraisal gave birth to a new approach which became known as the 'structured form of audit'.

Like most innovations, this process has by now become one of the accepted audit techniques, but in the mid-1960s it was startlingly new. Records were improved to keep abreast of the change in approach and the foundations were laid for a management system which has continued to expand to meet changing demands. The initial implementation of the structured audit meant a departure from the previous methods of attempting to cover all aspects of an audit at each visit. This had resulted in spreading the available resources thinly over a wide variety of tasks.

The new approach drew attention, by the overall review, to heads of income and expenditure that seemed to require special attention; it listed those essential tasks that needed to be performed as a priority at every audit; and it reserved a proportion of the time available for the examination of the items spotlighted by the overall review,and an in-depth audit of other matters which was conducted on a cyclical basis.

Part of this new approach had its roots in an earlier attempt to probe beneath the surface in what was known as 'deep auditing'. This had begun in the mid-1950s when attempts were made to select a number of items of income or expenditure at each audit and subject them to close examination, looking at every stage in the transaction, involving decisions of members and

officers, the systems and controls in force, security, and the safe custody of assets.

From these early attempts grew the technique of 'value for money' auditing, which began to flourish in the mid-1960s as part of the new structured audit approach. However, value for money auditing was not greeted with universal approval by either auditors or local authority chief officers. Some auditors took the view that such enquiries were outside their statutory duties, while some chief officers were more forthright and declared that auditors were enquiring into matters that

19/4 The computer.

were none of their business. Fortunately, this opposition subsided when auditors began to demonstrate that considerable savings could be made as a result of their recommendations.

In the late 1960s two other innovations were introduced. Both involved the formation of special audit teams working under the direction of audit headquarters and both teams visited selected audits anywhere in England and Wales.

The first team consisted of specially trained computer experts whose purpose was to visit local authorities that had installed a computer and to review their systems and offer advice of a practical nature. This team was an outstanding success. It was a revelation to the local authority chief officers to see auditors who could, *inter alia*, devise retrieval programmes, operate their computers and produce results which seemed, at the time, little short of miraculous. The work done by this team did much to enhance the reputation of the district audit service.

The second team's task was to carry out an appraisal of the quality and effectiveness of the audit work undertaken by the individual auditors and their staff at selected large authorities. The visits by this team could not be called popular – they were regarded by some as an unwelcome intrusion. The audit team under review were required to submit their files to scrutiny, and the management and direction of the audit was closely examined. It may be wondered what special qualifications the members of the appraisal team possessed, other than the benefit of hindsight. It was clearly necessary for them to keep a sense of proportion, not to look for perfection, and to bear in mind the

difficulties under which many directing officers had to work. The members of the inspection team were changed from time to time, and the daunting thought was that, one day, the biter might himself be bit!

It will be clear that during the quarter century from 1945 to 1970, the audit service was subject to great changes and pressures. Some of these have been mentioned, but others, too, deserve a passing reference. Many techniques enjoyed a brief popularity and some proved of more permanent worth. There was planned programme budgeting, cost benefit analysis, critical path analysis, discounted cash flow, and the joys of random sampling applied usually to expenditure vouchers. It seems a long time since anyone carried tables of random numbers to an audit! But the greatest trial of all was the perennial problem of staff complements. Not only were the staff numbers rarely up to complement, but the complements were inadequate.

The practical difficulty of running a section must not be dismissed lightly. The problems began with the compilation of the annual programme. It resembled the piecing together of a jigsaw puzzle. The section might consist of two directing officers with four or five staff. The workload for the section might typically include 30 or so medium or small audits of borough, urban and rural councils, numerous parishes, assistance with the county council audit and a number of joint committees and boards. All the staff would be required to state their major leave requirements for the full year before planning could begin.

The programme planned for each directing officer and the sharing out of staff would have to have regard to those few authorities known to be capable of presenting balanced accounts early; the size of the audit accommodation available, which clearly affected the number of staff assigned to each audit; the local authority treasurer's leave arrangements and the availability of cars or public transport.

When either directing officer was on leave, all the staff of necessity would have to work together. If each section had only one car available, then the absence of a car owner could be critical. If an audit were scheduled to be completed within a short time, say a week with a staff of two or three, then an unforeseen day's sick leave or an urgent need for a day's annual leave could delay the closure, maybe for some time because of the practical difficulties and diseconomies of a return visit.

The accumulation of a number of outstanding audits was deceptively easy and it was disproportionately time-consuming to deal with them. Strenuous efforts were therefore made to prevent audits overrunning.

19/5 Final discussions.

It was always necessary for the directing officer to keep a tight control over the daily progress of each audit and to deal promptly with any tendency to allow the timetable to slip. If an audit were timed to last one week, there was no time to spare. During those five days the audit programme had to be drafted and work allocated to each officer with quite precise indications of the time available for each job.

The directing officer would usually reserve to himself, as a minimum, the reading of the minutes, the examination of the ledger, the checking of the claims on government departments, the day-to-day supervision, the collation of matters for discussion, the final discussions with chief officers and, of course, the certification of the accounts. The tempo of these audits was quite different from that of a county council where time lost one day could be made up later.

At these small audits, it was essential that the planned tasks were fully completed – not nearly completed – by the end of the final day. The only exception to this golden rule was when serious irregularity or fraud occurred or was suspected. The last afternoon was quite hectic with a number of jobs nearing completion, while the directing officer was preparing to discuss the matters arising from the audit with the chief officers.

Another problem in rural districts was the audits of the attendant parish councils and meetings. Parish clerks in scattered rural communities often had difficulty in attending the audit other than on market days, when more local public transport was usually available. The parish accounts had to be audited in time to meet that deadline, whatever the difficulties.

After the audit had been concluded, there was still a lot of work for the directing officer to complete. The audit notes had to be assembled in a rational order and indexed; the notes and matters agreed with chief officers had to be redrafted in the form of letters to those officers; the draft audit report was prepared; certified claims recorded and assembled for despatch and various district internal control forms completed. This work was usually done at home so that no intrusion would be made into the time allotted to the following audit.

It was not uncommon for the chairman of the council or of the finance committee to attend for a discussion of the council's financial position; but it was rather exceptional to meet the full council or all the members of a committee. This usually occurred only when there were serious matters of major importance to discuss and almost certainly would involve the presence of the district auditor.

To be a successful directing officer it was necessary to exercise disciplined control over audits, and this had to be maintained week after week. There was nothing to be gained other than worry and frustration if a timetable was not adhered to.

However, it must not be thought that it was only the audit service that was under pressure and suffering from a variety of shortcomings. The staff employed at many small local authorities, even at the highest level, were to a large extent unqualified other than by experience. It was not unusual for directing officers to be relied upon to help with the preparation of statutory forms – notably the Epitome of Accounts and the Statutory Financial Statement – and the claims on government departments.

Between audits it was also quite usual for treasurers to telephone the directing officer often in the evenings at home for advice. This was perhaps an indication of the close working relationship that existed between the treasurer and the auditor, and it can be taken as a compliment that a treasurer should feel able to turn to the auditor for help.

It may be of interest to reflect on the small size of many local authorities before the 1972 reorganisation. During the 1960s, the author's programme included a small rural district council, with one parish, which was run, as a part-time job, entirely by one man who was also a part-time solicitor's clerk. Another small urban council had a total staff of six – a clerk, a treasurer and a surveyor each with one assistant. These were exceptional cases, but a combined clerk and chief financial officer's department of six or less was very common.

There was practically no mechanisation of accounting records in those offices and every financial record was completed manually. It is perhaps difficult for those

19/6 The close

who have not experienced it to imagine that every receipt issued, all the collectors' records, the posting of receipts from rents, rates, sundry debtors and housing advances, the records relating to salaries and wages, the entries in the cash book, the drawing of cheques and the analysis of expenditure were all manual operations.

With such small staff numbers, the smaller authorities had no internal audit and very limited possibilities for adequate separation of duties or internal check. Opportunities to commit fraud were, therefore, freely available, but, given the circumstances, surprisingly few frauds appear to have been committed. Details of discovered frauds were circulated then as now, and they appeared to occur in cycles – a series of income frauds giving way to a succession of expenditure frauds.

There was a temptation to follow the trends and to switch the major audit effort from income to

expenditure and back again – and this had to be resisted. Most frauds were very simple, being based on some form of misappropriation of cash collections, the falsification of wage records or the insertion of false or duplicate invoices. The more elaborate and ingenious frauds usually occurred only in the larger authorities.

In spite of all the difficulties that beset auditors prior to the 1972 reorganisation, the officers serving in the field, who made up the core of the Service, must have performed their duties well and have been held in high regard by local authority members and officers. For when the Local Government Act 1972 required each new local authority to choose the form of audit they preferred, the final result was overwhelmingly in favour of the District Audit Service. Without that massive vote of confidence it is debatable whether the Service could have survived to play its part in the events that lay ahead.

A R HARRIS

Started out in the National Insurance Audit Department but, after war service, transferred to district audit in 1947. Retired in 1981 as District Auditor in Chester. Has a great fondness for the Lake District and also enjoys touring abroad.

Experiences of Fraud

D F Kelley

'And now', said my chief, 'you must find a fraud'.

I had just passed my final qualifying exam and was basking in a glow of relief at clearing a dreaded hurdle. Failure could have brought down on my head the ultimate sanction: banishment to the Department. District audit was an elite service. Admission to it required a high pass in the civil service entrance exam. In return, it offered an interesting career in a field far removed from Whitehall and carrying a degree of independence unlikely to be found in the Department. It was this independence which had first attracted me. But to stay in the Service one had to pass the stiff qualifying exams; if not at the first attempt, certainly at the second. Otherwise, the Department.

With the exam and three years' hard study behind me, I was looking forward to a rather more relaxed time. Heeley's warning came as a most unwelcome jolt to my complacency.

'You're expected to find one from time to time', he added.

He handed me a copy of the latest half-yearly fraud report, detailing the recent cases. It looked a modest list. A mere dozen cases. Twelve frauds in six months from the entire country. I cast my mind back over the many faces which had come before me in the past three years. No rogues there, I decided: every one a model of rectitude, palpably honest. How could I expect to find a fraud among such a saintly lot?

However, to seek them out, if they existed, was now evidently an important part of my duties. Hopes of a more relaxed approach to my work faded, soon to vanish altogether – and never return. Auditors, I found, were always under pressure: so much to do, so little time to do it in. Not that I minded that: better to be pressed than bored.

But how on earth was I to fulfil this duty to find frauds? A police officer did not first have to find the crime he investigated: it was presented to him, ready committed. But we on district audit had this far more difficult task of first finding our fraud before we could investigate it; finding it, moreover – if indeed it existed (which it probably did not) – from amongst a daunting mass of documentation and figures. A difficult task and, seemingly, an impossible one, short of phenomenal luck.

And yet – such is life's unpredictability – I was to find myself within three months with three frauds on my hands.

They were found – like so many frauds, as I later learned – not by individual brilliance but by teamwork; teamwork, and the judicious application of special checks when the books seemed not to be giving the correct or the whole story.

My special partner in these early cases was Derrick Turpin, who had joined the Service straight from school shortly after I came to it from war service. It was Turpin who unearthed the first, a relatively minor case of a school catering assistant failing to bank all her school meals takings. In checking the possibility of other Plymouth schools having similar problems, we noticed that a large secondary modern school was accounting for weekly meals collections far below the level one would expect for a school of its size.

20/1 "You're expected to find a fraud from time to time".

We called in the meals registers detailing the pupils taking meals each day. Not many seemed to be taking them. The registers, we noted, were all in the same handwriting, and there were innumerable alterations. We asked for the statutory attendance registers which, being kept by individual class teachers, were likely to provide some check on the meals registers. To our surprise they were brought in by the Head Teacher, who, it turned out, kept the meals registers himself. A long session with him failed to resolve the confusion, and it became apparent that some sort of direct check would be necessary. Letters were accordingly sent to all parents requesting details of meals taken and amounts paid.

After several days not one letter had come back. Our fears that we might have real trouble on our hands looked like being confirmed. We decided to call on parents in some of the more baffling cases. At my very first call suspicion became certainty. I learnt that the Head Teacher had assembled the whole school and instructed pupils to collect our letters from their parents and bring them to him. It also became clear, at that first call (and confirmed by others), that money had been paid which had not been accounted for.

Late that night I phoned Heeley, and the three of us presented ourselves outside the Head's study the following morning before he arrived. At least, that was our intention. in fact at 8am he was already sitting at his desk, writing up fresh meals registers.

Heeley had met this sort of situation before and knew exactly what to look for. We searched the Head's study – and found what he expected: rough notebooks setting out the true facts of what had been paid to the Head for school meals.

That school was in the poorest part of Devonport, and the monies paid to him (and largely pocketed) had been hard earned by parents much worse off than him. Our sympathy when he was fined, dismissed and stripped of his pension was therefore muted. But it was sad to see a man in his position and so near retirement stooping to such deceits.

Financial pressures had clearly got the better of him. We found much evidence of this in his study, including boxes of cigarette ends, picked up who knows where, from which he was wont to roll his own cigarettes.

The first serious fraud taught me many things, and two in particular. First, that fraud can arise in the most unlikely places (and what more respectable quarter than a school?) and be perpetrated by unlikely people (this was a civilised, likeable man, patently anxious to help). In local government, when fraud reared its head, we were dealing not with hardened reprobates but with ordinary people for whom temptation allied with opportunity (and stimulated perhaps by financial pressures) had proved too much; people not wicked, but weak.

The other lesson was the importance, when we had doubts about the rightness or completeness of the records before us, of applying direct checks so devised as to resolve the doubts, one way or another. And timing of the checks was often vital. If Heeley had not moved in that morning, the unofficial (true) records would almost certainly have been destroyed. While this would not have frustrated detection of the fraud, it would certainly have complicated the calculation of the amount.

Which brings me to the third case. It was an unusual one. Years later I realised it was one of the very rare instances of corruption which were found at audit. It occurred, in fact, before the meals frauds but had somehow – perhaps because of its unusual nature – not registered with us as a fraud. Only when I was preparing the report on the Devonport case did I realise that this one too ought to have a wider circulation.

Down in West Cornwall there was a small cemetery controlled by a joint burial committee. Its day-to-day running was in the hands of a superintendent-sexton – a typical one-man show. We had had problems with him in the past, chiefly to do with the carrying out of private work in official time. At our suggestion the Committee had expressly forbidden this and had defined his duties more clearly.

As with most cemeteries in that part of the country, the local monumental masons operated not from small yards sited near the entrance, but from granite quarries many miles away. They were largely dependent for their business on recommendations from the sexton. But they also put their names in small black lettering at the foot of the more elaborate memorials.

The usual audit tour of the cemetery produced a crop of queries concerning memorials by one particular mason, who seemed to be getting the lion's share of the business. I drove out to the quarry with my list of points and knocked at the door of the small hut which stood duty as office. The boss was away but his clerk received me courteously. He produced his petty cash book, from which the memorial fees due to the Committee were paid. They seemed in order, but some entries in another column aroused my curiosity.

'What', I asked, 'are all these other payments to the sexton, in the "travelling expenses" column?'

'Oh, that's what we give him for bringing us the business.'

That delightful but damning admission would of course never have been made had I been dealing with the boss rather than with an innocent young clerk. The payments were simply bribes: sweeteners to recommend this mason rather than a rival. There were dozens of payments, one for each memorial and sometimes of quite large amount; in one case of an elaborate Italian marble statue, the equivalent of a week's wages.

Case law required that the bribes be paid over to the Committee, and this was done, together with lesser amounts of similar nature paid by a local undertaker. What happened to the sexton I no longer recall. But the case itself often recurred to me when we were dealing with the much more serious cases of corruption associated with the Poulson affair in the late sixties. Detection and proof of this type of fraud are exceptionally difficult, and lucky breaks such as I had in that Cornish quarry did not often come our way.

Corruption, of course, was a form of fraud which, in our audit world, I interpreted as embracing any case of loss to a local authority which stemmed from dishonesty on the part of a person or persons with whom the authority had a close relationship. This included not only members, officers and servants but also contractors, who were in a peculiarly strong position to defraud because their overcharges could so easily be made to appear accidental and therefore innocent.

More often than not when contractors overcharged, the

evidence would not sustain a charge of fraud, and we had to be content with a refund of the amount overcharged. In many cases the overcharges were, indeed, genuinely accidental, or stemmed from differing interpretations of the provisions of the contract. But some were undoubtedly deliberate. I recall one such at Portsmouth, some 30 years ago, which touched off a whole series of other investigations involving the same method of overcharge. It relied simply on a mis-statement of the tare weights of vehicles used to supply goods in bulk to the Council.

A coal merchant at Portsmouth supplied coal in bulk to a number of schools in the city and also to an old people's home. At the entrance to the home was a weighbridge, on which the vehicles delivering coal were weighed both on arrival (loaded) and on departure (empty); the difference between the two weights being the net weight of coal chargeable to the Council. The schools, however, had no weighbridges. Supplies to them were weighed on the weighbridge at the railway yard where the merchant had his depot. Weightickets showing the gross, tare and net weights were provided in all cases. Besides the weights, they gave the number of the delivering vehicle and, usually, the deliverer's name.

A comparison of the weightickets for the old people's home with those for the schools revealed that the tare weights on the former were consistently about half a ton higher than those on the schools' tickets. The higher weights, having been taken on the home's weighbridge, were believed to be correct. A reference to motor tax files for the vehicles concerned reinforced our suspicion that the tare weights shown on the schools' tickets were – making due allowance for items not included for tax purposes (fuel, tools etc) – about half a ton less than they

should have been. A visit to the railway weighbridge confirmed that tare weights were merely 'stated'. And, it seemed, were being consistently understated – with resulting overstating of the net weight of coal for which the Council was charged.

15 council officials 'fiddled' mileage

Express Staff Reporter

FIFTEEN officials—mostly women — employed by Kent County Council have been caught out " fiddling " their car-mileage returns.

Three of them—two midwives and a home nurse—have been sacked. Another woman, a senior assistant in the health department, has been ordered to repay £27 out of her salary.

Last night a council spokesman said: " The cases concerned officers using cars owned by the county council. They failed to pay the council for private mileage.

" Officials have been allowed to do 2,500 miles on private trips providing they pay the council a mileage rate."

BOMBSHELL

One of the midwives, who has been prosecuted, admitted she had claimed £53 for professional mileage which was private.

The other midwife and the home nurse—neither was prosecuted—were involved in sums of £108 and £45.

The expenses " bombshell " was dropped yesterday in a report by district auditor Mr. Arthur Vale. It was immediately made available to the public and may be debated at next Wednesday's council meeting.

20/2 "15 council officials 'fiddled' mileage": A report from the Daily Express, 22 February, 1964.

COUNCILLORS TRAVELLED 'THIRD'—CHARGED 'FIRST'

SURCHARGES totalling £288 7s. 8d. on members and officials of Bedlington, Northumberland, all-Labour council have been imposed by the district auditor, Mr. H. L. Stevens.

In a report, published yesterday, Mr. Stevens criticises what he terms "gross over-spending, inefficient administration and financial control," during 1949-50.

Of the total sum surcharged £132 15s. 2d. has been marked up against sixteen councillors and nine officials for incorrect expense claims.

The report says: "Expense claims from members and officials were found to be incorrect in the following respects:

"First-class fares had been claimed when actual journeys were made third-class;

"Fares had been claimed which had not actually been incurred; subsistence allowances had been claimed for days and periods when absence from home was unnecessary

"Financial loss allowances had been claimed when no loss was suffered and for absences in excess of the necessary periods."

Mr. Stevens also criticises the lack of proper action to recover rate and council house rent arrears.

20/3 "Councillors travelled 'third' – charged 'first' ": A report from the Daily Mirror, 23 February, 1951.

At this stage I called in my Chief, John Kendrick, later to be head of the Service. He had had experience of serious coal overcharges in London some years before, and – like Heeley in the earlier case – knew exactly what to do. He called in the firm's books and matched up purchases from collieries with supplies to the Council and other customers. The railway records of wagon loads arriving at the yard for the firm were also examined. It was abundantly clear that more coal had been charged out to customers than had been purchased; and that a major factor in this overcharging was the consistent understating of tare weights in all cases where the vehicles were not weighed empty.

As auditors we had no doubt that the overcharges were made deliberately with a view to defrauding the Council and other customers. The firm was a small family business, its half a dozen lorries all driven by members of the family. They undoubtedly knew what they were doing and why they were doing it. However, to establish *mens rea*, or guilty intent was never easy where firms, rather than individuals, were concerned. The Chief Constable and the Council's law officers advised against prosecution. The firm was required to repay the overcharges and was removed from the Council's list of approved suppliers.

This difficulty of knowing whether to prosecute a contractor who has overcharged was always with us. Most such overcharges arose from technicalities in complex building contracts, and even an auditor – who, I found, develops a powerful sense of right and wrong – would be hard put to it to determine whether it was deliberate or accidental.

After the Portsmouth affair, many more cases were unearthed where bulk suppliers of coal or roadstone were understating tare weights. No prosecutions were made, but all were required to refund the sums overcharged, and most were removed from the councils' approved lists.

Sometimes the mis-statements were the other way. If the contractor was buying goods from the Council (rather than selling goods to them) the temptation would be to overstate the tare weight; then the net weight would be understated and the contractor would pay the council less than he should.

This arose particularly with salvage collected from council depots. At Guildford a scrap merchant collecting baled waste paper in bulk from the council was found to be consistently overstating his vehicle weights. He, too, had to restore a substantial sum to the council. We found he was also understating the weights for motor tax purposes, and the resulting underpayments had, again, to be made good.

Another case which one felt was deliberate but which did not lead to prosecution concerned the painting of white lines on roads. My keen young assistant, Roger Carrier, later to be a very young council treasurer, spotted suspicious features in bills for the painting of these lines on roads in west Surrey. Dimensions of the lines were prescribed by statutory instrument, and failure by the contractor to conform strictly with the specification could result (as a recent case had shown) in failure on technical grounds of prosecutions for certain road traffic offences. So there was more to the matter than mere possibility of overcharge.

To resolve the queries Carrier and I, with officers of the Highways Department, spent a pleasant morning trundling a measuring wheel along a selection of road

lengths through the west Surrey countryside. The line in most general use was a hyphenated one in which the painted 'dashes' were required to be 15 feet long.

We found that in all cases they were 14 feet long!

Other, lesser, 'underlinings' had occurred, and once again there was a useful repayment to the Council.

One case in the late sixties which did lead to prosecution concerned some small-scale building contractors, who, with the Council's own direct labour force, shared the housing maintenance work in the City of Westminster. It had earlier become evident that, in the recently reorganised London boroughs, housing repairs expenditure was going to be a troublesome field for audit. At the previous audit, Camden, there had been substantial overclaims of bonus by workmen of the direct labour organisation. Cliff Scott, a shrewd investigator and never one to be put off by specious explanations, had burrowed deep into the DLO accounts. By matching timesheets and bonus sheets against the independently prepared works orders and stores issues, he had established that in many cases bonus had been claimed for work which could not possibly have been done. Visits to the houses and flats concerned had confirmed the overcharges.

These investigations into large numbers of individually small overcharges involve thousands of documents and much field work. When we moved on to Westminster I offered Scott a choice of the same housing repairs field or some less demanding area of the accounts. After the long and exhausting Camden investigation he had earned a break, and we could properly defer housing repairs till the following year: in the aftermath of reorganisation, there was much else of potential importance awaiting our attention.

Much as I privately expected, Scott decided to give Westminster the benefit of the experience gained at Camden, while it was fresh in his mind. Once again, he was joined by Derek Whalley and Don Maguire, who had done much of the detailed work at Camden. The same approach was called for – matching timesheets and overtime claims against independent records.

Within days, Scott was running into trouble. As at Camden, jobs had been charged for which could not have been done. Here, however, it was overtime rather than bonus which was the suspect field. Even the basic hours appeared in some cases not to have been worked. There was similar trouble with the contractors, who were charging on a dayworks basis at so much per hour worked by their men.

The investigation which followed surpassed even the Camden one for duration and sheer fatigue. In addition to thousands of Council documents, we had to examine the books, timesheets etc of half a dozen contractors. Many months passed before it was all wrapped up, the offenders dealt with and repayments made.

One contractor was successfully prosecuted, another narrowly escaped that fate. All were removed from the Council's approved list. Workmen and supervisors were disciplined and, in the more flagrant cases, dismissed. Very substantial reductions in overtime were achieved as soon as the investigation got under way. And there were fundamental changes in procedures to ensure better control for the future.

Among many interesting, and sometimes amusing,

features of that investigation, several come readily to mind. A common practice of the contractors was to charge for a mate when none was used or needed, the tradesman (plumber, carpenter etc) managing perfectly well on his own. In some cases the mate named had left the firm's employment, a fact which calling for the insurance card helped to uncover. One contractor on whom I called on a Friday and on whose wages book I raised a number of queries, produced on the Monday when I went back a wages book superficially similar but with subtle differences here and there in the contents. When I challenged him (on the strength of the notes I had made from the earlier book) he broke down and confessed everything. He had spent the whole weekend writing up the fresh but false record – just as that head teacher had started to do, twenty years before.

Another contractor produced, among other records, jobsheets which had ostensibly been prepared by workmen for each separate job done. Close examination revealed that the original pencil entries by the workmen had been overwritten in ink. The most important entry was the one on the basis of which the charge would be made on the Council: the number of hours worked. By holding the job sheet at a certain angle to the light, it was possible to trace the slight indentation made by the workman's original pencil entry. It could be clearly seen that in many cases the subsequent inking in was at a higher figure than the original entry.

The head of the firm was away and his two clerks professed ignorance of the matter. Local gossip had it that the head, who had just taken over from his father, was pursuing a lifestyle far above what might be expected of a small-time builder. The police were, however, unable to pin the fraudulent alterations on him or on anyone else, and there was no prosecution, only a recovery – of substantial amount.

I took many close-up photographs of these and other documents which were keys to the detection and evaluation of these funds. With an appropriate text they made an interesting conference paper which was later used at headquarters for training purposes.

The Camden and Westminster frauds, and other lesser ones which followed, were, I believe, one of the less happy consequences of the major reorganisation of the London authorities which had taken place a year or two before. The investigations brought me in to close contact with employees at all levels, from the workmen on the ground, through foremen and lower management, to the upper echelons in City Hall.

MYSTERY OF A LONDON MESSENGER

EDMONTON police are searching for a member of the staff of the Edmonton Borough Council who disappeared to-day after calling at a bank and collecting for wages a sum believed to be about £1700. He did not return from the bank, which is only about 100 yards away.

Colleagues

Watch For Man With £1,700

SEA and air port authorities were asked by the police last night to look out for John Lloyd Phillips, a Londoner, missing with £1,700 in notes.

Phillips, an Edmonton Borough Council employee, vanished after leaving Barclays Bank in Edmonton Broadway.

He had only a few hundred yards to go to his destination, the Town Hall.

Phillips was one of three men who went to collect about £2,000 for Council staff wages.

The cashier handed him £1,700 in notes and he went out, leaving the other two men behind to collect the silver and copper.

When these men returned to the Town Hall and found that Phillips was not there, the police were informed.

Later another cheque was cashed to cover the missing money.

20/4 Newspaper clippings from June 1938 reporting the case of J L Phillips who disappeared with £1,700 of Edmonton Council wages.

20/5 Newspaper clippings covering the corruption case against D H Turnock Smith in 1962.

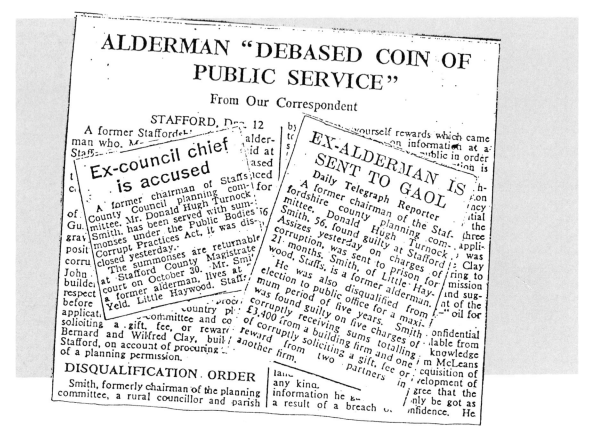

ALDERMAN "DEBASED COIN OF PUBLIC SERVICE"

From Our Correspondent

STAFFORD, Dec 12

A former Stafford alderman who...

Ex-council chief is accused

A former chairman of Staffs County Council planning committee, Mr. Donald Hugh Turnock Smith, has been served with summonses under the Public Bodies Corrupt Practices Act, it was disclosed yesterday.

The summonses are returnable at Stafford County Magistrate court on October 30. Mr. Smith, a former alderman, lives at Yeld, Little Haywood, Staffs.

soliciting a gift, fee, or reward from Bernard and Wilfred Clay, builders, of Stafford, on account of procuring a planning permission.

DISQUALIFICATION ORDER

Smith, formerly chairman of the planning committee, a rural councillor and parish...

EX-ALDERMAN IS SENT TO GAOL

Daily Telegraph Reporter

A former chairman of the Staffordshire county planning committee, Donald Hugh Turnock Smith, 56, found guilty at Stafford Assizes yesterday on charges of corruption, was sent to prison for 21 months. Smith, of Little Haywood, Staffs, is a former alderman.

He was also disqualified from election to public office for a maximum period of five years.

Smith was found guilty on five charges of corruptly receiving sums totalling £3,400 from a building firm and one of corruptly soliciting a gift, fee or reward from two partners in another firm.

Everywhere one was conscious of the remoteness of the men from the centre of management. The men, too, were well aware of this. The malpractices, starting no doubt in a small way, had been quick to spread. Loyalties were, I believe, loosened by this increased managerial remoteness, which had stemmed from the general upgrading, all through the management pyramid, of supervisory staff with whom the men had previously been in close contact. The best performers had gone on up the tree, leaving the weaker vessels behind to carry on the day-to-day supervision. Declining standards in the permissive society possibly aggravated the situation.

There were other 'ground-floor' frauds in London in the years following reorganisation. Car park takings were a common field, both among directly employed staff and among employees of agent operators. At Westminster a very serious fraud was perpetrated by one of the itinerant teams of parking meter collectors. As often happens with collusive frauds, detection was hastened by an anonymous letter to the police, although internal audit were already hot on the scent through their comparisons of the different teams' collections. When the police intercepted the suspect team's armoured van, on its way back from a collecting round, they found the entire team sitting in the back sharing out a proportion of the contents of the meter boxes. They had discovered a way of extracting cash from the supposedly thief-proof boxes.

That fraud, it was estimated, amounted to some £50,000: a figure fully supported by the high living styles of the members of the team, apparent when the police searched their homes. Shortly afterwards, a similar case occurred at Kensington and Chelsea, in which internal audit was again prominent.

Getting one's first clue to the existence of fraud was always a challenge. One method was to make statistical comparisons designed to isolate the potential wrong 'un. Given this starter, one could apply more penetrating checks to the suspect transactions including, if necessary, direct fieldchecks. Inner London after the 1965 reorganisation was a perfect field for such comparisons: 12 similar authorities in a compact area and all under the same audit umbrella. So was born the *Blue Book*. The name, I hasten to add, derived from the colour of the cover, not from the character of the contents – although the book did lay bare a lot of interesting features which might otherwise have escaped attention.

The *Blue Book* was directed primarily to the pinpointing of possible cases of loss or waste, rather than to the detection of fraud. It gave, in separate columns for each of the inner London boroughs, an appropriate 'unit measure' for all those items of income and expenditure which, because of their size or their susceptibility to loss or waste, were of special interest to the auditor. Refuse collection costs, for example, were expressed as so much per ton of refuse collected, separately for labour, transport and other costs; expenditure at residential homes for children or old people as so much per person-day for wages, food etc. And so on.

Many areas of potential savings were pinpointed. One borough, for instance, was out on its own on street-lighting costs – due, it transpired, to slowness in switching from the old-type mercury-vapour lamps to the much more economical sodium lamps.

Another was exceptionally high on refuse collection costs – due chiefly, we found, to restrictive practices dating from the days when the collection was done by private contractors. (Interestingly, that authority has since reverted to private collection.)

At least one case of fraud was, however, thrown up by the *Blue Book*. Cost figures for children's homes showed that at Tower Hamlets the food costs were unusually high. Breaking the costs down between individual homes showed that one in particular was responsible for the overall high cost. Deeper enquiry revealed that the housemother was buying most of her food at the local Tesco supermarket, and that she was including in her cost-record not only the genuine 'check-out' lists given her by the Tesco cashier but many others, discarded by other customers, which she had picked off the floor outside the check-outs. A quite substantial fraud had thereby been perpetrated.

Some incipient similar frauds were subsequently nipped

in the bud in other boroughs.

The frauds I have described were some of the more interesting ones, in the investigation of which I had some part in the fifties and sixties. There were many others. Lest, however, a wrong impression be given of standards of integrity and efficiency in local government, I add two further thoughts.

First, the detection and investigation of fraud was by far the most dramatic part of our work as auditors. The finding of the first vital clue, the excitement of the subsequent chase, the final – often harrowing – denouement, these all impressed themselves indelibly on the mind of the investigator. Seven years have passed since I retired. In that period, active in a totally different sphere, I have barely spared a thought for my former audit life. Yet, when invited to write these notes I find that these and other frauds, occurring 15 to 35 years ago, can be recalled as easily as if they occurred yesterday, without recourse to notes.

They were the highlights of one's career. Although some were long in the solving, they took up, as a whole, a very small part of one's day-to-day life. They are remembered not merely for their dramatic quality, but because they were, indeed, so rare. A vast field of the accounts of many authorities was covered every year without a suspicion of fraud.

Secondly – and very much on the same tack – we were dealing, in our daily round, with transactions in money or moneys-worth in which many thousands of local authority employees were concerned. Measured against these numbers, the few who unhappily succumbed to some fatal combination of temptation, opportunity and personal financial problems constituted an infinitesimal proportion of the whole.

Since my retirement I have been involved with many people in walks of life very different from those I met in local government. Comparisons can be odious, but I say without disparagement to those others that I have, since retiring, been strongly confirmed in the view I always held, that standards of integrity and efficiency are extremely high in local government.

To err is human – and human nature does not change. I believe that much of the credit for these high standards lies with district audit, and in more recent years with increasingly effective internal audit. The best safeguard against fraud is fear of detection. The unrivalled experience and skills of district audit in uncovering fraud has, I believe, acted as a powerful deterrent to potential wrongdoers.

Fraud in public funds, raised largely by compulsory impost on taxpayers and ratepayers, is a far more serious matter than fraud in the commercial world. I venture the hope that it will always remain at a trifling level; and that, to this end, district audit and internal audit will always direct a significant part of their activities to its detection and prevention.

D F KELLEY

Went to school at Plymouth College which has provided many recruits to district audit including two Chief Inspectors. Saw war service as an officer in the Indian Army. Retired as DDA in 1978, and spends his time researching into the life-history of bass on which he has published numerous articles in scientific journals.

Random Recollections of Audit Cricket

V G Claydon

There was a time when a recruit to the District Audit Service could have been forgiven for believing that advancement in his chosen career was dependent as much on a knowledge of the laws of cricket as on a mastery of those relating to local government. An aptitude for ignoring them at the right moment was believed to be even more efficacious. The anecdotes which follow have been collected from survivors of that era, and although they may have gained a little in the telling, they do tend to support these beliefs.

It was not uncommon in those days for the new entrant, making his first appearance before his district auditor, to be asked not 'Do you incline towards accountancy or the law?', but 'Do you bat or bowl?' One unfortunate, having confessed his inability to do either, volunteered in a moment of panic that he might nevertheless be able to keep wicket. Some weeks later his bravado was rewarded with an invitation to do just that at the first post-war match between London and No 9 AD. Off the fifth ball of the game he found to his surprise that he had held the first and only catch of his brief playing career, only to have his appeal peremptorily turned down.

During the tea interval the umpire took him on one

side. 'Young man' he said, 'the first and most important thing you need to know about district audit is that Mr Hurle-Hobbs is never out in the first over.' Needless to say, the wicket keeper never made DA; but the umpire went on to become a Deputy Secretary in the Ministry.

A recently retired DA delights in telling a similar story of how in 1961 he made his future promotion prospects secure by giving his DA not out three times in the first over in response to ever more fervent appeals for lbw. He also claims to be the only umpire ever to be applauded all the way to the pavilion at the end of a match, admittedly only by the supporters of the winning side from his own district.

But if further evidence is needed of the value of cricket as an aid to promotion, the photograph of the Surrey team, taken in 1938, provides it. It features one current and three future DAs, as well as four future Inspectors or Chief Inspectors; and there can be little doubt that, but for premature death or resignation, the other seven players would have reached equal heights. For the photo we are indebted to Reg Jones (third from the left, front row), whose happy smile was no doubt accounted for by

21/1 Recollections of audit cricket: London v Essex 1950 Hurle Hobbs (left) goes out to bat.

21/2 Inset: From the same match Hurle Hobbs (centre) returns to pavillion after another fine innings.

the fact that, with 58 not out, he was the top scorer in the match. It goes without saying that it was only with great reluctance that he was persuaded to part with the certified score sheet revealing this.

The origin of this preoccupation with cricket is not known, but it probably started in the thirties when 'Daddy' Weigall reigned as DA in Maidstone. Such was his enthusiasm for the game that he arranged the audit fixtures, whenever possible, to coincide with the Kent county cricket weeks. After a brief visit to the audit room, he would retire to the members' tent on the ground, but not before inviting each member of the staff to join him during the afternoon 'to discuss problems'. The sort of problems he had in mind were not audit ones but, for example, whether Chapman should put on Tich Freeman before or after the tea interval; and anyone foolish enough to mention work would have been instantly banished to the hard benches on the popular side of the ground.

In 1938 and 1939 the Surrey School organised a number of matches against local authority teams. The most memorable was against the staff of Graylingwell Mental Hospital in West Sussex, where a large crowd of excitable patients turned up, all rooting strongly for the audit side. The match ended in a tense draw, Graylingwell playing out time with only one wicket to fall. This result did not please the spectators and Nobby Clarke, who was umpiring, had to beat a hasty and undignified retreat to the pavilion pursued by patients seeking to convince him that he should have allowed another over.

This is the last recorded instance of impartial umpiring to be found in the audit archives, for in the immediate post-war period there emerged a generation of umpire-DAs whose meticulous administration of the laws of the land was surpassed only by their total disregard for those of cricket. Pre-eminent among this breed was A S Higlett, an austere and upright character of the utmost moral rectitude, who was the regular umpire for No 8 AD. In the last over of a needle match against the London District side (captained by Hurle-Hobbs), the game could have gone either way, and the London batsman attempted a short run. The fielder skilfully threw down the wicket (wisely, at Higlett's end). Not only did the umpire's finger go up, the umpire's hat was thrown high in the air with a cry of 'He's out, and we've won!'

There was another occasion when one, Neighbour, then the mainstay of the London side, was laid low for some minutes on being struck in a most sensitive part by a fast bouncer. Great sympathy was expressed by his sporting opponents, and admiration when he eventually and courageously decided to carry on batting. Unfortunately, it was then found that Higlett had already given him out lbw. It should be added that Neighbour was an extremely tall man.

It is not surprising that at this time the No 8 team was all-triumphant, but eventually they met their Waterloo on the playing fields of Brentwood School. These idyllic surroundings were made available for audit matches only by virtue of the influence of Tom Graty, without whose double-bass playing the school orchestra would have been in dire straits. Although well on in his sixties, Tom was still captain of the No 10 team, who were currently wooden spoonists of the audit cricket world. On this occasion, however, the No 10 opening batsmen collared the bowling from the outset, and neither their

21/3–21/6 Top left, top right, centre and bottom left: More recollections of the London v Essex match from 1950.

21/7 Bottom right; Sports Day, 1951.

21/8 'And so to battle' Les Baker (left) strides confidently to the wicket during the London v Essex match.

players nor their umpire was able to avert an ignominious defeat for No 8. Nobody seemed to recognise these opening batsmen, however. It emerged that Tom's influence at the school had extended to recruiting as temporary acting ADAs a couple of former Cambridge Blues from among the schoolmasters.

Some years later, No 10 were themselves victims of a similar act of unofficial recruitment to the audit service. This was at Sidcup, where No 9 AD, finding themselves one short, cast around for anyone to help them out. Occupying the bench which was required for the scorers was a scruffy, long-haired youth who appeared to be playing hookey from school. To kill two birds with one stone he was invited to play and was in due course appointed CO for the afternoon.

No 10 batted first and amassed 175 – a formidable score in audit matches. Whether from an understandable reluctance of the others to face the fast bowling of Martin Sims (then at his devastating best), or out of gratitude for his help, the new member of the staff was allowed to open the batting for No 9. The massacre of the innocents then commenced – but it was the bowlers, not the batsmen, who were slaughtered. No 9 won a resounding victory, thanks to an innings of 126 not out from the 'recruit' who, having taken a four and four sixes from the last over, nonchalantly put down his bat, resigned from the Service, and ambled quietly away.

Despite all the gamesmanship, audit did produce some very fine cricket and a number of first-rate players during this period. For several years running, a team was entered for the Curtis Bennett competition, open to all government departments, and on one occasion the semi-final was reached – no mean feat for such a small service. Inter-district matches proliferated. London, Nos 9, 10 and 13 Districts all played each other annually; in the heart of the Pennines, Nos 2 and 3 refought the Wars of the Roses each year; and the pre-war practice of arranging games against local authority sides was resumed.

These dangerous exercises in public relations not only gave disgruntled accountants a chance to strike back, literally, at the audit staff, but produced at least one umpiring treasurer who could have out-Higletted Higlett. Reckoned to be worth at least two wickets to his side, he was even more deadly in the pontoon school which generally followed the cricket, his ability to add up quickly but not always accurately being far superior to anything that audit could do in that respect.

The highlight of the season, however, was the North v South match which was played almost every year from 1950 to 1980. In its heyday this event, which took place at Peterborough, attracted spectators from as far apart as Sheffield and Brighton – London even used to hire a coach – and each side could field a first and second team. There being no bar on the ground, liquid refreshment was unobtrusively brought in in audit bags, but for many years the capacity of the spectators exceeded that of the receptacles.

This problem was eventually solved with the introduction of the new, jumbo-sized black bags, which, if skilfully packed, were found capable of accommodating 2¼ gallons of canned beer – a record which still stands to this day.

But it was not the ale or even the cricket that pulled in the crowds – it was the gargantuan teas prepared by

21/9 London Audit District team, 1950 taken at Hertford.

21/10 Ian Gardner, Hugh Gwyther, Alex Smith and E D Clarke discuss tactics during the London v Essex match.

Mrs Martin, whose husband Colin organised the event. These spreads were calculated to slow down even the fastest of bowlers, and it was a rare thing for the side in the field for the evening session to win the match. It was suggested by one eminent player that the usual practice should be reversed and that there should be two sessions of tea, with an interval for cricket.

It is said that cricket has now been replaced as the 'in' audit game by skittles – played at night on licensed premises. This deplorable and retrograde step has but one thing to commend it – it allows full participation by the female members of the staff. But the price paid for this sexual equality has been a heavy one. What chances now of catching the DA's eye with a fine spell of real bowling? What incentives to try for a new record in the audit bag beer-carrying competition? And, above all, what opportunity is there for a budding Mrs Martin to earn the affection of generations of auditors by producing unforgettable teas?

V G CLAYDON

Was fated from birth to a close association with district audit. Started his career unofficially at the age of 8, audit-stamping vouchers at his father's audits. In 1945 married Miss Monic Burdge, daughter of W H Burdge ADA, and joined the Service officially in 1947 on his father-in-law's section. Has three daughters and one son, Paul, who is currently an SADA. Has a fondness for cricket and a good malt.

Clay Cross

Ron Mason

Clay Cross Urban District Council wrote itself into the law relating to district audit by the opposition of its members to the implementation of the provisions of the Housing Finance Act 1972. Clay Cross, a small mining town in Derbyshire, was governed by an Urban District Council of only 11 members. The area of the district extended to just over 2,000 acres, equivalent to 3.125 square miles; its population was just under 10,000, and the Council owned 1,340 houses. Unemployment was high.

Long before the Act received Royal Assent, the Council informed the Department of the Environment that it had resolved not to put into operation any of its provisions. The Act, which came into operation on 27 July 1972, required rent increases to be made towards 'fair rents', the operation of a rent rebate scheme and an allowance scheme. Continued refusal to implement the provisions led to the Secretary of State making an order declaring the Council to be in default, and a few days later a direction to the district auditor to hold an extraordinary audit of the Housing Revenue Account for the period 1 April 1972 to 16 November 1972.

The district auditor Mr C D (Bill) Lacey held a public

THE STAR, SHEFFIELD, MONDAY 30 JULY/73

£9,000 bill, the crunch for 11 Rent Act rebels

THE "Clay Cross Eleven"—the rebel Labour councillors who refused to put up council house rents under the Governments rent laws must personally pay £6,985, three High Court judges ruled today.

The sum was a surcharge imposed by the District Auditor. On top of that the eleven — miners, foundry men or other low-paid workers — now also face a £2,000 legal bill.

"It is bankruptcy for all of us," said one of the 11, David Nuttall, after today's hearing.

Local Labour MP Mr. Tom Swain said that today's dismissal of the councillors' appeal against paying the

22/1 Clipping from the Sheffield Star, July 1973 covering the case of the Clay Cross councillors who refused to put up council house rents in accordance with the Government rent laws.

hearing on 7 December 1972 which was adjourned to 4 January 1973. All 11 members were present and were represented by Mr Tom Swain, then MP for North East Derbyshire. The district auditor decided that a loss of £6,985 to the Council's funds had been incurred and he surcharged that sum jointly and severally upon the 11 members of the Council on the grounds of their negligence and misconduct. In his statement of reasons issued on 22 January 1973 the district auditor concluded that the loss had been incurred through failure to carry out duties imposed by the provisions of the 1972 Act; that this failure was the direct result of the Council's resolution of 4 September 1972, viz:

> "that this Council will not operate any of the provisions contained in the Housing Finance Act 1972, and that the Electorate shall be informed of this decision together with all the reasons for coming to this decision, and that the Officers of the Council be instructed not to make any preparation for implementation of any of the provisions of the Act, nor to act on behalf of the Conservative Government as a Commissioner.";

and that the action of the 11 members of the Council who voted in favour of the resolution amounted to negligence and misconduct.

In due course the members appealed against the decision on the grounds:

(i) that the decision not to operate the provisions of the Housing Finance Act 1972 did not constitute 'negligence or misconduct' within the meaning of section 228(1) of the Local Government Act 1933;

(ii) that the loss to the ratepayers was occasioned not by the fault of the councillors, but by the failure of the Secretary of State to appoint a Housing Commissioner under the provisions of the Housing Finance Act 1972;

and

(iii) that the failure of the Council to increase the rents pursuant to that Act did not result in a 'loss or deficiency' within the meaning of section 228(1) of the Local Government Act 1933.

The Court of the Queens Bench Division which heard the appeal dismissed it with costs to the district auditor and confirmed the surcharge.

Bill Lacey retired at the end of May 1973, the last few years of his career being very eventful. He had to suffer threats of physical violence and much by way of unparliamentary and even defamatory language. The new district auditor, Bert Harrison, was soon baptised with an originating summons served by the 11 surchargees on the 29 October. The case was heard in the Chancery Division of the High Court by Mr Justice Megarry, his judgement being delivered on 21 December 1973.

The main purpose of the action was to obtain a ruling that the Secretary of State's direction to hold the extraordinary audit 'was punitive in intent and/or was made solely or principally to secure some object (which the Plaintiffs cannot specify) other than the recoupment of moneys lost by the Plaintiffs' default and was *ultra vires* the First Defendant', and, then, a declaration that the district auditor might not lawfully take action to recover the existing surcharge.

In finding against the 11 surchargees, the judge said 'this seems to me to be plainly a case in which the proceedings against the [district auditor] are vexatious as being an attempt to re-litigate a matter which has already been decided by the Divisional Court and has produced a certificate which by statute is conclusive evidence of the plaintiffs' liability.'

In commenting that the relief sought consisted entirely of declarations and that the making of declarations is discretionary, he added:

"Those who are elected to a local authority and who flatly refuse to carry out statutory duties which include securing reductions of rent for the poor have little claim to discretionary relief in respect of the same subject-matter; in such cases the Court may properly take account of matters

22/2 "But I'm the auditor." Cartoon from No. 11 AD annual dinner, May 1973.

Recognising the law

THE High Court has decided that the 11 Clay Cross councillors who refused to put up council house rents "quite deliberately broke the law."

And that, apart from the possibility of a further appeal, is that. If the law of the land has any meaning at all, you cannot set out to break it and expect to get away with it, however sincere and unselfish your motives.

Britain is not a federation of urban district councils, it is a centrally-governed nation in which Parliament is supreme. And the Clay Cross political protest against the Housing Finance Act is now over.

It has now moved into the realm of legal interpretation, and the judges were in no doubt that the councillors acted illegally.

Whatever one might think of the Act, or indeed any actions of Parliament or Government, is a subject for political debate and action, and is strictly beside the point. The Act is a fact and the only way to defeat it is to get it repealed.

This

22/3 Clipping from Sheffield Morning Telegraph reporting on the verdict against the Clay Cross rebels, July 1973.

of a moral or ethical nature: see *Re Freeman-Thomas Indenture [1957] 1 WLR 560 at 563,* per Harman J. I do not for a moment say that such considerations would necessarily bar the plaintiffs from relief: I do say that they are or may be of relevance. However, in this case they merely go to reinforce the clear view that I have formed quite apart from them. For the reasons that I have given, I feel no doubt that this statement of claim must be struck out and the action dismissed."

The 11 surchargees lodged an appeal against Mr Justice Megarry's judgement and it was heard in the Court of Appeal before the Master of the Rolls (Lord Denning), Lord Justice Orr and Lord Justice Lawton. In passing it is worth noting that Lord Denning recognised that the district auditor held a position of much responsibility, his duties going far beyond those of a company auditor. In delivering judgement he said:

"These proceedings are, in my opinion, an abuse. These Councillors are seeking, by one shift or another, to escape the consequences of their own wrongdoing. The time had come when they must be told quite firmly that the law must be obeyed. Their disobedience cannot be tolerated. They are disqualified. They must stand down. Others must be elected in their place – others who will fulfil the duties which these eleven have failed to do. I trust that there are good men to be found in Clay Cross ready to take over. I would dismiss the appeal".

On the question of the Secretary of State's direction to hold an extraordinary audit, the principle was enunciated that his decision could not be challenged unless it had been made in bad faith, or was frivolous or vexatious. The appeal was dismissed with costs.

In view of this long-drawn-out series of legal proceedings, it was not surprising that none of the audits for the years from 1 April 1971 had been concluded. Two local government electors made certain objections to the accounts. Those objections were incorporated into four heads of account which the district auditor identified as calling for his consideration of disallowance and/or surcharge:

(i) increased bonus payments made to the Council's employees for the period from 17 September 1973 to 11 November 1973 £3,250

(ii) stand-by payments made to the Council's employees for the period from 5 December 1973 to 31 March 1974; £7,754

(iii) payments of increased wages to wardens of old people's grouped dwellings for the period from 8 June 1973 to 31 March 1974; £11,205

(iv) expenditure on wages of the Council's employees in the three years 1971–1972, 1972–1973 and 1973–1974 to the extent that more workmen may have been employed than were necessary for the efficient discharge of the functions of the council; £30,000

Total: £52,209

The first three items represented increases in pay in excess of those permitted by the current legislation controlling prices and incomes. To arrive at the fourth item the district auditor concluded that the growth in the number of employees from 42 at 1 April 1971 to 93 at 31 March 1974 without a proportionate increase in the Council's functions was so excessive as to be unreasonable. After making generous allowances for some increases in numbers, he calculated that the cost in wages of the unreasonable and therefore unlawful element was not less than £30,000.

There was a public hearing on 4 February 1975; and it was evident, from the statement put in by members at the hearing, that from the coming into operation of the Housing Finance Act 1972, they had been determined to defy any legislation introduced by 'the Tory government' in so far as it sought to control or limit the activities of local authorities.

After due consideration, the district auditor issued certificates of disallowance and surcharge in the total sum of £52,209 on 16 April 1975.

It was not by accident that the district auditor's statement of reasons ran to 228 paragraphs. The district auditor's powers of disallowance and surcharge were contained in section 228 of the Local Government Act 1933. To make the numbers coincide was too much of a temptation for a highly numerate district auditor to resist.

As part of a general conclusion the district auditor said:

> "In my opinion the misconduct involved in each of the matters in this statement and in the failure to implement the Housing Finance Act 1972, is relevant to each of the other matters because they display a common defiance of any law which was not to the liking of the Council members; and of reckless disregard of the advice of officers as to the legal and proper courses which ought to have been followed."

One complication was that the original 11 members of the Council had become disqualified as a result of the first surcharge, the final legal proceedings being concluded in the Court of Appeal on 31 January 1974. A new Council consisting of the 'second eleven' was elected on 2 March 1974; but the new members had the avowed intention of continuing with the policies of the 'first eleven'.

The Clerk advised the new Council at their first meeting on 4 March that certain decisions needed to be reconsidered. Amongst them were the recently introduced stand-by payments to employees and the increased pay for wardens. The Council completely ignored the Clerk's warning and continued to implement the decisions of its predecessor.

The Clerk and the other officers came out on strike when the new Council refused to accept the proffered advice, whereupon the new Council, with only three weeks of its life remaining, appointed a new Clerk. Not inappropriately, in all the circumstances, their choice fell upon the young lady who at the time was leader of the pre-school play group.

The district auditor concluded that their reckless disregard of their chief officer's advice constituted misconduct causing loss to the funds of the Council. The amounts for which he apportioned responsibility to the new Council totalled £2,229 and he surcharged that sum jointly and severally upon ten of the 11 members. The eleventh member had sufficiently demonstrated his opposition to the continuance of the questionable payments.

The remaining £49,980 was surcharged upon members of the old Council, £46,730 jointly and severally upon all eleven of them and £3,250 upon ten of them. One member had voted against the proposition to increase bonus payments and had requested his vote to be recorded. Thus he was excluded from any liability in respect of those payments. None of these 'first eleven' appealed or made application to the Court for relief.

Recovery of both the Lacey and Harrison surcharges was painstakingly pursued to the point of obtaining judgement orders. Some of the surchargees made public statements about disposing of their assets to defeat the recovery process. Eventually the district auditor instituted bankruptcy proceedings and receiving orders were made.

In 1980 six of the surchargees applied for and were granted their discharge. In financial terms the exercise was a failure. Negligible sums of money were recovered, in fact only £409.47p in total from three of the surchargees. But, of course, all 11 were disqualified from being elected or being members of a local authority, not only because of the surcharge but also because of the bankruptcy.

The ten surchargees from the 'second eleven' appealed to the High Court against one element of the surcharge amounting to £899; and also sought a declaration in relation to the full amount of £2,229 that they had acted reasonably and/or in the belief that their actions were authorised by law, and that therefore they ought to be excused and relieved wholly from personal liability. The Court found against them, Mr Justice Kilner Brown in the course of his judgement saying:

> "In my judgement this is not a case in which a deep sense of social injustice can enable councillors to say 'we will do as our predecessors did because we are only here for three weeks and no more'. In my judgement, these councillors are caught by the provisions of the Local Government Act 1933 . . . In my judgement, it is impossible to say that they acted reasonably, and I would not only dismiss the appeal insofar as objection is made to the surcharge for the amounts in respect of old people's homes, but I would find it impossible to say that this is a case in which relief should be granted . . ."

PAGE 10

Daily Mail

Rent rebels must pay

£9,000 bill will bankrupt us all says Clay Cross councillor

ELEVEN rebel councillors who refused to put up rents now face a £9,000 bill, to be paid out of their own pockets.

Nearly £7,000 of this is a surcharge imposed by the district auditor on the councillors of Clay Cross, Derbyshire, for failing to increase council house rents.

On top of that the 11 — are miners —

judges in London had ruled that they must pay the surcharge.

Mr Nuttall said the decision also meant that all the 11 councillors would be banned for five years from holding office, including membership of the newly-formed North East Derbyshire which

with, was an obscene law and should never have got into the Statute Book.

Clay Cross population 9,726 had 1,386 council-house tenants and was an area of high unemployment.

Dismissing the

moral obligation, and no matter whether this was a matter of policy or politics, the inescapable fact is that they quite deliberately broke the law.

bound, to make the surcharge he made.

Lord Justice James said the 11 councillors sincerely regarded themselves as pledged to their electorate not to carry out any measures such as those contained in the Act.

They felt themselves under a moral obligation to carry out their

Kelvin

THE SUNDAY TIMES, AUGUST 12 1973

Defiant 11 say: This is only the start

By Tom Shaw

THE Clay Cross rebellion against the Conservative Government's policies will outlive the local council itself. Leaders of the Labour group which will control the new North-East Derbyshire District Council taking over the area next year have already decided that they, too, will defy the Housing Finance Act.

It was similar defiance which first landed the 11 Clay Cross urban district councillors in trouble with the courts. They refused to increase council house rents and now face a High Court order to pay nearly £7,000 for failing to do so. Last week they remained defiant: planning an appeal to the House of Lords, then breaking the incomes policy Phase Two norm with pay rises for their 80 manual workers.

Clay Cross is a declining mining community south of Chesterfield in Derbyshire. It has a population of about 10,000. It also has 1,600 council houses where no rent is higher than £1.80 for which, they boast, there is no waiting list.

Since being ordered to pay £6,985, with £2,000 legal costs, the 11 Clay Cross councillors—10 men and one woman—may have to go into bankruptcy. The saga might have been expected

to come to an end when the existing council is merged into the new North-East Derbyshire District Council.

John Dunn, a member of the ruling Labour group, has declared however: "The new district council will have a similar policy. It has been decided by the temporary co-ordinating committee of the Labour Party, which will control the new council, that there will be no more rent increases and that any increases that have taken place as a result of the Housing Finance Act will be rescinded and the tenants reimbursed." In addition to Clay Cross, the new council will cover Chesterfield rural district, which has about 8,000 council houses and Dronfield.

The 11 "rebel" councillors

The Clay Cross rebels: facing bankruptcy, but not budging

hope that the new authority will also show the same "enlightened" attitude towards its employees as at Clay Cross, where pay increases of between £4.50 and £5 awarded to manual workers on Thursday have brought their pay up to about £25 a week — backdated to June 18.

The council meeting which decided this was something of a showpiece in the drab town. The council first sat in committee, while crowds of ratepayers joked as they waited impatiently in the narrow corridors. Eventually Jim Simpson, shop steward for the manual workers, opened the door to ask the council to speed things up. "Just a few minutes more," he was told. When the door did open nearly

10 minutes later people fell over eachother to find a seat.

Even then the pay rise was nearly killed by a slip of the tongue. The chairman, Mrs Eileen Wholey, who works as a cook at a local school, banged the gavel and said: "I declare the meting closed." There was a roar from the crowd and, in confusion, she said: "I mean, I declare the meeting open."

Councillor David Skinner argued that the Clay Cross Council had saved £70,000 in rebates by not implementing the Housing Finance Act and that the pay award was fair. He has declared in a Marxist paper: "If all the Labour councils followed the example of Clay Cross it would be impossible to carry out the Housing Finance Act."

Key: 1) David Nuttall, 34, miner; 2) David Percival, 30, foundry worker; 3) Charles Bunting, 47, unemployed foundry worker; 4) David Skinner, 29, storeman; 5) Terry Asher, 33, foundry worker; 6) Arthur Wellon, 34, bridge engineer; 7) George Goodfellow, 63, school caretaker; 8) Graham Skinner, 30, clerk of works; 9) Mrs Eileen Wholey, 52, council chairman; 10) Graham Smith, 35, railway clerk; 11) Roy Booker, 33, coke plant worker.

22/4 Top: Clipping from The Daily Mail, July 1973 with the report that the Clay Cross rebels would have to pay the surcharge for failing to put up rents. Bottom: Clipping from The Sunday Times, August 1973 reporting the intention of the Clay Cross rebels to fight the verdict of the court.

22/5 Clippings from Sheffield Morning Telegraph (top and bottom) and The Guardian (centre) covering the Clay Cross rebels decision to fight on.

SHEFFIELD "MORNING TELEGRAPH" MONDAY 6 AUGUST 1973

Rebels plan last stand in Europe

Morning Telegraph Reporters

The 11 rebel

Tuesday July 31 1973

Rent councillors unrepentant

By Lindsay Mackie and Martin Adeney

● Mr Tom Swain, MP: The dismissal of the appeal proves that the 1972 Act is the most vicious on the Statute Book

THE 11 Clay Cross councillors who refused to put up council housing rents under the Housing Finance Act yesterday lost their appeal against a decision to make them personally liable for a £6,985 surcharge imposed by the district auditor.

Each councillor must now pay around £635 as a share of the surcharge—and the three High Court judges who heard the appeal yesterday also ruled that the councillors must pay legal costs of £2,000.

After the hearing, Councillor Graham Smith one of the nine councillors who travelled to London for the appeal said : "We just won't be able to pay costs. We'll be having a group meeting to decide what to do. We have got a support fund, but there is only a few hundred pounds in it.

Councillor David Nuttall, a miner, said : "We are disappointed by the result, but we were not really expecting anything else." Mr Nuttall said that although the result meant bankruptcy for all of us, the councillors would do the same again.

Seven of the councillors for Clay Cross, which has a population of 9,726, are married with children. As a result of the Appeal Court decision none of the 11 will be able to hold office on the council for five years, nor will they be able to serve on the new North East Derbyshire authority, which is to take over the Clay Cross Urban District Council next spring.

Mr Tom Swain, Labour MP North-East Derbyshire, said night that the dismissal of appeal "proved that the Housing Finance Act was the vicious act on the statute book

councillors would not only be out of pocket, but would also be debarred from office as councillors for the next five years. "These councillors have made no personal gain out of their stand," Mr Lyon said.

But Lord Justice James dismissed the costs plea, saying that in the circumstances there was no way of avoiding an order for costs.

Last night the future of the Clay Cross council remained in doubt. Derbyshire County Council, which may have to install a caretaker council to run the urban district until Local Government reorganisations next April, said the next step would depend on the action taken by the Clay Cross councillors.

...land the Secretary of State,
...mpbell, threatened to
...rnment housing sub-
...ouncils which do not
...y implement the next
...increases by October 1,
Edinburgh, Aberdeen,
...ydebank and Midlothian
...y decided against rent

...se of Glasgow, the amount
... at stake is more than
...s.

...npbell's latest warning is
... be the subject of heated
...n Glasgow tomorrow when
...ual estimates and rates are
...ed by Mrs Ellen McCulloch,
...y Treasurer, at a meeting of
...eral finance committee.

Labour administration will
...nly be challenged by the Con-
...tives on maintaining a higher
... of rates than necessary by
...sing to increase rents. The threat
... ost or at least delayed subsidy
... add strength to the Opposition
...ument.

(SHEFFIELD) MORNING TELEGRAPH, Thursday, August 2, 1973

Replacing the rebels

Elections for a new Clay Cross council are likely to be held this autumn unless the 11 "rent rebel" councillors appeal against their five - year ban from local government and win.

The law rules out by elections to councils involved in next April's reorganisation, but the Government seems to have found a loophole.

Though Clay Cross will be swallowed up by the new North - East Derbyshire council, the present urban district council will remain in being as a "successor" parish council.

According to the Department of the Environment, this means elections could be held to replace the 11 barred councillors this autumn. Successful can-

The eleven "rent rebel" councillors of Clay Cross face surcharges and legal bills totalling more than £9,000 as the price of having refused to implement the Housing Finance Act. Meanwhile the people of Clay Cross may be soon be going to the polls to elect a new council. Our Municipal Correspondent, NICHOLAS COMPORT, reports . . .

didates would act as Clay Cross Urban District Council until the change over, and then become parish councillors.

"The council's powers will change, but the personnel and the area it covers will not," said a DoE spokesman yesterday.

"Given this continuity, there is no reason why the councillors cannot be replaced if they are disqualified from local government."

Unless there was an appeal the disqualifications would take effect when the

28 days' notice of appeal expired or when the councillors stated they would not be appealing.

It would then be up to the clerk of Clay Cross council, as returning officer, to work out details of the election in consultation with the Home Office.

Clay Cross Labour Party has already announced that it has 11 candidates ready to fight fresh elections if they are called — and ready to continue the policy of refusing to implement the Housing Finance Act.

And Mr Justice Watkins included this important passage:

> "If a matter is brought to the notice of a Councillor who of course bears public responsibilities which indicates to him in plain terms that he will break the law by either action or inaction, he is not behaving reasonably if he ignores it. He is behaving in wilful disregard of properly tendered advice. The plain fact of the matter here is that the Councillors at Clay Cross, although only in harness for a little short of a month, deliberately chose to ignore the [Clerk's] letter and its contents. In my judgement that is sufficient effectively to dispose of this application."

The ten members of the 'second eleven' took no further legal proceedings themselves and avoided recovery proceedings against them. Before the appeal period had expired the full amount of the surcharge was paid in to the new North East Derbyshire District Council, which had been set up under the Local Government Act 1972. It was understood that at least some of the money was raised on a sponsored walk by some of the members and their political friends.

The final episode was played out against the provisions of the Housing Finance (Special Provisions) Act 1975. The purpose of that Act was to prevent the making of surcharges arising from failure to implement the Housing Finance Act 1972 and to substitute other means of making good losses or deficiencies. In circumstances where he would have issued a certificate of surcharge, the district auditor had to issue a 'rent loss certificate' specifying the sum which and the persons whom he would have surcharged. Normal procedures had to be followed by serving notices on those at risk and affording them opportunities to be heard. It was of course the 'first eleven' members who were called to account for the period following that covered by the

Council surcharge upheld

Asher and Other v Lacey

Before Lord Justice James, Mr Justice Kilner Brown and Mr Justice Boreham

A district auditor is entitled under section 228(1)(d) of the Local Government Act, 1933, to make a surcharge in respect of the amount of the loss or deficiency of rental income from a council's dwellings brought about by the negligence or misconduct of the councillors in refusing to make rent increases required by the Housing Finance Act, 1972.

Their Lordships so held when dismissing an appeal by 11 members of Clay Cross Urban District Council, under section 229 of the 1933 Act, against a surcharge of £6,985 imposed on them jointly and severally by the auditor on January 17.

Mr Paul Baker, QC, and Mr Alexander Lyon for the councillors ; Mr David Widdicombe, QC, and Mr Michael Fitzgerald for the auditor.

LORD JUSTICE JAMES, reading the judgment, said that on September 4, 1972, the council, being aware of the duties imposed by the Housing Finance Act to make " increases towards fair rents " and to bring into operation a rent " rebate scheme " and an " allowance scheme ", and being aware of the consequences likely to flow from failure to do so resolved not to operate any provisions in the Act. The Secretary of State made an order declaring the council to be in default, and on November 16 he directed an extraordinary audit of the council's housing revenue account. The auditor, Mr Lacey, decided that a loss of £6,985 had been incurred by the councillors' negligence and misconduct, and on January 17 he issued his certificate certifying the surcharge.

Section 228 of the Local Government Act provided that " (1) It shall be the duty of the district auditor at every audit held by him . . . (d) to surcharge the amount of any loss or deficiency upon any person by whose negligence or misconduct the loss or deficiency has been incurred ; . . . "

The auditor was entitled and, indeed, bound by section 228 (1) (d) to make the surcharge. Section 247 of the Public Health Act, 1875, was its forerunner and the headnote in *R v Roberts* ([1908] 1 KB 407) read in part : " An auditor appointed by the Local Government Board under section 247 to audit the accounts of a metropolitan borough council is authorized and required to decide whether any member or officer of the council has been guilty of negligence or misconduct in relation to the accounts whereby loss has been occasioned to the council, and to assess the amount of the loss."

That statement represented the law today. The audit of the council's housing revenue account would have shown an item in respect of rent received. The law required that the rent be increased in accordance with the Housing Finance Act, and the account would have shown a shortfall of rents received from the rents which ought to have been received; the auditor could not be blind to that. If (d) was restricted to loss or deficiency in respect of expenditure there was no power under section 228(1) to recoup the loss or deficiency which had occurred. It was not material that the Secretary of State had a different course open to him under the 1972 Act.

The decision of September 4 constituted " negligence or misconduct " within section 228(1). No matter how sincerely the councillors believed in the course they followed, no matter how strong were their feelings of moral obligation and no matter whether it was a matter of policy or politics, the inescapable fact was that they quite deliberately broke the law. The loss or deficiency found by the auditor did not result from any failure by the Secretary of State, who was under no obligation to appoint a housing commissioner, but from the councillors' decision to break the law.

Solicitors : Lewis Silkin & Partners ; Clifford-Turner & Co.

22/6 Clipping from The Times. The appeal against the surcharge is dismissed by the courts.

Lacey surcharges.

In assessing the rent loss the district auditor adopted the formula used by Bill Lacey in assessing his surcharge of £6,985. The process on this occasion went as follows:

(i) calculate the total additional rent which would have been due to the Council between 1 October 1972 and

31 March 1974 if the Council had applied the statutory increases of £1 per week in October 1972 and 50 pence per week in October 1973;

(ii) deduct –

(a) the increases that would have been uncollectable in respect of empty dwellings;

(b) the saving which accrued to the general rate fund as a result of the Council's failure to grant rebates;

(iii) deduct the amount of £6,985 already surcharged;

(iv) deduct the sum of £17,108 which was the total increase which the Housing Commissioner was required by the Order to charge, with effect from the first rent week in January 1974, leaving £87,959 as the rent loss.

Formal hearings were held in December 1975 and February 1976. Only two members attended and only one of those made submissions. At the later hearing he was represented by Mr Tom Swain MP.

The submissions were that:

(i) the amount of £87,959 in the proposed rent loss certificate should be reduced by the amount of the loss which accrued after 12 October 1973 when the Housing Commissioner was appointed;

(ii) the district auditor should surcharge the Housing Commissioner or name him in a rent loss certificate in respect of his failure to increase rents with effect from the first week in January 1974;

(iii) for the period from 17 November 1972, following the end of the extraordinary audit, up to the date of the appointment of the Housing Commissioner (12 October 1973) responsibility for the rent loss should attach to the Secretary of State because he did not appoint a Housing Commissioner at an earlier date;

(iv) the amount of the rent loss certificate should be reduced to reflect this responsibility of the Secretary of State; and

(v) the Secretary of State, like the Housing Commissioner, was subject to the jurisdiction of the district auditor under section 228 of the Local Government Act 1933, and loss due to his negligence or misconduct should therefore be surcharged upon him.

In his statement of reasons, the district auditor dealt with each of the submissions rejecting them on the grounds:

(i) the Housing Commissioner had no power to increase the rents until the first rent week in January 1974 and could not be responsible for an earlier period;

(ii) the decision in *Re Dickson (1948)* restricted the persons who were subject to the district auditor's jurisdiction under section 228 of the Local Government Act 1933 so that the Housing Commissioner and the Secretary of State were excluded;

(iii) as had been decided in the Court, there was no obligation upon the Secretary of State to appoint a Housing Commissioner and therefore no responsibility could be attached to the Secretary of State.

The rent loss certificate was issued on 7 April 1976 in the sum of £87,959 covering the two years to 31 March 1974 and naming the 'first eleven' as the persons who would have been surcharged but for the passing of the Housing Finance (Special Provisions) Act 1975.

In accordance with its discretion under the 1975 Act,

the North East Derbyshire District Council, on which there were, of course, members representing the Clay Cross area, decided to make good the losses by increasing the rents of the Clay Cross houses. Tenants were charged an extra 24 pence on their rents from 15 November 1976 and after some five and a half years the full amount of the losses had been recovered.

Thus it was ultimately the tenants of the houses between 1976 and 1982 who had to make good the amounts which should have been collected from the tenants at the proper time in accordance with the provisions of the Housing Finance Act 1972.

The total amount of the surcharges and the rent loss was just short of £150,000 – a colossal sum in the early 1970s for a small authority with a penny rate product of just over £1,000 and governed by only 11 members.

RON MASON

Joined district audit in 1949 after war service in the RAF and the Border Regiment and a short spell with the Ministry of National Insurance. An honours finalist in the CIPFA examinations, he progressed to become Deputy District Auditor in 1975 and District Auditor in 1981. Retired in 1986 and golf is his principal hobby.

Computer Audit – The Beginnings

Alan Edmonds and Chris Hurford

Early in the 1960s it was appreciated that training in computer accounting would be needed, so a select number of largely very senior auditors from each audit district were sent on short courses at Kingston Polytechnic. These turned out to be something more akin to workshop sessions and a common fund of best practices evolved. Clearly, in order to keep pace with developments, some specialised training was desirable, and three officers went to the Treasury's systems analysts course. Their experience indicated that what was needed was training in programming, since the principles of systems analysis were in effect already being practised by every experienced auditor.

So, in 1969, Bob Hutchings was seconded to Leicestershire County Council for training as a programmer. Bob and Alan Edmonds, who had privately acquired programming training, were sent on a trial audit to a county borough in the North west. Coincident with this, ICL had just released a new type of utility program for retrieving information from computer files.

Using this program – FIND 1 – the team produced an extract of audit information. It was the first time that the Service had used a computer for this purpose and it is much to the credit of Stuart Collins, the then Chief Inspector of Audit, that the significance of this albeit rather limited display of the use of retrieval was fully appreciated. Very soon after, the two officers formed a specialist computer audit team and began to visit local authorities all over the country by invitation. ICL issued the very much more powerful FIND 2, and the team began to make an impact in both audit and computer circles of local government.

Asked to speak to a mixed local government audience in Bradford at that time, the team leader was roundly attacked by a senior auditor for tinkering with local authorities' computers. Two computer managers stood up to defend us, asserting that, having experienced a visit from the team, it was welcome to enter their computer rooms at any time.

One early achievement went largely unnoticed at the time. A test on a rating file reported that some owner-occupiers had received owners' discounts to which they were not entitled, although a validity check of the input should have rejected them. This must have been the first time that district audit had detected a programming error by computer.

It must be said that progress in audit retrieval on other than ICL 1900 machines was very much slower. Utility retrieval programs were not part of the philosophy of the other manufacturers, and although a program was available for the current IBM machine, it was so cumbersomely large that only two authorities had machines big enough to accept it at all and none could accommodate it within their normal processor partitions. Neither were the computer managers willing to indulge district audit by pre-empting their entire computer power for our use!

However, it transpired that Derbyshire County Council were developing a retrieval program and an invitation to pay them a visit was quickly sought. A rewarding dialogue took place and the team secured the very fine program called FISH for general use at authorities using IBM computers. About the same time, the Honeywell company released a program known as CRESTS, originally developed by Courtaulds. Some success was achieved with this too, but the program was, to say the least, touchy about the version of the operating system it chose to obey – or ignore, as the case may be!

The FIND 2 program, although an excellent general purpose retrieval program, was not created specifically for auditors, but it did contain 'user entry points' at which proficient users could insert their own coding, thereby interrupting the operation of the program to perform routines of their own design. Bob Hutchings used the technique to expand FIND 2 to become an audit tool of exceptional value, using Leicestershire County Council's computer. The program, renamed DART – District Audit Record Transmogrifier – was

23/1 Alan Edmonds loading and interrogation program.

made freely available to local authorities and greatly increased the prestige of the District Audit Service in the computer field and the demand for the services of its specialists.

It was a matter of policy at this time that, aside from blatant security risks (such as the computer manager who shouldered aside his operations manager to run FIND programs to alter operational tapes), pretty well all the activities of the specialists centred on retrieval. It was clear that retrieval, being spectacular and beyond the capability of all but a very few internal auditors, was having a powerful impact at a time when district audit was having to face 'choice of audit'. Furthermore, our ability to get urgent changes made to computer systems was enhanced by retrieval reports which identified errors and failures, or supplemented management information which made the task easier.

The scarcity of experienced auditors capable of identifying fields for retrieval work and of carrying out such work, however, was so marked throughout the public sector that in a period of approximately 12 months between 1971 and 1972 the service lost half its specialists to other bodies in the public sector. District auditors who had recommended staff for computer training must have found it a frustrating exercise!

The mid-seventies brought a number of changes to the development of computer audit within the District Audit Service and this was influenced, not surprisingly, by the signficant changes in local government computing.

Since the installation of the first computer in local government during the mid-sixties, technological development of business computing had been relatively slow. Mainframes needed enormous inputs of programming time and the construction of special air-conditioned operating suites, and their capabilities were restricted by their small memory and limited local authority experience in their use. An authority which had upgraded from an 8K to a 16K machine was thought to have sufficient capacity to last it a decade The specialists who could program and operate these monsters were in short supply and they were often rated according to the ingenuity they could muster in maximising the limited memory which the computers possessed. Analysis skills were undeveloped and few systems were documented.

At one authority with imperfect documentation, tests had been written to check the validity of a program. However, the tests could not be run without the co-operation of the programmer concerned (little having been committed to paper). The programmer said he would have to check in the computer room whether the requisite tape was still in existence, and we were obliged to chase him there to be sure that his intention was not to destroy it before we could get at it.

The storage facilities on the early machines were also a limiting factor and they reflected the evolving technology, with most computers relying on magnetic tape, some using magnetic card and a few bearing the expense of magnetic disks. Inputting data into the computer relied upon paper tape or punched card and the VDU screen was far too futuristic to be a commercial proposition.

To illustrate how much easier it became for us to retain disc storage for our own use, the first exchangeable disc provided for us was valued at £140 and could store 8 million characters of information. Five years later the same authority provided a 64 million character disc at a cost of £100.

In retrospect it is difficult to imagine how any benefit could be forthcoming from such apparently unwieldy machines. Even more surprising was the confidence of the external auditor that he could grapple with this emerging technology and demonstrate the virtues of such machines as an audit tool.

One of the problems which, as trailblazers, the early computer auditors had to overcome was that computer managers generally were sceptical about the whole idea of auditors actually being able to use their beloved machines. One such manager demonstrated his scepticism by agreeing that we could use his computer provided that we could operate it ourselves. Quite unaware of the pitfalls that awaited us, we blithely accepted the challenge.

Promptly at 5pm that afternoon the computer staff went home and the auditors took over. Unfortunately the machine – which the auditor is still convinced had escaped from an episode of Dr Who – possessed no console typewriter. Instead it had a huge display of illuminated push buttons through which all instructions, in machine code, had to be fed. It also had fiendish magnetic tape decks which required the operator to place precisely the correct footage of tape into the vacuum that existed between the drives. Too much tape and the drives refused to acknowledge the presence of the tape; too little and the tape ended up with nasty stretch marks. Four long hours later the auditor achieved a major breakthrough; the first program was successfully loaded. The following day

they triumphantly produced their solitary exception report, carefully omitting to mention at what time they had gone home.

Another example of the problem of coping with older technologies arose where an authority replaced an Eliott computer with an ICL 1900. Eliott binary representation of characters was different from that of ICL, though ICL had provided the authority with a conversion package to enable them to continue using their old Eliott programs. For some reason this package could not be used with the DART retrieval package and the first use of DART produced nonsense output: instead of letters, the output was a series of "!?=,:!. This problem was resolved by adding or subtracting 26 from the output data immediately prior to printing. The computer manager was very grateful because he had already seen the potential of the DART package, which, prior to the audit visit, he had concluded was unusable.

The stories surrounding our early use of retrieval software are legion, but the following true accounts are probably classics.

With the use of computer interrogation software, problems are always likely to arise unless the parameters are very carefully thought out. If you want to find just the exceptions, then the parameters must clearly reflect this. On one occasion, the parameters were correctly devised but the logic was back to front. So instead of searching for the one in 10,000 ratepayers where perhaps too much rate relief had been given, details were extracted of the other 9,999 cases!

The Welsh caused us not a little embarrassment also. One of the regular computer audit tests was an extract from the student grants file of any student receiving two

23/2 The auditor and computer language: Total corporate amnesia.

grants. For this test it was useful to combine the computer files of perhaps two neighbouring authorities and the interrogation was based on finding two records with identical Christian and surnames. This worked perfectly well for us until in Wales we found that the 'exception' reports were full of 'Gareth Davies' and 'David Jones' We were asked more than once in those early days to provide our own wheelbarrow to carry the output back to the audit room, or could they please turn off the computer as they wanted to go home!

The cost of computing in the early seventies was such that the larger county boroughs and county councils tended to be the only authorities who could afford computing. The development of suitable telecommunication facilities, however, provided the ability to connect users who were physically remote from the computer centre. This meant that a smaller authority could input data to a card reader within its own offices and transmit that data to the mainframe where it would be processed and the results sent back to a printer at the remote authority. Now computing was available to a much wider market and the county took on the role of a provider of systems and services for district councils, alongside those developed and provided for their own use.

The reorganisation of local authorities in the mid seventies created larger units of government, particularly at district level, several of which felt more able to invest in their own computing facilities. The arrival of this new market for business computing coincided with developments in computing itself which had arisen from the technology which was essential for space travel. Smaller yet more powerful processors were vital for the space programme to succeed and the concentration of design effort on this problem was to have dramatic repercussions upon the business community worldwide.

The first commercial effect of this was the arrival of the mini computer which had as much memory as some of its older mainframe brothers, and could cater for data to be input through VDUs linked to the mini and held on a magnetic disk. Data could be captured more readily and amended more easily and the user could be made more responsible for his computing needs. Such minis could be used as stand alone computers – provided the systems were not too large – and could also be linked as terminals to a remote mainframe.

Computing now began to arrive for the smaller organisation and many authorities were not slow to grasp the potential which the computer offered. The new district councils who had no previous computing experience – particularly where they were formed from an amalgamation of several smaller rural and urban districts – could now consider an in-house computer which provided the opportunity both for connection to a larger mainframe and completely independent computing.

In the early days the use of retrieval software by auditors was limited to the larger authorities, and fraught with difficulty. The increased use and experience of and dependency on computing in local authorities meant that the auditor could now, and indeed had to, look at the computer as a help and not a hindrance. The opportunity to apply audit tests to all the data within a few minutes at most authorities represented a dramatic improvement in the efficiency of audit.

It was against this background of a change in the nature

of local government computing that the organisation of computing within the District Audit Service deserved review. Demands were being placed on the few computer auditors then in post to widen their responsibilities and extend them beyond the development and use of programming techniques for audit retrieval. With more authorities embarking upon computing, there were not only more installations to cope with, but also the time had arrived to extend the scope of computer audit. There were assessments of installation security to be made, a proliferation of computerised systems to be reviewed, and more authorities were asking for advice on the appropriateness of hardware and software to satisfy their particular needs.

Clearly more resources were needed. Not only had we lost many of our experts, but also the specialist retrieval teams, after years of living out of suitcases, had mutinied. So the number of specialists was increased, and the decision was taken to deploy these resources within audit districts rather than maintain centralised support units.

Because of the high profile that the computer auditors were enjoying, there was an expectation that all of their efforts would produce successful results which would demand the full attention of the senior auditors and of the senior staff within the authority as well.

On one occasion when the computer auditors were visiting an authority for the first time, no one knew what to expect and it was, therefore, with some trepidation that they were accompanied by the district auditor to the computer room to give him a demonstration of their skills. The trepidation turned to outright fear when he requested the pleasure of the

company of the Director of Finance. Much to their lasting surprise and delight the interrogation of the Rates file worked first time. The delight was cut short by the district auditor's stentorian voice announcing that the list which had just been extracted, of ratepayers in arrears where no summons had been taken out, contained the name of the Director of Finance. Fortunately the Director announced, much to their relief, that the interrogation *had* worked properly – he had only recently arrived in the authority and had received a late demand sent out just before the end of March.

These high expectations had remained throughout the changing computing scene, but now not only were more resources needed but also the demand began to grow for other skills, in addition to using the computer to extract information. The presence of a computer expert in the audit district meant that he could now comment upon the authority's decision to install a new computer and the adequacy of controls in a newly computerised payroll system, as well as the appropriateness of staffing levels in the computer section.

Inevitably, the lone computer auditor could not satisfy all of those who bid for his skills, and this demonstrated a need to rethink the responsibility for coping with computers and the competing demands being placed upon the one individual within the district.

This shift in approach marked a change in emphasis for two different reasons. On the one hand, it was necessary to establish who was responsible for auditing the computer, and, on the other hand, the District Audit Service needed to continue to demonstrate its skill and knowledge in computing matters across a wider front.

The potential for using computers for audit had been demonstrated by the computer team, but now it was necessary to establish the technique as an audit tool available to audit at large. This meant that local skills had to be developed and more users of the new techniques had to be found.

It was difficult then – and indeed now – to specify precisely what qualities the new breed of computer auditor had to possess and, even assuming that these could be identified in abstract terms, how they could be translated into effective guidelines for selecting the right people.

Great reliance was placed upon the computer programming aptitude test and likely candidates were exposed to a day of eleven-plus secondary school entrance examination-type questions which seemed to be far removed from the then 'white heat technology' associated with computers.

The successful candidates having been selected, the next step was to give them programming training. Here the Service was particularly fortunate in being able to use the generous services of several local authorities who, equally anxious to see their external auditors become familiar with their computer, willingly provided varying periods of secondment to their computer programming departments.

There is little doubt that this training period was very valuable, and the benefits of learning how to program in a real environment were recognised by auditor and auditee alike. Perhaps one of the most useful lessons, over and above those of a technical nature, was the opportunity to experience the dilemma of managing a computing department and matching the oft ill-defined demands of the user with the scarce resources of the programmer and analyst.

Such experience, however, did have its funny side, like discovering what happens on the night shift when computer operators appear to prove that it's chips with everything in more senses than one!

Training was not, however, restricted to specialists in computer audit, and it would be a pity not to tell of the much wider programme of training that was carried out in this field. In the late sixties and early seventies over 250 members of the Service had attended courses on general computer appreciation at Kingston Polytechnic. By the late seventies it was clear that auditors generally needed training in basic computer audit, and it was decided to launch our own internal courses. But by this time the reputation of the Service in the use of computers for audit and the audit of computerised systems was becoming firmly established and several local authorities were looking to the Service to provide much needed training for their internal auditors, so we opened our doors to them.

The pilot course (memorable and also forgettable), was held in late 1977 and coincided with the publication by the Service of one of the earliest set of guidelines for computer audit. Over the next five years 26 such courses were run and attended by a mixture of over 300 members of the Service and an equal number of internal auditors from the public sector.

At first the courses were held in Bristol, but in the autumn of 1979 we exchanged the flesh pots of Bristol for the more spartan regimen of the DOE residential training centre at Cardington in Bedfordshire, which still bore the hallmarks of an RAF reception camp There, course members enjoyed the doubtful pleasures of military-style accommodation and mess halls, and not a few brisk trots through the rain to and from the wooden classrooms over half a mile away. They did, however, appear to enjoy the rural delights of early morning jogging, football and conkers, or just sitting on the grass in warm sunshine. They also enjoyed countryside walks, for on one occasion, when told to take a break and go for a walk, it took over half an hour to get the course members back from the fields and lanes of Bedfordshire.

23/3 The auditor and computer language: liveware.

Certainly they worked hard and played hard and enjoyed the social atmosphere of the country pubs or residents' bar, enhanced by the very mixed and varied company. On which note we shall leave them and return to the computer auditors, save for one comment. The value and prestige of the courses was due in no small part to the fact that they were based on practical and, sometimes, painful experience of computer audit in the field.

Having experienced some months of programming, the newly created computer auditor was then thrust upon the unsuspecting audit district and local authorities. Everyone had high expectations of these auditors, and the sustained training and long spell away from the audit room suggested to the other staff that these individuals had amassed a vast amount of knowledge of all things to do with computers, and would be able to unravel the mysteries of these hideously complex machines, allowing the rest of the audit team to work in splendid isolation from them in the earnest belief that the machines would eventually disappear as quickly as they had arrived.

Nothing proved further from the truth! Indeed, many computer auditors then realised that they faced an uphill struggle to convince many of their colleagues that computing was here to stay and that their impact on audit was certain to be significant. The most daunting prospect facing the computer auditor, though, was the problem of coping with the wide range of computing facilities which local authorities were installing. The specialist auditor had indeed received training, but perhaps in the ICL low-level language PLAN which was quite alien to the IBM and Honeywell computers which were scattered throughout his territory. He also faced the dilemma of a range of retrieval packages, some developed by authorities themselves with names such as RUPERT, GRASP, REINS and PUSSCAT; some proprietary packages such as FIND and FILETAB; and in some cases an absence of any such software and, therefore, a need to write the audit tests in a programming language, if that was possible.

But computer audit has always had its lighter moments. One computer auditor at the end of a long day found himself alone and locked into the computer suite. In trying to get out he inadvertently tested the security system by setting off the alarms. The only response was from a passer-by who looked in to see that his friend, the cleaner in the outer office, was safe and well!

Computer audit thus proved to be a challenging and exciting activity for those early pioneers. Those first heady days may have passed, but the scene is still an enthralling and rewarding one with much to learn and develop. Indeed, sometimes the world of computer audit must seem like that of Alice in *Through the Looking Glass* where you have to keep running merely to stay in the same place.

ALAN EDMONDS

Joined the Service in 1937 under Hurle-Hobbs. Captivated by a computer's speed at a business exhibition in the late fifties, he learned computer programming at evening school. Headed the first DA computer team in 1969 and was responsible for the initial development of computer audit in the Service – particularly in retrieval techniques. Became the computer specialist in Met AD, retiring in 1980.

CHRIS HURFORD

As Associate Director in the Audit Commission, advises on computer audit strategy, the provision of resources and training as well as the overall management of computing facilities. His involvement in computing goes back to 1973, and his interest in the subject extends beyond the local government sector through his activities with CIPFA.

Choice of Auditor: The Local Government Act 1972

S V Collins CB

The decade 1962 to 1972, which began with the preliminaries leading to the London Government Act 1963 and ended with the Local Government Act 1972, saw the minor skirmishes between those advocating district audit and those in favour of professional audit for local government develop into a real battle.

Prior to the 1963 Act, the challenge to the district auditor had been confined mainly to newly established boards, for which authorities the right to choose had, on several occasions, been conceded. District audit had, however, been applied compulsorily for most of the services considered by Parliament since World War II.

The proposal for London that district audit should be applied to all the new authorities led to representations by the accountancy profession, culminating in a letter from the President of the Institute of Chartered Accountants in England and Wales to *The Times* in which he argued that those authorities should have a right to choose their auditor and added:

> ". . . it is proposed that an important right now possessed by 43 boroughs should be taken away, for no better reason than a departmental desire for uniformity."

The President's letter was misleading in several respects — only seven of the 43 authorities concerned had chosen professional audit — and it dealt with the issue in an altogether over simplistic way. Responses by the Honorary Secretary of the District Auditors' Society and others referred to the advantages to the ratepayers of the special code under which district auditors operated and to their lengthy experience of this particular field. The Honorary Secretary of the District Auditors' Society wrote in his letter to *The Times*:

> "The Institute [of Chartered Accountants] is pre-eminent in the commercial field; in the local government field, the District Auditors with their 118 years of service have played the major role. They have also made a substantial contribution towards bringing the standard of local government accounting up to its present high level.

> The apparent simplicity of the choice suggested by Mr Carpenter hides the real issue in this matter. Mr Hurle-Hobbs has already pointed out (April 2) that the District Auditor has special powers in the way of disallowance and surcharge and special duties over and above those of other auditors. It would be natural that many authorities, given freedom of choice, should opt for the more limited form of audit. A choice for professional audit would, however, mean the end of the independently appointed auditor and the end of the ratepayers' rights to question in a simple manner whether the funds they have

provided have been properly and lawfully applied."

The Honorary Secretary concluded by pointing out that, as long ago as 1864, a Select Committee of the House of Commons had stressed that authorities should not appoint their own auditors.

The Times took up the issues raised in the correspondence and examined in great detail the organisation and methods of the District Audit Service. In a fourth Leader they wrote:

". . . those who are neither accountants nor auditors nor councillors nor local government officers, just electors and ratepayers, may well conclude that the essential principle of the district audit is open and rigorous examination by independently appointed auditors in a form appropriate to the expenditure of tax revenues by politically controlled authorities; and that this system appears to, and probably does, protect the private citizen's interests better than any other at present available".

24/1 "Well that's sorted out the tea making arrangements!"

In the event, the Government stuck to the proposal that all the new London authorities should be subject to district audit and the 1963 Act enacted accordingly.

As reorganization of local government in the rest of the country loomed on the horizon, the question of the audit arrangements again began to attract debate. The widespread boundary changes proposed meant that many authorities partly audited by professional auditors were to be joined to others wholly audited by district auditors. Short of making all the new authorities subject to district audit, which in the climate of opinion at the time was not a practicality, the solution was far from simple.

The 1972 Act had, of necessity, to resolve this problem but it also provided an opportunity to deal with a number of criticisms of the audit code which had become apparent during the nearly 40 years since it was last substantially overhauled.

Elective audit was a subject of one such criticism. The auditor was not required to have any accounting qualifications or indeed experience, and by and large they were ineffective. And because district auditors were professionally qualified, it was misleading to use the expression 'professional audit' in contrast with district audit.

Under section 228 of the Local Government Act 1933, the district auditor had a duty to disallow expenditure contrary to law and to surcharge the amount disallowed upon those responsible. He had a duty also to surcharge any sum not duly brought into account, upon the person by whom that sum ought to have been brought into account and the amount of any loss or deficiency upon any person by whose negligence or misconduct the loss or deficiency had been incurred. The person involved had a right of appeal to the High Court and, in some limited cases, to the Minister.

The Minister's jurisdiction on appeals conflicted with the Government's declared aim to reduce central government involvement in local affairs. And in fact, the appeals procedure had not worked well – delays were considerable and the Minister's decision was not always regarded as sound in law. Appeals ought to be to the courts alone.

It had long been felt that questions of illegality were better determined by the courts in the first instance and that members and officers who had incurred illegal expenditure in good faith ought not to be surcharged and have to appeal to obtain relief. The very words 'disallowance and surcharge' had become emotive and the district auditor's role, instead of resulting in a decision having legal effect, should be one of initiating proceedings to enable the court to reach a decision at first instance. And the court should have a discretion on the question of disqualification.

The auditor's jurisdiction over losses arising from negligence had, since the *Pentecost* case in 1955, been understood to cover losses arising from negligence in its ordinary legal sense and not necessarily involving moral culpability. In this respect, the liability of members and officers of local authorities was unique. In no other field were individuals subject to possible penalty under statute law, it being left to the body or persons damaged to take such disciplinary action or pursue such remedy under the general law as they thought fit. There was much to be said for abandoning the special rule applicable to negligence in local government.

So far as losses arising from items not brought into account and misconduct were concerned, the district auditor was considered to be well placed to make the detailed investigations required to assess the sums due and identify those responsible. No substantial change in the auditor's duty was required but 'misconduct' was thought to be better qualified by 'wilful', perhaps unnecessarily.

Certain aspects of the auditor's general duties were in need of clarification. In particular, some leading treasurers had challenged the auditor's right to raise matters which they regarded as their prerogative as managers. After much consideration and debate, there was general acceptance of the words:

". . . the auditor shall be under a duty to consider whether, in the public interest, he should make a report on any matters arising out of or in connection with the accounts, in order that those matters may be considered by the Body concerned or brought to the attention of the public",

which more or less expressed the well-established practice of district auditors as approved by the courts. There was also need to strengthen the law regarding publicity for the report.

Experience had shown that other matters needed attention. The question of facilities for the auditor and current audit had both given difficulty in the past. And it was very desirable that district auditors should have a right to obtain explanations from persons holding or answerable for documents.

Although there was much discussion about the detail of the foregoing proposals for the improvement in the district audit code, there was general acceptance of

THE RIGHT TO CHOOSE

RESPONSIBILITY FOR AUDITING

TO THE EDITOR OF THE TIMES

Sir,—Under the London Government Bill it is proposed that an important right now possessed by 43 boroughs shall be taken away, for no better reason than a departmental desire for uniformity. I refer to the right to choose whether to have district auditors (i.e. civil servants) or professional auditors.

There will be 32 London boroughs under the reorganization, of which 19 will be wholly or mainly the successors of those authorities which at present have the right to choose. Yet the Bill proposes that district audit shall apply compulsorily to all the London boroughs.

This "closed shop" principle is proposed in the Bill notwithstanding that

(a) it would remove an existing right, which some of the boroughs have exercised in favour of professional audit

(b) outside the London area the county and non-county boroughs (some 400 authorities) have the right to choose and about 60 per cent of them have chosen professional audit

(c) on no less than six occasions the accountancy bodies have successfully contended before committees of both Houses of Parliament that the right to choose should be allowed to various statutory boards and on the last occasion a *committee of the House of Lords reported that "when a point has been decided against a Minister five times, he should no longer persist in making recommendations to the contrary"*.

Accompanied by the Presidents of the Institute of Chartered Accountants of Scotland, the Institute of Chartered Accountants in Ireland, and the Association of Certified and Corporate Accountants, I have waited upon the Minister of Housing and Local Government with a view to the amendment of the Bill in order to preserve the right

24/2 Clipping from The Times, March 1963. A letter to the editor expressing the views of P F Carpenter, President of the Institute of Chartered Accountants in England and Wales, on the right of choice of auditors by local authorities.

them, and in due course they were incorporated in the Act or Regulations made under it.

To return to the principal question regarding the division of work between the district and professional (henceforward to be called private) audit, the Local Government Bill as originally drafted attempted to preserve the existing position, under which certain authorities could chose between district audit and private audit for some of their accounts, whilst other authorities had no such discretion. Although district auditors had considerable experience in the local government field compared with their private counterparts, none could deny that private audit could make a valuable contribution and the somewhat arbitrary decision as first proposed was anomolous and could not be defended.

One solution that was floated was that an independent audit commission, comprising representatives of central government, local government and the accountancy profession, should be responsible for the appointment of district auditors and private auditors as it thought fit.

Such an arrangement would have been a further step towards achieving the Government's aim of ridding itself of direct involvement in local government affairs and it would have helped to remove the central government image which some saw colouring the District Audit Service. It would incidentally have greatly eased the district audit staffing problem. But this solution did not receive support.

Initially the tide moved towards choice for all authorities, including London. The best estimate of the consequences of such an arrangement, if nothing more was done, was that the District Audit Service might suffer a reduction in workload of some 40 per cent and would be so thin on the ground in certain areas as to raise operational difficulties. It was clear that to ensure that choice was fairly based, certain conditions had to be introduced.

First and foremost, authorities should not be able to avoid the rigours of the district audit system – involving members and officers in liability for certain illegalities

24/3 "How the other half lives".

and losses – by choosing private audit. There had to be some means of bringing the district auditor into the area of a private audited authority where matters arose for the possible exercise of their powers. This could be done conveniently through a direction for an extraordinary audit. And local government electors ought not to lose their right of inspection of accounts and of objection when private audit was chosen.

Then it was important that auditing standards appropriate for the audit of public funds should be maintained, and to this end it was proposed that the appointment of private auditors should require the approval of the Secretary of State. As the Secretary of State said, 'it [would] be very difficult for a firm that does not specialise . . . to satisfy [me] that it is capable of doing the work'. The Secretary of State would be empowered to withdraw his approval, and the work of the private auditors – henceforth to be known as 'approved auditors' – should be reviewed on the same basis as the work of district auditors was already reviewed. In order that auditors might know the standards they were expected to meet, a Code of Practice

should be prepared.

As a further measure to ensure the maintenance of satisfactory standards of auditing, the Secretary of State would prescribe minimum fees, albeit with provision for flexibility in particular cases.

It was an essential part of these new proposals that there was to be a single system of audit. Whether the accounts were audited by a district or an approved auditor, the general duties of the auditor were to be the same and the accounts subject to the same special safeguards. These proposals, which in due course found their way into the Act and the Regulations made thereunder, eliminated the concept of two different systems of audit, and made it clear that the choice to be exercised by local authorities was the choice of an auditor rather than a choice of system.

It is satisfactory to note that when the dust had finally settled and all choices had been made, overall the district audit share of the workload increased from about 85 per cent of the local government transactions before reorganisation to about 95 per cent afterwards.

S V COLLINS CB

Became District Auditor for London and Hon Secretary of the District Auditors' Society in 1958. Appointed Deputy Chief Inspector in 1965 and Chief Inspector of Audit in 1968. He was closely involved in the audit innovations introduced under the Local Government Act 1972. Retired to the West Country in 1977, and can now be found most summers sailing the Brittany coast of France.

Performance Measurement and the Use of Statistics

Jack Sprigg

The auditor's work is essentially a review of performance: in his examination of the accounts, he compares what he finds with what he expects to find. The latter may be an amount of money, a statutory requirement, a system of control, a standard or some other criterion. In public administration the auditor's writ is wider than that of his commercial counterpart: he has to satisfy himself not only that the accounts present the auditee's transactions fairly, but also that adequate arrangements have been made to secure value for money. The manager in local government, too, needs to be able to satisfy himself, and those to whom he is accountable, that the activities within his responsibility are providing the public with value for money.

This cannot be done convincingly without the maintenance and proper presentation of financial, statistical and other management information. Management information in turn provides performance indicators which enable comparisons to be made internally over a period of time or externally with other similar bodies.

The differences which such comparisons reveal provide both auditor and manager with reassurance that the organisation is on course or with warning signs that all is not well.

Financial and other statistics have been used increasingly by auditors as the size and complexity of the organisations they review has grown. Over the years there has been a steady development from comparing this year's balance sheet with previous years', this year's expenditure and income with last year's and with those forecast in the budget, to a wide-ranging statistical review of performance across the whole of local government.

The district auditor has been fortunate in that firstly, although each local authority has its own individual characteristics and problems, the services it provides are the same as those in every other authority in the same class. Secondly, he has been well served for many years by the publication of a wide range of statistics by the Chartered Institute of Public Finance and Accountancy, the Society of County Treasurers and others, including, in many cases, county councils who have produced statistical reviews for district councils within their areas.

The local government auditor uses statistics in three ways. Firstly, as a means of optimising the short time he has available, he carries out an overall review of a local authority's accounts and other data to identify areas where he ought to direct particular attention. For example, if the trend in the expenditure or income of an activity is out of line with that of other authorities or with the trend in the scale of the activity, the auditor will make further enquiries to ensure that there is a satisfactory explanation for the apparent anomaly, rather than management inefficiency or some more sinister reason. Secondly, he uses statistical analysis as part of his more searching enquiries into specific services or functions. Thirdly, the auditor is often able to use statistical information in support of the audit findings he presents to the council.

In his review of a council's management arrangements the auditor expects to find that managers also are using financial and other management information in similar ways.

The practice of making statistical comparisons between one authority and others has gradually developed from being generally unacceptable (if not impossible) to one that is widespread, and the strengths and limitations of which are well understood.

An early example of a more systematic approach to inter-authority comparisons took place in 1976 at Epping Forest and four other district councils. Here, in co-operation with the five local authorities, the District Audit Service set out to measure the performance of each authority in comparison with the other four, both in respect of each service and as a whole. The study aroused widespread interest, some approving, some critical.

Briefly, the study involved identifying and giving a value to outputs for each service and dividing the quantified outputs by inputs (expressed as employee

25/1 The code of practice: "An Auditor must be concerned not only with the form of accounts but also with the issues of substance arising therefrom."

costs and man years) to give performance indicators. The results of the study led to internal reviews of particular services by the authorities themselves. For example, one council was surprised at the relative costs of its swimming baths. A more detailed review led to the better matching of staffing levels to demand throughout the week. At another authority the management services programme was changed to give priority to a review of housing management, whilst at a third the comparisons made upon a consistent basis (ie. ensuring that the bases for allocating expenditure were the same) showed that the refuse collection service was much more expensive than had been thought.

Later the technique was extended to a number of other authorities at the auditor's or council's request with similar results.

The Epping Study was primarily a comparison of efficiency and economy based upon a review of unit costs. Whilst it led in some instances to an examination of effectiveness, it did not in itself provide any direct effectiveness indicators. There is much argument as to the precise meanings of the three terms and their relationships in the process of performance review. However, efficiency is generally taken to reflect the relationship between output and input (ie. productivity).

The difficulty of identifying and quantifying the true output (and its value) from bodies providing a public service is often quite serious and may also lead to profound disagreement, since one person's perception of good value is a complete waste of money to someone else. For that reason, 'intermediate' outputs are often used in the measurement of efficiency, eg. a planning application, a council dwelling, an inspection, a pupil, or a student.

Economy relates to the acquisition and maintenance of assets (the main asset in local government is manpower).

Evaluating effectiveness is more difficult, since it is concerned with the impact of a service upon the public and the achievement of policy aims and objectives. Effectiveness may sometimes take years to measure. For example, high-rise system-built flats were once regarded as a highly effective means of dealing with the housing shortage. Views have changed since then. Some services provide more ready measures of effectiveness. For example, the reduction of atmospheric pollution is not only evident but measurable. So are examination results, student retention rates, the incidence of crime, or the growth or decline of local industry and employment.

The district auditors' attentions have helped to promote an awareness of the need for performance review and to overcome resistance to the acceptance of performance indicators. This has been achieved by persistence and steady developments rather than some startling breakthrough.

Until 1977, auditors were generally left to their own initiative in their use of statistics for their work. In that year, however, the District Auditors' Society set up a Statistics Panel which first reviewed the availability, value and limitations of statistics, as well as current practice and expertise in their use. Two years later the Society, with the co-operation of the Audit Inspectorate, began to produce statistical tabulations derived mainly from the published data, which included the highlighting of 'out of line' levels of expenditure and income. Other statistical reviews employed more refined

For example Profile of ABC County Council:

	Expenditure (£000s)	£ per head	Average for all similar authorities	Difference (£000s)
Education	74,300	293	223	17,619
School Meals and Milk	3,250	13	9	955
Personal Social Services	27,459	108	63	11,511

methods, such as regression analysis and a presentation based upon standard costing techniques.

One of the statistical approaches which proved to be particularly useful was the local authority profile. This was developed from an earlier experiment in No 1 Audit District and enabled the expenditure of one authority to be compared on a service-by-service basis with other similar authorities and for the financial consequences of the differences revealed to be quantified (see table above).

Needless to say, this approach was merely a starting point for more detailed analysis, but it did help to focus attention on specific services.

Naturally, the statistical approach to performance review was not at first universally welcomed in local government, but as its value has been demonstrated and the techniques developed, there is now a wide acceptance of its validity and many authorities closely review the results for their own benefit.

The demographic and economic characters of authorities vary greatly and the need to compare like with like was reflected in the production of a classification of local authorities based upon a technique known as 'cluster

analysis'. This grouped authorities by their similarity in relation to over 40 variables. The classification was subsequently updated following the 1981 census and used a wider range of demographic and other variables.

The Audit Commission has built upon the District Audit Service's foundations for its local authority profiles, which provide a comprehensive statistical picture of each authority in relation to authorities in the same 'family' or 'cluster'. The profiles have been further developed as 'logic trees', which are systematic service-by-service analyses of expenditure and income.

Statistics, like accounts, have never been and never should be considered as ends in themselves but their use has greatly helped the auditor in his task. Much more importantly, their wider use has brought both better accountability and public awareness of the performance of local government services. The Code of Practice on information for the ratepayers is an example of development in this area.

More accountability puts pressure upon managers to measure their own performance and thus creates a requirement for accurate, relevant and timely management information. This in turn leads to improved motivation, control and performance. The District Audit Service can claim to have played a leading part in this path to better management control and accountability.

JACK SPRIGG

Joined the Service in 1964. Has worked in a number of audit districts, but his particular interests are in statistics and value for money auditing. Recently has been doing some pioneering work in the audit of colleges and polytechnics, and is writing a handbook on performance measurement in local government.

Comparative Studies

M H Langley

In the mid 1920s the courts referred to one purpose of district audit as being 'to ensure wise and prudent administration', and the public have for a long time required that the audits of local authorities' accounts go beyond regularity checks and detection of fraud, and that the auditor should be alert to the wasteful use of resources. Public feeling in this regard was recognised in the Local Government Audit Code of Practice, published in the early 1970s, which required the auditor to be concerned with 'issues of substance arising therefrom (the accounts), such as the possibility of loss due to waste, extravagance, inefficient financial administration, poor value for money, mistake or other cause'.

To carry through their duties economically, district auditors commonly made use of published statistics. They knew from experience that many of the transactions before them at audit were unlikely to require detailed attention, and statistics helped to locate the areas of operation where their efforts might best be concentrated. Published statistics, usually only highlighted areas for examination, and to investigate the cause for variations required the collection of more information, not only at the local authority then under audit, but also at other comparable authorities.

However, the limited audit resources meant that comparisons could only be made over a small number of authorities of similar character, and enquiries were usually confined to narrow fields of activity for which costs and explanations for differences might be reasonably easy to define.

Despite their limitations, the comparisons often served a useful purpose for the client authorities. Audits are based on enquiries into administrative and operational systems, and auditors' investigations enabled them to refer confidently to systems which were working economically, efficiently and effectively. As a result of audit recommendations, local authority officers were encouraged to consult with their professional colleagues elsewhere and so to profit from their experience.

The Layfield Committee, set up in 1975 to enquire into local government finance, considered the audit effort in relation to what was going on at the time; that is, against a background of the after effects of a wholesale reorganisation of local government. The Chief Inspector of Audit at that time referred to the period as a difficult and demanding one, with many problems arising from the sheer volume of local authority staff movement. He reported that audit staff had been in constant demand from newly formed authorities for guidance, not only on the preparation of the old authorities' accounts, but also on the introduction of financial control systems and on the countless day-to-day problems of the new authorities. The district auditors had, without exception, informed him of the very severe pressure on their staff at all levels, particularly at directing officer level.

26/1 The specialists are coming.

The Layfield Committee, in its report in May 1976, stated 'we believe that the best way of promoting efficiency and securing value for money by external means is through the dissemination of comprehensive but intelligible information on the methods employed by local authorities and the results they achieve'. So attention was drawn to a need for the development of comparative studies. The Committee accepted that the District Audit Service had already done work along these lines, but as the auditors' duties under their Code of Practice were necessarily directed towards the audit of each individual authority's accounts, any exercises involving comparisons were controlled by the auditor's own need for additional information relevant to the particular audit.

The Committee thought there was a need for wider-ranging comparisons with better dissemination of information on best practices, primarily for the information of local authorities but also to allay public disquiet, as they had received numerous complaints of alleged waste in local government. The Committee referred to the value of a limited number of comparability exercises which had been undertaken through the Chief Inspector of Audit's office, but considered such comparisons should be undertaken on a more regular and systematic basis. They concluded that this could best be achieved through a reorganisation of the District Audit Service with the addition of more resources.

The Government's Green Paper on Local Government Finance, issued in response to the Layfield Committee, endorsed the Committee's recommendations only in part. The Government agreed there was a need for more comparative information about costs and practices to enable performance to be more easily judged, and they accepted that district audit should extend their work in the value for money field. However, they did not accept a reorganisation of the District Audit Service, nor their need for more resources.

The Government looked instead to local authorities to finance comparative studies through the Local Authority Management Services and Computer Committee (LAMSAC) and other agencies. The Government's Green Paper did, however, propose 'that a new advisory body on audit should be established which would consider general questions on efficiency and value for money in local authorities' and said that 'the proposed institution should be able to work independently and its reports should attract a measure of public attention'.

The Advisory Committee on Local Government Audit was set up following the Government's Green Paper proposal. Its terms of reference required the Committee to consider the annual report of the Chief Inspector of Audit, and to invite information and submissions on comparative and other value for money studies from local authorities and their associations, and from other agencies concerned; and in the light of these and other information, to advise on the need for such studies and arrangements for carrying them out.

The Committee, therefore, had to look mainly outside the District Audit Service for work on comparative studies. However, in its consideration of the Chief Inspector's annual report, it provided a channel for wider dissemination of information about problems and issues in local government, which had arisen from audit work at individual authorities, but which had a general relevance. The Chief Inspector in his second report to the Advisory Committee, for the year ended 31 March

1979, suggested that the auditor's most useful contribution to comparative studies might be in the identification of aspects for investigation, and this might well evolve as part of the process of drawing together findings and experiences for report to the Advisory Committee.

In the same report, the Chief Inspector referred to five exercises which were in the nature of comparative studies and which had been carried out by the District

26/2 The specialists arrive.

Audit Service during the year. Two of the exercises were based on data supplied by local authorities to central departments:student/staff ratios in polytechnics, and various cost heads in the police service. Two other studies had been made of data collected by the auditors at a large sample of local authorities by means of the completion of specially prepared questionnaires.

One set of data was analysed to show the differing costs of the many methods used by local authorities in paying salaries and wages to their employees. The analysis showed clearly that there was scope for substantial administrative savings by reducing payments in cash, and by encouraging greater acceptance of cheques and bank credit transfers. There were similar results from the other study, which examined methods of collection of the main sources of income in local government, viz from rents and rates. It showed savings could be made in administration by greater use of the banks' services, particularly from obtaining payments by direct debit arrangements.

The fifth study, based on work in the audit districts, examined deterioration in systems of control of building contracts at a number of local authorities and made suggestions for improvements.

The publication of the Chief Inspector's report prompted many local authority officers to seek more detailed information from the Audit Inspectorate, so that they could assess the possibility of changes in procedures at their authorities. The later consideration of the report by the Advisory Committee and their own enquiries and report prompted action in central government departments, as well as in local authorities.

The manpower and other resources available to the District Audit Service were controlled by the Department of the Environment, although paid for by local authorities through audit fees assessed on the statutory scale. For the period immediately before local government reorganisation, in 1974, and for several years afterwards, the Department of the Environment, operating through the Civil Service Commissioners, failed to provide sufficient staff to the audit service to meet the assessed requirement for the work the district auditors had to do to complete the full range of their duties, statutory and otherwise. From 1979 onwards, the staffing position deteriorated through the imposition of arbitrary cuts.

The income, however, did not reduce at the very least it kept pace with inflation. To ensure a proper return to clients from the fees they paid, the Service developed audit methods which facilitated working with professionals from accounting and other disciplines, employed on a contract basis. Furthermore, within the fee income it was possible to expand the central support section in the Chief Inspector's office in those areas for which there was the most demand:computer auditing, and in the provision of a statistics service.

Expansion of statistical work highlighted the need for the development of comparative studies. Local government opposition to such studies, except under the direct control of authorities themselves or their associations, was partly related to a fear that the studies might produce league tables of costs without sufficient regard to quality of service or local circumstances, or that results might be published in a way that provoked unacceptable comparisons.

The Audit Service was well aware that an analysis of cost variations was at best only a starting point, and that a comparative study required much deeper investigation of the underlying reasons. For such investigations the District Audit Service decided teams of mixed talents were required. Essential to each team was knowledge of local government functions and administration, investigatory skills, and familiarity with methods and systems and with the work of officers at each authority taking part in a study. All of this the District Audit Service could provide. Other skilled help, however, was required in the examination of management processes. For this the District Audit Service engaged specialist assistants from firms of management consultants.

The requirement was different from the normal consultancy put to such firms, and was more a selection of individuals from the staff of the firms, having regard to their experience in the needs of each particular job and their ability to work within a team which was essentially audit orientated. Discussions on the requirements took place with the leading firms and all were willing to participate. The people selected, from those made available by the consultancy firms, worked under the auditors' directions, so ensuring that each study was conducted within the purpose of the audit function. Finally, each study required input from professional officers engaged in that local government activity – in general terms, this was available at each authority but it had to be seen to be unbiased. Therefore, arrangements were made for advice and monitoring of each study by the appropriate professional association of officers and by the local authorities associations' professional advisers.

The participation of the associations of professional

officers and local authorities associations, in an advisory capacity at the earliest stages of each study, had the effect of bringing to light possible difficulties, and enabled adaptation of proposed methods of study to avoid them. Furthermore, when it was known to local authorities that the nature of the studies had been discussed with the local authorities associations, they were more willing to take part.

The comparative studies first undertaken touched on three major areas of local government activity: the fire service, further education, and social services. The fire service study examined, at a sample of fire authorities, the mechanics of working from Home Office guidelines on the assessment of fire risk to the requirement for men and appliances, and touched on other activities for which there were no manning guidelines, such as fire prevention. The study of further education concerned three aspects of management control of colleges of further education: courses, academic resources and control information. The social services programme areas were ambitious in covering four aspects: care of children, care of the elderly, care of the mentally handicapped and the administration of services.

The aim of each study was to produce a methodology to assist auditors in their work, and to explore and publish information about how different practices at authorities affected economy, efficiency and effectiveness. The studies extended over two years, and not all had been completed before the creation of the Audit Commission for Local Authorities in England and Wales and the reorganisation of the audit service under the Local Government Finance Act 1982. Several other areas of study had also been started, but either they had not been completed or the results had not been published before the Audit Commission took over the work.

The studies, for which results were published, aroused considerable interest in local government, and many authorities were moved to review their practices to ascertain how they might benefit from methods employed elsewhere.

Apart from the activity prompted in local government by the published results of comparative studies undertaken by the District Audit Service, there was benefit to the Audit Commission in being able to take over a working organisation experienced in undertaking comparative studies and a volume of research work in a number of areas of local government. Furthermore, procedures for consultation had been developed with associations of professional officers and with the local authorities associations. These consultations and the results of the studies had moved local government opinion towards enthusiasm for this area of the Audit Commission's activities.

M H LANGLEY

Served in district audit from 1948 to 1983. Like most members of the Service, he worked in a number of different audit districts, but has the unique experience of having served under 11 district auditors and, in eight years at Audit Headquarters, under four Chief Inspectors and Cliff Nicholson as Under Secretary (Audit). Appointed District Auditor in Chester in 1974 and Inspector of Audit in 1978.

The Society's Annual Golf Meetings

In 1952 certain members of the District Auditors' Society suggested that on the occasion of the Society's Conference that year an endeavour should be made to arrange a golf meeting. Sufficient support was canvassed and the first annual golf meeting took place at Pinner Hill Golf Club on 29 October 1952, attended by 12 playing members and four supporters. Since that date a golf meeting has been held each year on the day preceding the Annual Conference of the Society.

In 1954 a George III flagon (by Francis Crump, London 1773) was presented by Mr C R H Hurle-Hobbs for competition at the annual golf meeting. This trophy, which is known as the 'Hurle-Hobbs' Flagon has been held by the winner of the Singles Competition in each year from 1954 onwards.

Ron Lloyd took on the job as golf secretary in the late 1950s and continued for some 13 years until his retirement. He had no interest in golf, he says, but was landed with the secretary's job only because he happened to be a willing option near enough to Stuart Collins to fall victim to his incisive persuasion.

At the time, Ron did not even have any golf clubs and at his first meeting used a spare set of clubs belonging to Collins. For his first game as a 'rabbit', Ron Lloyd did very well. The following year, Stuart Collins let him use the same clubs again, but this time he kept missing the ball all around the course. At the end of the day, Collins, with a wry smile, told him that the clubs had

27/1 ". . . the clubs had been shortened for his young daughter."

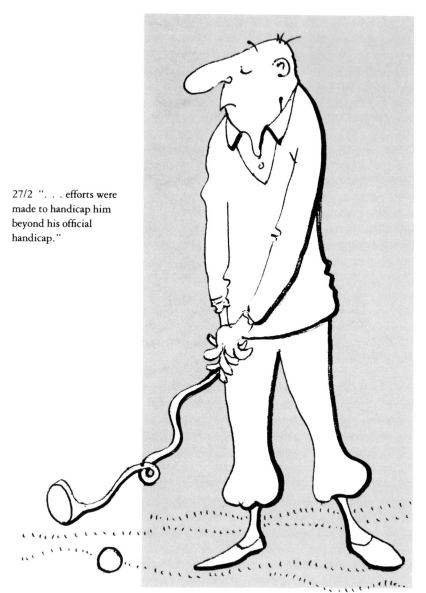

27/2 ". . . efforts were made to handicap him beyond his official handicap."

all been shortened for his young schoolgirl daughter. Thereafter, Ron acquired his own set of clubs, but avers that he never did master golf: instead he did the next best thing and handed his clubs on to his grandson.

Ron has said that his one satisfying recollection is that year after year during his period of office as golf secretary, the weather on those golf days was always good. It has become something of a joke to record the number of times Stan Pude has won the Hurle-Hobbs Trophy, despite the efforts made to handicap him beyond his official handicap – unthinkable to the dedicated golfer!

Fixing the handicap for new recruits joining the annual competition went to such lengths to encourage new members to participate that no matter how ineptly they played, they would end up with an encouraging total of points on their score cards. Such was the flexibility of the Stableford competition rules that it reached a pitch where the more of a 'rabbit' one was, the better chance one had of gaining a prize. Ron recalls that the one who seemed to qualify most for the booby prize was himself!

In the recollections of most members, the annual golf meetings will be remembered more for their camaraderie than their golfing achievements. What better preparation for a two-day conference than a day spent on a golf course with morning coffee and biscuits, lunch and tea and two rounds of golf (morning singles and afternoon pairs), with an even chance of holding the Hurle-Hobbs trophy and winning the 'captain's prize', plus even a booby prize (for effort) – all for between £2 to £3!

As Ron said, Stan Pude won the Hurle-Hobbs Trophy more times than any other player – nine times in all up to 1982. Stan Pude recalls that 'in the good old days, it was customary for CIAs and DCIAs to take part, whether they could tell one end of a golf club from another. Bates and Kendrick used to struggle round manfully and, I believe, Alan Wilson. There was one occasion when we had played our morning round and had had lunch when it was realised that two of those named had not appeared. Search parties were about to be sent out but they materialised on the eighteenth just in time'.

Stan refused to comment on the style (or lack of it) of many of the illustrious personages who took part in the yearly competitions, but added, 'the sight of Stanley Hills stroking the ball (with a golf club, of course) with all the respect due to a newly laid egg is one which I cannot forget'.

Stan hoped that some tribute could be paid to Stuart Collins, remarking 'it was due to his energy and determination and enthusiasm that the meetings were started and kept going over the years. He was the best golfer we had, making up for lack of length with deadly accuracy when the greens were in range. It is a pity that he never won the Hurle-Hobbs Flagon (I think) though I understand he won the initial competition before Hurle-Hobbs presented our magnificent trophy. I remember playing as his partner many years ago in the subsidiary foursomes competition. Although only a casual or very occasional player, he had a games player's instincts and showed a steadiness around the greens which enabled us to win by some enormous margin.'

The winners of the Hurle-Hobbs Flagon are listed below.

1954 E Feith	1969 W D Munrow CBE
1955 S D Pude	1970 S D Pude
1956 S D Pude	1971 G F S McMillan
1957 N S Middleton	1972 G F S McMillan
1958 T Peel	1973 S D Pude
1959 P A Chater	1974 D Wilkinson
1960 L A Walmsley	1975 P A A Court MM BEM
1961 N S Middleton	1976 A Long
1962 P A A Court MM BEM	1977 A Long
1963 S D Pude	1978 L Y Cond
1964 I M Pickwell	1979 R C Jackman
1965 G F S McMillan	1980 S D Pude
1966 S D Pude	1981 S D Pude
1967 W D Munrow CBE	1982 D Wilkinson
1968 S D Pude	

Sundry Memorabilia

One of the great pleasures in compiling this book was the receipt of letters from a number of retired and serving members, recounting old memories and impressions which had lingered and which they obviously still savoured. Another source of delight was the discovery of amusing and revealing passages in old official records and the like.

Among these was an extract from the minutes of the Birmingham Board of Guardians, which reflects the great apprehension felt by many in 1844 about the proposal by the government to appoint independent auditors to audit the Poor Law accounts:

> "On 23 April 1844 your deputation together with the deputations from Brighton, Bristol, Coventry, Hull, Plymouth and Southampton accompanied by Mr Dugdale and Mr Newdigate, Warwickshire MPs, Messrs Scholefield and Muntz, MPs for Birmingham, Lord Clive, Lord Harvey, Sir Walter James, Sir John Mannar (and numerous other listed MPs) proceeded to the Home Office and were received by Sir James Graham the Home Secretary. The attention of Sir James Graham was drawn to the proposed appointment of auditors with such extraordinary powers calculated to cripple the efforts of the Guardians, to deprive the representatives of their rights and give opportunity for improper interference in the government of the poor."

Mr O Barraclough recalled the days when a district auditor, once appointed:

> "was independent and answerable to no one – not to the Ministry, since it was to that body that appeals against his decisions in some cases would lie. This independence resulted in a tendency to autocracy; the district auditor was a little king. He sat on a raised dais and handed down decisions. The 'quasi judicial' function of audit was much emphasised. This attitude lingered on a long time. I remember in the late 1920s when industrial depression was resulting in large and growing rate arrears, the DAs from Lancashire asked the old school DA for North Wales, Mr Easterby, what line he was taking in his district about rate arrears. 'I have given instructions that there are to be no rate arrears,' he replied. There wouldn't be! Many rate collectors in his district would pay the few arrears themselves, hoping to recoup them later rather than face the wrath of the auditor.

> It was, I believe, Carson Roberts who really began introducing accountancy and proper auditing. Somewhere in the early 1920s – before my time, but I heard of it – he took a small, picked team of auditors into Wales, I think, and turned out fraud after fraud by the use of simple audit methods – mainly getting paying-in slips from the bank and identifying the cheques thereon".

Another retired member, Mr L T Butler, wrote of two particular district auditors whom he still recalls as colourful characters:

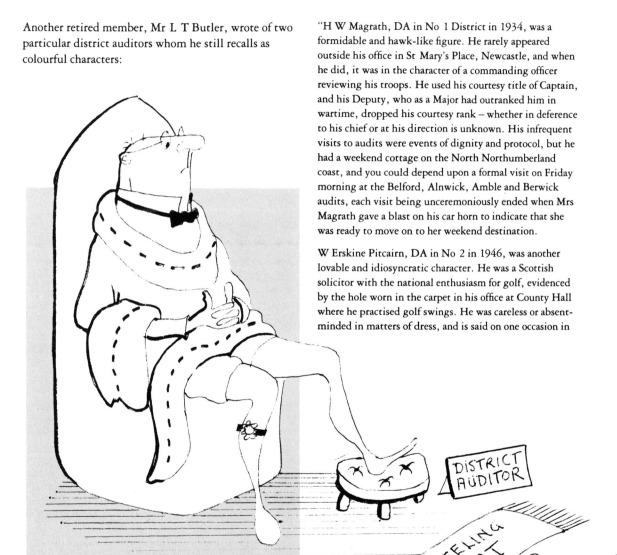

"H W Magrath, DA in No 1 District in 1934, was a formidable and hawk-like figure. He rarely appeared outside his office in St Mary's Place, Newcastle, and when he did, it was in the character of a commanding officer reviewing his troops. He used his courtesy title of Captain, and his Deputy, who as a Major had outranked him in wartime, dropped his courtesy rank – whether in deference to his chief or at his direction is unknown. His infrequent visits to audits were events of dignity and protocol, but he had a weekend cottage on the North Northumberland coast, and you could depend upon a formal visit on Friday morning at the Belford, Alnwick, Amble and Berwick audits, each visit being unceremoniously ended when Mrs Magrath gave a blast on his car horn to indicate that she was ready to move on to her weekend destination.

W Erskine Pitcairn, DA in No 2 in 1946, was another lovable and idiosyncratic character. He was a Scottish solicitor with the national enthusiasm for golf, evidenced by the hole worn in the carpet in his office at County Hall where he practised golf swings. He was careless or absent-minded in matters of dress, and is said on one occasion in

28/1 ". . . the District Auditor was like a little king."

28/2 ". . . having attended the office wearing two overcoats but no socks."

the depth of winter to have attended the office wearing two overcoats but no socks. After one staff conference at Wigan at a time when pedestrian crossings were still a novelty, he held up traffic in the main road by occupying the crossing, brandishing his walking-stick and declaring to a lorry driver, whom he considered to have been too eager, that he would die defending his rights on a Belisha crossing. The lorry driver, who was blameless, did not oblige."

Les Butler has a lively wit and a gift for writing parodies and wickedly satirical sketches which enlivened many a district's annual staff dinner. In the following passage he captures something of the spirit of those gatherings:

"Over the years the pattern of audit dinners changed. In the early 1930s, at Newcastle, the annual dinner took the form of an all-male 'smoker', with a formal meal and after dinner speeches, followed by social chat. Entertainment was casual and was limited to occasional vocal solos of 'The Road to Mandalay' variety and to funny stories, usually off-colour. 'Uncle' Ted Thomas, the DDA, could be relied upon to retell his apocryphal story of the parish councillor complaining of the poor jet of water produced by the village fire brigade at a local fire. 'I could have urinated as far' he said. The Chairman ruled that the speaker was out of order. 'I know I am' he replied, 'otherwise I could have urinated twice as far'.

After the war dinners became less formal, with the employment of female staff and the general loosening of the rank divisions. Entertainment became more adventurous with the introduction of comic sketches, mock conference papers, home-produced songs and the like, most of which poked gentle fun at audit subjects, practices and personnel. It was the occasion for staff to let their hair down and indulge in some quiet ribbing of their elders and betters.

Old members of No 2 District will remember Neil Middleton miming to a Carmen Miranda record while dressed in exotic female clothes and wearing a two-foot high head-dress composed mainly of fruit. On another memorable occasion at Preston, a Whitehall messenger was interviewed behind a mock television screen. He explained that it was his job to flag the staff disposition map in CIA's office. CIA's belief was that a man who was contented with his own life would not be good at finding fault with others, so, to keep an efficient audit staff, one kept auditors miserable and harassed by frequent, unheralded transfers. CIA was, the messenger added, out on an inspection at the moment and was no doubt writing down names in his black book, ready for a general stir-up on his return. Alan Wilson, then CIA and not noted for his sense of humour, was in the audience – and was highly amused.

By the mid-1970s, annual dinners in No 7 District had reverted to formal events without any organised entertainment, but, for the first time, wives and husbands were invited. This pattern was also followed in No 12, and whilst the move made for a more colourful and sophisticated occasion, it doubled up on cost to individual staff members and tended to freeze out the younger members on economic grounds."

These annual dinners, as now, were helpful in engendering a corporate spirit in each district, and some districts went further in organising sporting events within the district and with neighbouring districts. Les recounts that:

"In the 1950s the Lancashire District had more or less regular annual cricket fixtures with other districts and occasional matches within the district on a North v South basis. The needle inter-district game was the 'Roses' match against Yorkshire and this usually took place at the delightful Gargrave ground near Skipton. Two other sports were tried out as district events. A tennis afternoon was held at Whalley near Clitheroe, and whilst this was a very pleasant occasion from a social point of view, it produced few tennis players. Surprisingly, a district football match between North and South teams at Bolton produced two full teams, although most of the players had not kicked a football for many years. The game took place in appalling conditions with continuous, horizontal sleet and mud so deep and sticky that it was difficult to move the ball more than a foot or two except near the corner flags. The only concession made to the weather was to restrict the game to 30 minutes each way with no half-time interval. After the game it was found that no hot water was available in the changing room. To the surprise of all present no-one suffered any ill effects, but significantly the fixture was not repeated."

Securing suitable office accommodation for himself, his deputy and secretary was often a problem for a district auditor. Sometimes, if he was fortunate, he was able to beg the use of unwanted office space from an obliging

28/3 Trophies won by London AD at the Ministry of Health Sports Day 1950.

local authority: otherwise, he had to rely on the Ministry of Works finding him a garret in an old commercial block or shabby Government building. The service generally seemed to get the left overs!

Perhaps something of the despair felt by many district auditors may be gleaned from the following minute to the Chief Inspector of Audit, written by a district auditor in the 1970s on taking up his appointment on transfer to a new district. (Perhaps it should be recorded that the district auditor in question is a keen amateur sailor and of comfortable girth):

"1. You will recall that the office is situated on the first floor of a detached block (formerly the sanatorium) in an orphanage now occupied by the Department of Employment and Productivity. One half of the sanatorium is used by the Civil Service Sports Council as changing rooms and in the other half the DEP occupy the ground floor for storage purposes and we occupy the first floor.

2. The surroundings of the office are pleasant and there is adequate parking space. This is all that can be said in its favour. The exterior of the sanatorium is dilapidated and the approach to my office distinctly Hogarthian. We share

28/4 District Audit Cup Winners, Ministry of Health Sports Day, 1950.

28/5 The District Audit Athletics team at Ministry of Health Sports Day, 1950.

28/6 District Audit 'A' Medley relay team, Ministry of Health Sports Day, 1950.

a stone staircase with the Civil Service Sports Council and although I have seen better mud in the Medway we are disadvantaged here in that it is never covered by the incoming tide.

3. The furnishings do nothing to dispel the initial impression (my armchair collapsed and deposited me on the floor soon after I arrived and this typifies the whole set up).

4. In addition, in spite of a special effort by the DEP's Premises Officer (who is most co-operative) the offices are depressingly dirty and it is difficult to see how they could be made otherwise. They are also inconvenient. My secretary works in a small cubby hole and the two DDAs share a room measuring $8' \times 12'$. There is inadequate storage space and what there is is grossly inconvenient.

5. I do not need to spell out the disadvantages which stem from the occupation of such offices in trying to develop an efficient organisation. What is required is an office located in a position which does not bring the service into disrepute . . ."

The Chief Inspector, who knew the DA well, sought to cheer him up, and in his reply to this plea for his support in obtaining improved accommodation wrote as follows:

"1. I think you ought to examine very closely the advantages of your present office before looking elsewhere. I confess I can see little benefit for you in an orphanage, but to be able to spend much of your time in even an ex-sanatorium must help your general well-being. You can obviously make good use of the changing rooms and put your boating gear in the store. You could even winter your boat in the ample grounds.

2. I regret the accident with the chair but would suggest that you keep within the weight limit in future. I would be happy to let you have a couple of screws — we have surplus here.

3. It also grieves me that your two deputies have to spend their days in such discomfort. Would it not be possible for them to breathe in and out alternately?

4. However, since we are approaching Christmas and the season of goodwill I have decided to support you in your aim to secure more suitable accommodation . . ."

Disallowances and consequential surcharges were common in the nineteenth century. In connection with the Local Authorities (Expenses) Bill in 1887, the President of the Local Government Board stated that there had been 3,500 disallowances in the previous financial year. Such occurrences are much rarer today.

Perhaps the earliest example recorded of a disallowance and surcharge appears in a book entitled *The Parish Chest* by W E Tate, published in 1947 by the Cambridge University Press. Before 1834, allowance of Poor Law accounts was the duty of the Justice, and the following is an entry in the parish book of Laxton, Notts, dated 7 June 1739:

"Whereas complaint was made unto me one of his Majesty's Justices of the Peace . . . by several inhabitants of the Parish of Laxton against ye accounts of Thomas Skinner and Gervas Cullen in ye last three preceding pages of this book, particularly against the two last articles of forty shillings and three pounds pretended or said to be paid to John Hunter & Mr J Keyworth, and whereas it appears to me upon a full hearing of ye said Inhabitants Skinner and Cullen that ye said sums are not justly charged, the same being paid by them upon their own acts only and not upon act of ye Inhabitants or by or with their consent and privity. I do therefore disallow of the sd two articles and adjudge that they are Debtors to the sd Inhabitants upon ye balance of ye sd Accounts ye sum of four pounds six shlgs and fourpence farthing, and do order them to pay ye same to ye present Overseers of ye poor.

E A W Becher"

In their report for 1881–1882 the Local Government Board, with some touches of dry humour, give examples of appeals against certain classes of disallowed expenditure which seem to have been common a century ago:

"In our last report we gave some examples of disallowed expenditure which was especially open to objection as representing an outlay for eating and drinking by officers or members of Local Authorities. In dealing with appeals against disallowances of this description we are fully assured that the law and public opinion are in complete accord. Feasting at the cost of the rates is an abuse for which few defenders would nowadays be found, and it is also one which, by its comparative variety, is particularly striking. There were during the year several instances in which our attention was drawn to expenditure under this head.

A succession of bills of fare submitted for examination in connection with an appeal by members of a Local Authority showed that at frequent intervals during several weeks it had been the practice to provide a substantial repast for a considerable number of persons. The bills made mention of soup, fish, meat, poultry, grouse, pastry, cheese, salad, and dessert, and the beverages seem to have been ale, stout and brandy. It is hardly necessary to say that our decision on this appeal is not likely to encourage the continuance of these entertainments.

In another case we were told that a Local Authority, 'at the urgent solicitation of the inhabitants who were very enthusiastic on the occasion, and with a view of doing proper honour to the Chairman' had resolved to celebrate his wedding day by a 'suitable demonstration'. This took the form of an illumination in which an array of ten devices in gas was described as having given 'universal satisfaction' . . . .

We were nevertheless unable to accept the conclusion that this 'unqualified success' was one which could properly be attained at the expense of the ratepayers."

Few members of the Service would dispute the proposition that the worth of the district auditor has never been properly recognised, nor the extent of his duties and the personal qualities required for their discharge. The early district auditors were up against this when, in 1860, they presented a memorial to the Poor Law Board to show that their salaries were 'not sufficient remuneration for their service'. The Honorary Secretary and a handful of members of the District Auditors' Society were called to give evidence before the Poor Law Relief Committee of the House of Commons on 16 July 1882. The following passages are extracts from the evidence given by the Honorary Secretary to the Committee:

"8898. You say that the scale of remuneration is too low? – Yes, a great deal too low.

8899. Is that the feeling of the Association of District Auditors? – Yes, and my own conviction is very strongly the same.

8900. The position is eagerly sought for, notwithstanding that, is it not? – I know of no public office of which that cannot be said, from highest to lowest; I dare say you might reduce half the salaries of all public offices in the Kingdom, and yet if you put them up to competition there would be candidates for them; I do not think that is a fair way of putting it, especially when you consider what the qualifications of an auditor are.

8901. Do you observe, as a consequence of the district auditor being too lowly paid, that he is not so vigilant as he might be? – Not at all; simply that he is a sufferer unjustly; that is the only consequence that I refer to. I do not think that I should do my duty better if I were well paid, nor do I think it would be the case with any gentleman I know, nor do I think that he would do his duties worse if you took off half his salary; so far as I know the gentlemen of our

society, they are upright and intelligent men, and very zealous and anxious in the performance of their duty.

8914. . . . .You see he must be a lawyer; he must be competent to judge, he must know how to take evidence, he must know how to judge upon that evidence, he must know how to construe Acts of Parliament; he must have, or ought to have, a great deal of discretion and patience, and then he must be an accountant, to understand the books and accounts, and to be able to check them."

Not everyone, especially not officers or members who had suffered at the hands of the district auditor, thought as highly of him. There is still extant on the audit files for an Essex authority a letter from a superannuated former clerk to the authority. He was of some longevity, and in replying to a request for a 'life certificate' he wrote complaining that he was feeling his years, and of being unable to sleep. His letter continues:

"Much of my disability stems from the crazy antics of Auditors more than 50 years ago when, and for many years, all officials met with the most abusive, profane, brutal and inhuman treatment at their hands. The language of some would have won a prize at Billingsgate. Their usual attitude was that of a VERY bad tempered schoolmaster. One such Auditor was so horrible that the Council threatened to have the subject discussed in the House of Commons. The Clerk to the Council resigned because of it and said he would never again speak to a L G Auditor. In the end that Auditor was called to book for mutilating my General Ledger with livid green ink, saying that the A/Cs were all wrongly built up and the Ministry saying I was right. He was dismissed. I received a personal apology from the Minister but that is poor consolation when so much damage had been done and recorded for ever.

Another inhuman beast narrowly escaped death at the hands of a tormented official who, a little drunk, threatened to shoot the Auditor but we saw the butt of the revolver sticking out of his pocket and relieved him of it in the nick of time . . .

Maybe your present auditor would be interested in reading this letter. He would at least know that I am very much alive to write it in spite of old age, so much disability and so near to 'the Great Divide'.''

28/7 R K Edwards behind the wheel of a Vitesse 6 at Oulton Park, 1964. Perhaps the only DA to have driven in competitive races.

Audit Fees

David C Smith

The assessment and collection of audit fees would seem to be a prosaic matter, but it is a subject full of interest in the period 1844 to 1983 when the office of district auditor was a statutory appointment. During this period fees were determined not by the auditor, nor by the body audited, but by central government through administrative departments, specialising initially in the poor law and subsequently in local government generally, with titles appropriate to the functions and fashion of the time – including the Poor Law Board, Local Government Board, Ministry of Health and Housing, Ministry of Housing and Local Government, and Department of the Environment. It was this control of the fee arrangements by a central government department which was the determining factor in deciding what form those arrangements should take and when they should, or more usually should not, be changed.

Historically, the reason for control of fees by the centre is not hard to find. Abuse of the poor law rate and national concern at its ever-growing burden had led to the Poor Law Amendment Act 1834, a decade before the district auditor appeared on the statute book. This empowered the Poor Law Commission to secure the appointment of paid officers, including auditors, by the local administering authorities, the overseers and guardians. Moreover, these officers were subject to dismissal if the Commission considered them unfit for or incompetent to discharge their duties, or if they should refuse to comply with the rules and orders of the Commission. By regulating the level of audit fees paid by the authorities, the Commission believed that an effective audit might be carried out, a belief not entirely without foundation in that poor rate expenditure fell by a quarter by 1840.

In so far as audit fees were concerned, the Poor Law Amendment Act 1844 substantially re-enacted the 1834 legislation which it replaced, the Commission continuing to determine the salary of the auditor to be met by the overseers or guardians from the poor law rate. However, to overcome the Commission's uphill battle of the previous decade against the invidiousness of local patronage, the legislation provided for the appointment of 'auditors for districts', the districts being defined by the Commission, and the auditor being chosen by the chairmen and vice-chairmen of the boards of guardians within the district. In practice, a significant proportion of the 1844 appointments were persons recommended by the Commission!

The 1834 legislation made possible an appropriate level of audit effort; the 1844 legislation provided a means by which truly independent auditors might be appointed. Together, they laid the foundations of the District Audit Service. The 1834 legislation proved to be inadequate because appointments of auditors were left to local patronage. The 1844 legislation might have been equally ineffective, had it left auditors' salaries to be determined by the chairmen and vice-chairmen of the boards of guardians, or, worse still, by the individual boards. The central determination of fees was a key factor in establishing a local government auditor removed from local influence.

Throughout the period 1844 to 1878, poor law authorities and the various other bodies to which district audit was applied – local boards of health (subsequently urban and rural sanitary districts), highway districts, school boards – were obliged to pay the district auditor from local funds. Fees were assessed and invoiced by individual auditors. An example of an invoice raised on a local board of health appears at Fig 1.

The hallmark of the era was a resolve by the Commission, and by its successors the Poor Law Board from 1847 and the Local Government Board from 1871, to improve the standards of local administration. Regulations and instructional letters to auditors poured out from the centre, and from 1868 the Board took over the appointment and payment of district auditors, who thus became civil servants. The bitter pill of increased audit costs was deflected from authorities by costs being met roughly half from the centre, half locally, by 1878. The broadly similar audit fee arrangements which applied to the different types of authority then subject to district audit were rationalised by the District Auditors Act 1879.

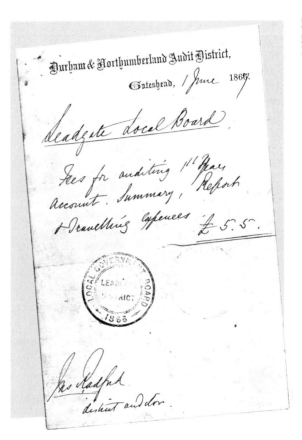

Fig 1: Audit fee invoice payable by the Leadgate Local Board of Health.

The 1879 Act provided for the salaries and expenses of district auditors to be paid out of moneys provided by Parliament and a scale fee to be charged on every local authority subject to district audit for the purpose of *contributing* to the cost. The scale was set at a rate which would recover roughly half of those costs and was based on expenditure audited. Apart from increasing the fee scale above its then maximum of £50 to accommodate the county councils in 1888, the arrangements operated uneventfully until shortly after the 1914–1918 War.

At that stage, the newly formed Ministry of Health, as successor to the Local Government Board, embarked on a major reorganisation of the District Audit Service, including the appointment of superannuable civil servants who, over a period, were to replace the clerks formerly appointed personally by the individual district auditors. Alarmed by the resulting increased costs, the government, in the Finance Act 1921, transferred the full burden to local authorities, the Treasury being empowered to fix a scale of fees 'sufficient to meet the costs' of district audit.

An order of the same year achieved all, in fact more, than the Ministry had sought. Fee income rose from £64,000 in 1920 to £183,000 in 1923. The legislative changes of the Local Government Act 1929 led to a fall in fee income from £200,000 in 1927 to £185,000 in 1930, but even so, it was 1938 before the accumulated surplus had been 'returned' to local government and a new, fully redrawn scale was introduced. This scale, like its 1974 and 1982 successors, was based on the aggregate of audited income and expenditure, rather than on expenditure alone.

The 1938 scale produced £300,000 in its first year of operation, £465,000 in 1950, £905,000 in 1960, £1.9 million in 1970. Total costs and fee income being broadly in line, the Treasury was unwilling to initiate a review of the scale, but the taper in the scale and rapid increase in local government expenditure in the 1960s resulted in larger authorities being overcharged and smaller undercharged. As an extreme example, a small authority with expenditure of £50 or transactions of

£100 in 1973 was charged a fee of £1, precisely the same as in 1879. No wonder there was to be an outcry when the fee rose to £6 under the 1974 and £11 under the 1982 scales. Only in 1972 when curtailed audits of the larger authorities scheduled for abolition seemed likely to produce windfall profits did the Treasury relent and permit the Department of Environment to authorise reduced fees based closer to cost.

The 1974 scale, unlike its predecessors, was the responsibility of the Department of Environment rather than the Treasury, and applied to 'approved' as well as district auditors, that is, to firms of accountants appointed by authorities with the approval of the Department. The level of audit effort which would be needed for the new, larger authorities was uncertain, and in fixing the scale, the Department made clear that auditors should seek approval to reduce fees if audit costs warranted it. Although some £1.5 million fee reductions were granted, this was due mainly to truncated audits to clear the backlog of audit work resulting from local government reorganisation, rather than any defect in the scale.

The fee scale was, in fact, cast on the low side. Inflation was to increase fee receipts from £5.6 million in 1976 to £8.4 million in 1981, but by then the taper in the scale resulted in a failure to recover district audit costs. The results were twofold: a patched-up new scale – though still inadequate – in 1982 increasing fees overall by 16%, and a determination by the newly formed Audit Commission to fix fees on a basis other than the scale value of audited transactions.

By casting the 1974 scale on the low side, the Department set in motion the train of events which contributed to the establishment of the Audit

Commission. The 1974 district audit staffing complement was set at a level which would enable audits to be carried out within the scale. When civil service staffing policies depressed professionally qualified staff salaries below the market rate, staffing difficulties arose and were compounded by a virtual recruitment ban. The government filled the gap by authorising the employment of contract staff and by appointing firms to act as 'additional district auditors'. The Commission emerged as the means, ultimately acceptable to the government, department and auditors alike (although for widely different reasons), by which the problem could be resolved.

To ensure that each fee was assessed in accordance with the legislation, authorities were required to compile in duplicate a financial statement of their expenditure under the 1879 Act or 1921 Order, or of their income and expenditure under the later orders. Failure to complete the statement was an offence, subject to a £20 penalty from the outset. The auditor certified both copies as to the accuracy of the assessed fee, one copy being forwarded to the Department/Ministry/Board etc, the other being returned to the authority.

The format of the earlier statements was prescribed by order and hence, as statutory financial statements, they became known to generations of auditors as the 'SFS'. In the early part of the twentieth century, there were a large number of different types of statement, one for each type of authority, but these were gradually rationalised until, when the 1974 scale was introduced and the format of statements no longer prescribed, only three types were found to be necessary, one for principal authorities, one for parishes and one for the rest. Similarly, the excessive detail required in the earlier

statements was gradually relaxed, the seven pages of the parish statement of 1900 having shrunk to a single page by the time the system was abandoned.

The scales prescribed items which might be deducted in arriving at the amount on which the fee was to be assessed. The intention was to reduce the fee for items which were relatively easy to audit, and the 1879 scheme provided merely for exclusion of precept payments to other local authorities. Each succeeding scheme, however, became increasingly complex: the 1974 scheme, for example, provided eleven categories of deduction. When the aggregate of income and expenditure was used as the base figure with effect from the 1938 scheme, the greatest care had to be employed to ensure that there was no netting off of income against expenditure within the accounts which might serve to understate the audit fee.

The complexity of the scheme was such that, for many years, a committee of district auditors ('the stamp duty committee') met to determine how novel transactions should be recorded to secure equity of treatment between authorities in the assessment of fees. For the new principal authorities formed under the 1972 Act, the statements were drawn up from returns submitted to the Department for statistical purposes with the aim of simplifying the arrangements, but even so, compilation represented a good day's work for an accountant and checking about half that time for an auditor. The system destroyed itself in its search for perfection.

When the 1974 fees scale was introduced, audit fees were collected very much on the same basis as had applied prior to 1879 in that they were invoiced on authorities by auditors. In the case of approved auditors, the fees were payable to the firm. In the case of district audit, Department of the Environment invoices were used to secure payment to the Department.

During the previous 95 years, however, a different system applied. From 1879 to 1974 audit fees were collected by means of fee stamps and administered as a stamp duty by the Inland Revenue. This system covered the greater part of the period during which district auditors were civil servants and in which their fees had to be accounted for to the Exchequer to be applied towards district audit costs.

Stamp duties had been introduced originally as a form of taxation in 1694, being brought to this country by William of Orange, having been highly effective in the Netherlands. The legality of a document was made dependent on it being written on paper, to which a stamp denoting the value of the duty paid was applied by embossing machine. The stamping was carried out by the 30 or so Stamp Offices of the Inland Revenue, using embossing dies of various denominations, with multiple or multi-value stamping to make up the value of a duty where necessary.

Fig 2: Examples of early (first line) and later (second line) Minerva head embossed general duty dies, the shape of each value being retained when the dies were reduced in size.

The maximum stamp value was increased from time to time. The maximum was £5,000 in 1879 and £50,000 in 1974. The latter was adequate to cope with the largest individual fee under the system, being £200,000 for the GLC in 1974. Special dies were made for common duties, eg estate duty, but general duty dies were used for the majority, including audit stamp duty. The Stamp Office recorded the duty in respect of which the die had been applied, and accounted for the duty to the appropriate Department. By the time audit fees were made collectable by stamp duty, the impressions were invariably in permanent vermillion ink through which the text of the stamped document could be read, and incorporated the date of usage as a security device.

Although in the first few years of audit stamp duty some older coat of arms-type dies were still in use, the Minerva head pattern (Fig 2), which was of a different shape for each denomination, had been generally adopted, and apart from being reduced in size from the 1920s, remains in use to the present day, although not, of course, for audit fee purposes.

When district auditors became civil servants in 1868, impressed stamps were effectively the only option available for fee collection by means of a stamp duty; and the requirement to submit financial statements to Stamp Offices for the predominantly small authorities of that era put a stamp duty out of the question. Adhesive stamps for various revenue purposes existed, spawned by the introduction of postage stamps in 1840 and of their perforation from 1853. Very common duties, such as the stamp duty on receipts, were collected in this way, as were some duties for which relatively few stamps were used, for example, those of the various courts –

admiralty, common law and chancery. The cost of engraving dies from which stamps might be printed was high, however, and served as a deterrent to collection of duties in this way.

The breakthrough was to come with the design in 1872 by the firm of De la Rue of a set of dies of different face values up to £20, which by overprinting could be put to the collection of any number of different duties. Examples of unappropriated dies of the £5 value appear at Fig 3. De la Rue held the contract for printing the stamps, which were appropriated to district audit stamp duty throughout the whole period of their use, only marginally short of a century.

The District Auditors Act 1879, in setting out the scale of audit fees, required their collection by way of stamp duty. An Inland Revenue circular of 28 March 1879, issued to all distributors of stamps, notified the printing of adhesive audit stamps of the values of five and ten shillings, one, two and five pounds, payment being by means of general duty impressed stamp above that figure. A similar circular withdrew the adhesive stamps from sale on 29 August 1975. Apart from decimalisation to 25 pence and 50 pence in 1971, the values of the five adhesive stamps never varied.

The 1879 adhesives are reproduced at Fig 4. They were printed on watermarked paper as an obstacle to forgery, and in fugitive ink to make impossible the removal of the cancellation with a view to re-use of the stamp. Initially the shilling values were green and the pound values violet, but the violet gave way to lilac in 1882, probably because the violet ink was excessively fugitive. Green, violet and lilac were the only colours for which fugitive inks were available at that time, but were

retained for all later issues until the shilling values became blue on decimalisation.

Fig 3: Examples of De la Rue unappropriated dies for adhesive stamps. *(Courtesy of the British Library)*. The stamps printed from the dies were 'appropriated' to the collection of a particular fee or duty by means of overprinting.

Fig 4: 1879 issue of district audit adhesive stamps.

Fig 5: 1896 issue of
district audit adhesive
stamps. As previous
issue but additionally
surcharged to increase
the legibility of the
value.

It will be noted that although the designs of the various
denominations were similar, the engraving varied to
eliminate the risk of stamps being doctored to a higher
face value. Moreover, to facilitate identification of the
various values, the "district audit" overprints were in
distinctive colours, in ascending value, violet, red,
black, blue, green. To increase the legibility of the
value, the stamps were additionally surcharged in 1896
with their denominations in figures (Fig 5), both
'district audit' and the surcharge being in blue on all
values.

The reigns of Edward VII, George V and VI and of the
present Queen had a common design, varied only by the
monarch's profile (Fig 6), the district audit overprint
being in blue and engraving of the various values
continuing to differ. At decimalisation the 25p and 50p
were of the same design and the value and 'district audit'
in black (Fig 7). Emergency printings of the pound
values overprinted in black and in a variety of typefaces
(Fig 8) exist from the period when the stamps were on
the point of being withdrawn. The Inland Revenue saw
no reason to introduce new dies in haste, and those for
George V did not appear until 1918, George VI 1947
and Elizabeth 1960. As late as the 1960s, stamps from
all five reigns were in use, partly because of their late
introduction, partly because of low usage in some areas.

The collection of fees by means of stamp duty gave
authorities and auditors a number of original problems.

In certifying an SFS, the auditor confirmed the accuracy
of the fee calculation and, until 1974, that he had
completed the audit. Where completion of an audit was
delayed due to objection etc, the auditor was precluded
from collecting his fee.

Where collection was by impressed stamp, there was a
delay of a few days whilst the statement and a cheque
were passing to and from the Stamp Office. This delay
stretched to several weeks during and immediately after
the two world wars.

All certified SFSs were sent by auditors to the
Department which used them to agree the sum
accounted for by the Inland Revenue. Because some
authorities stamped their SFS months in advance of
audit visits, whilst others retained their Statements
until chased by the auditor, the Department had an

almost impossible task to establish an annual debit.

Adhesive stamps were available only from distributors of stamps, in practice from head post offices. They could be requested through sub-offices but with delays of up to a week. Because of the relatively low usage (only a total of 10,000 stamps per annum in 1970), purchasers from head post offices often had to wait for some time at post office counters whilst stocks were located.

The requirement to use impressed stamps where the duty exceeded £5 led to difficulties when authorities inadvertently obtained adhesive stamps for higher duties. The system required an erroneously stamped statement to be sent to the Stamp Office which overprinted the adhesive stamp 'Allowed' (Fig 6, £5 value) and applied substitute embossed stamps. Once cancelled and removed from the statement, no refund could be obtained for an adhesive stamp, stamp duty legislation regarding such a stamp as having been used. A refund for unused stamps could be obtained but this again involved application to the Stamp Office.

Similarly, postage, as opposed to district audit, stamps were sometimes affixed due to ignorance of or oversight by local government or post office staff, predominantly by parish council clerks. It was hardly surprising that, in spite of Stamp Office legislative penalties and Chief Inspector of Audit prohibition, there was collusion between auditors and authorities to find a market for unwanted stamps among other authorities with statements awaiting stamping. The audit kettle came into its own if stamps had been affixed!

Some parish clerks relied on the auditor to affix stamps

Fig 6: District audit adhesive stamps for four reigns. The dies, differing for each value, where unchanged throughout the period except for the monarch's profile. For example, compare the £1 value with that in Fig 8 below.

Fig 7: The 25p and 50p decimalisation issues, the same die being used for both values.

Fig 8: Emergency overprinting shortly before the stamps were withdrawn.

when the audit was completed, and enclosed the stamps with the records produced for audit in unmarked envelopes at the back of the accounts or along with the property deeds where the auditor was certain to find them. Alternatively, stamps might, or again might not, be brought along at the end of the audit. It was disconcerting to the auditor to discover an unaffixed stamp at the end of a day's work on several different parishes, and alarming to receive a stamp with a cryptic note saying 'please stick on financial statement' at the end of a three-week stint on 30 or 40 sets of accounts.

The 1879 Act and later orders required all stamps to be cancelled. It is puzzling why this should be, as the Stamp Office sought cancellation merely of adhesives. Pre-war auditors who had been faced with up to a dozen embossed stamps on an SFS must have blessed the introduction of ballpoint pens. The Stamp Duty Management Acts merely required cancellation by 'name or initials or otherwise', but 1909 instructions by the Local Government Board required the auditor to write across the stamp 'the name of the local authority, his signature and the date', guidance which unsurprisingly was modified in 1919 to a requirement that the stamps be 'effectually cancelled'.

Finally, from 1969 the Post Office levied a counter handling charge for each stamp sold irrespective of face value, the charge being 40 pence by 1974. This produces some interesting thoughts, for example when a £1 audit was stamped with four 25p stamps. With a final flourish, the Inland Revenue produced a £3 stamp which had been one of the most common fees for the previous 90 years. This, however, was to remain in the archives and never brought into use, for by this time the knell of the system had been tolled.

In retrospect, it can be seen that the stamp duty system was suitable for the small authorities of 1879, many of whom had no bank accounts and who found convenient the purchase of adhesive stamps through post offices. At this time the relatively cumbersome procedure of securing the embossing of fees over £5 (required because of Inland Revenue fears of forgery) was something of a rarity. What is surprising is that the system survived for so long, for the creation of larger authorities, the growth of local government services and inflation inevitably forced more and more authorities to seek embossing. Yet it was not until the 1960s that the Inland Revenue sought to abandon the system, and only their refusal to continue the arrangements when the 1974 order was introduced finally obliged the Department of the Environment to revert to invoicing arrangements and bring the chapter to a close.

D C SMITH

Was active in the field for 12 years until
sudden deafness in 1973 necessitated a move
to Audit Headquarters. His arrival coincided
with the winding up of the audit stamp duty
system giving him a unique insight into the
old and new arrangements from the
viewpoint of both the field and headquarters.
We are grateful for his authoritative account.

The Creation of the Audit Commission

J C Nicholson, CBE

Even so few years after the creation of the Audit Commission, myths and legends abound about its genesis. Was it the brainchild of the Layfield Committee, the Maynard Committee or Michael Heseltine? What was the driving force which brought it into existence? Certainly the return of Michael Heseltine to the Department of the Environment as Secretary of State in May 1979 started a sequence of events which led to the creation of the Commission. But the story starts very much earlier than that.

Probably the first seeds were sown during the District Audit Service developments of the late 1950s and 1960s. As the Service sought to rethink its role and priorities, a much greater emphasis developed in what we now think of as value for money matters. By present standards, those early efforts were puny in scope and resources, and often, too, they were shallow in content. But in spite of those limitations they produced results.

The work also sparked off a series of concerns both in local government and among auditors about the extension of audit activity into management. So much so, that at least one district auditor banned the use of the term 'management auditing'. Some prominent local government officers expressed rather deeper concerns

that the extension of auditing into value for money matters might bring the independence of the Service into question and create the danger of it becoming an instrument of central government.

In the late 1960s, these were the issues which much exercised the minds of Stuart Collins, the Chief Inspector, and his deputy, Laurence Tovell. By 1971, there were also other worries. Provincial local government reorganisation was in the offing and something had to be done about the audit arrangements. Even had it been desirable, maintaining the status quo was not a realistic option. Neither was the 'London solution' which imposed district audit on all the authorities created by the London Government Act 1963; even at the time, the passing of those audit provisions was somewhat surprising – and largely a matter of parliamentary chance.

Circumstances had also changed in that some of the auditing firms were aggressively keen to increase their share of local government work. At the same time, the traditional, overt support for the District Audit Service by local government finance officers was open to some doubt because of the proposals for the merging of the accounting profession, which implied a constraint against rocking the boat.

There really was a formidable array of problems. But as happens so often, at least in successful organisations, 'comes the hour, comes the man'. In July 1970, Stuart Collins, in a penetrating examination of the issues, proposed to the Department of the Environment that the local government audit function should be made the responsibility of an independent body – 'perhaps an audit commission appointed by the Minister with provision for nominations of some members of local authorities associations'. So far as I have been able to establish, that was the first expression of the proposition and the title.

Consideration of the proposal by the Department was somewhat tardy. But by July 1971 some interest was being shown in the idea, and Stanley Hills prepared a paper on how a local government audit commission might work. Some of the key ingredients were the use of auditors from firms as well as district audit, independence of auditors in carrying out their professional responsibilities, the role of a commission in promoting good audit practice, and the possible use of specialist audit teams to carry out assignments additional to the normal audit.

In the event, while the Department accepted that there were arguments in favour of a commission, they were not convinced. By August 1971, timing had become a critical issue with provisions urgently needed for the Local Government Bill to be introduced in the autumn. It was decided, therefore, to go for status quo provisions (later amended to the 'choice of auditor' provisions) and to have another look at the future of audit, in the course of which the idea of a commission could be explored in more detail.

The Scots, however, with rather different problems and a little more time before their reorganisation legislation, were less reticent. They saw a commission as an acceptable and viable way of improving standards and achieving cohesion in their local government audit function, while at the same time distancing it from central government. So it was that their 1973 Act set up the Commission for Local Authority Accounts in Scotland.

Meanwhile in England and Wales, a new slant on the commission idea was advocated by a *Local Government Chronicle* editorial in February 1972. This was prompted by a consultation paper on the establishment of the system of ombudsmen. What the *Local Government Chronicle* suggested was that there should be a permanent independent commission to administer both the audit system and the complaints machinery. There were consultations between the Department and the local authority associations on the idea but nothing came of them and, in due course, the legislation provided for the Commission for Local Administration to be concerned only with the complaints fulcrum.

Even before the 1972 Act had completed its Parliamentary process, Stuart Collins was further arguing the objections to, and the potential instability of, the 'choice of auditor' arrangements, and the advantages of having the appointments function in the hands of an independent commission. Things then went rather dead for a while. This was inevitable, since it was clear that it would take time to change attitudes, and in any event there were other pressing problems arising from local government reorganisation and the Housing Finance Act 1972 rents confrontations.

By the autumn of 1975, the commission idea was back

30/1 1983:. The birth of the Audit Commission.

EXIT

DISTRICT AUDIT

AUDIT COMMISSION

1983

...and the last

Tempora mutantur, et nos mutantur in illis ....

on the Chief Inspector's agenda, this time with added reasons – the need for a greater emphasis on waste and inefficiency, the failure to deal with district audit staffing shortages, and the consideration of the issues by the Layfield Committee. The response was still frustrating:

"Nor did the idea of an Audit Commission in itself have much attraction";

"Of course Mr Collins is wrong to think that a Commission would have the flexibility he has in mind on recruitment, and so on; but it is a common illusion".

Although one door seemed firmly bolted, another was opening up. The Layfield Committee asked for evidence, and a submission was made about local government audit, including the case for an independent body to appoint auditors and to administer the function. The Committee accepted the merit of the proposals and recommended in its report the creation of a 'higher institution' to run the audit function. But the battle was far from over. Government departments were still not convinced. In fact, they were not convinced about any of the Layfield recommendations, with their emphasis on a new financial structure for local government.

One by one, the recommendations were rejected until there was nothing left but audit. Something had to be done about the audit proposals to avoid rejection of the whole Layfield report. Even so, the idea of an independent executive body was still not acceptable; so there was a compromise. The Advisory Committee on Local Government Audit in England and Wales was brought into being.

The Advisory Committee had no executive role in the management of the audit function. Nevertheless, its terms of reference were interesting:

"(a) to consider the annual report of the Chief Inspector of Audit and any questions arising from it, which are of general public interest or concern, within the field of value for money or otherwise, and to make general recommendations to local authorities, and to central government as it thinks fit, and;

(b) to invite information and submissions on comparative and other value for money studies, from local authorities and their associations, and from other agencies concerned; and in the light of this and other information to advise on the need for such studies and arrangements for carrying them out."

In practice, in the two years or so of its active existence, the Advisory Committee, sometimes also known as the Maynard Committee after its chairman, Brian A Maynard, largely confined itself to consideration of the annual reports of the Chief Inspector.

Without being too critical of the Advisory Committee, the fact is that it had no means to achieve its ends, and this was noticeable in connection with the studies aspect of its terms of reference. It is also a fact that by May 1979 when it held its first meeting, the scene was becoming fast-moving and the Committee had no time to play itself in and develop its role. As I shall explain later, it did, however, have an important direct contribution to make towards the establishment of the Audit Commission.

The establishment of the Advisory Committee also gave rise to a valuable indirect development; since one of its duties was to consider reports of the Chief Inspector and to comment on them, it followed that those reports must be made public. So it was that we gained a shop window in which to display the achievements – and problems – of the Audit Service.

Other factors in that fast-moving scene included the report of three Parliamentary Select Committees – the Public Accounts Committee, the Expenditure Committee, and the Procedure Committee – over the period 1976 to 1979. The common theme of these reports was that since local government received substantial financial assistance from central government through the rate support grant and other grants and subsidies, there should be a direct Parliamentary concern to see that this expenditure was properly spent. The three Select Committees therefore thought that the Comptroller and Auditor General should have access to local authority accounts, that he should report on general local authority issues to the Public Accounts Committee, and that there was a case for merging the District Audit Service with the Exchequer and Audit Department.

In May 1979 then, the sequence of events leading to the creation of the Audit Commission was ready to move into its next phase. With the return of Michael Heseltine to the Department of the Environment, changes in the audit provisions were inevitable. Michael Heseltine had been a Minister in the Department at the time of the 'choice of audit' provisions of the 1972 Act. However, he had concluded that the provisions had failed because the firms had only 10 per cent of the work. But he had several other reasons for wanting change – a firm belief in the desirability of reducing the number of civil servants, the view that the relationship between district audit and local government was undesirably cosy, and a strong will to toughen up the audit function – particularly as regards value for money.

Perhaps the only surprise was that it was three months before he called for action in the shape of a paper setting out the options for the future of audit. The preparation of that paper was probably the most important task which fell to Peter Kimmance, Malcolm Langley, and me during our triumvirate. Our perception, and indeed the reality, was that it was the key opportunity to secure a sound future for effective and progressive local government auditing and, of course, for the District Audit Service. Although a number of options were explored – and honestly explored – in our view, only one met the requirements: an independent Audit Commission.

Discussions on the options continued until the autumn of 1979. They were examined from every angle, and also in the light of the pressures for a National Audit Office to include local government audit. Disclosure of those discussions must await the lapse of time under the thirty-year rule. For the moment, suffice it to say that the Audit Commission option soon attracted the support of Michael Heseltine – and he was the man who mattered. By the end of the year, he was sufficiently convinced to float the idea with the local authority associations, and for the first time the debate moved into the public domain.

At that stage, the proposals included the suggestion that LAMSAC might be part of the Commission. That issue met with no support. Indeed, the response to the whole proposal for an audit commission was somewhat bleak. The Institute of Chartered Accountants were early supporters, but there were few others. Local government was highly sceptical and, at a time of developing central/local government tension, took the view that this could only be some new device for their further chastisement. The Advisory Committee, on the other hand, expressed wholehearted support, and that support, together with the earlier Layfield Committee recommendations, were called in aid on many occasions in the lead up to the legislation and during its Parliamentary passage.

In spite of the generally cool reception, views about progress were still optimistic, and preliminary thoughts were that the Commission could be in place and in operation by April 1981. Looking back, it seems a further oddity of those early considerations that the Commission was to be the Accounts Commission; indeed, that provisional title persisted for quite some time. But the first optimistic timetable was not to be.

During 1980 and 1981, there were what seemed at the time to be interminable delays in progressing the proposals. One major reason was the contemporaneous consideration of the future of the Exchequer and Audit Department. Within the Whitehall establishment, attitudes polarised between the supporters of an independent audit commission, and those who favoured a National Audit Office which included the local government audit function. In an odd way, these delays probably tipped the balance. Local government did not want the Commission, but it wanted even less to be part of a National Audit Office, with an apparently direct line of accountability to Parliament.

30/2 "An unlikely marriage" the creation of the Audit Commission.

There were other effects of the delay. Michael Heseltine wanted to press on towards the new regime. He agreed to make money available – or rather to let the Service use some of its fee income – to engage consultants to undertake comparative studies. Work was carried out, most notably in further education and social services. The studies were valuable in their own right; even more valuable was the experience they gave us, and the proving of the approach which was to become the 'special studies' provision of the eventual legislation.

A further consequence of the delay, coupled with civil service recruitment constraints, was the decline in the staffing of the District Audit Service. In response to repeated representations about this, but perhaps more motivated by a desire to bring forward a greater share of the work of the firms, Michael Heseltine decided to appoint fourteen partners of firms as 'additional district auditors'. Local authorities which had chosen district auditors under the 1972 Act's 'choice of auditor' provisions found themselves with a different sort of district auditor.

Out of these considerations came the decision, announced in Parliament in July 1981, to legislate for an audit commission. The audit provisions emerged as Part III of the Local Government Finance Bill, introduced into Parliament on 6 November 1981. We would all have wished to have been spared our bedfellows in the Bill – the controversial provisions on rates and precepts in Part I, and on block grant in Part II. Indeed, so controversial were the rating provisions that the Bill was abandoned, and we reappeared as Part III of the Local Government Finance No 2 Bill on 16 December.

The Parliamentary passage of the Bill was somewhat tedious, although much of the flak was directed at Parts I and II. The debates on audit provisions tended to focus on a limited number of issues: pro and anti private firms arguments, the conflict of interest between auditing and consultancy, the differences from the Scottish provisions, fears of domination of the Commission by the Secretary of State, and fears of interference by auditors and the Commission in policy decisions of local authorities. Interestingly enough, the illegality and wilful misconduct provisions were never an issue. Finally, the Parliamentary process was completed, and on 13 July 1982 the Bill received Royal Assent.

In the meantime, preparations had been going on. Insofar as these related to identifying problems, they were useful; but where they attempted to provide ready-made answers for the Commission, those answers were too much the product of the Departmental approach to meet the Commission's needs. I cannot think of any of those ready-made answers which were actually adopted. But perhaps the most disappointing thing of all about the preparations for the Commission was the lack of progress in appointing the Members and Controller.

The idea in the first place was to have the Shadow Commission ready to start its work as soon as the Bill became law. In the event, it was not until December 1982 that the Chairman, Members, and Controller were appointed, with only three months to prepare for the most significant change in the history of local government audit. That those preparations were made, and that the Audit Commission was successfully established, is now a matter of record. It is also a further demonstration of successful leadership – by John Read,

John Banham and the Commission – and of their dedication and that of the District Audit Service to the ideals of effective local government auditing.

There is an epilogue – an incident of failure turned into success on the way to the Commission. During the preparations, Peter Kimmance and I strongly urged that on its merger into the Commission, the District Audit Service identity should be retained, but we failed, and pleas from Members of Parliament during the consideration of the Bill were no more successful.

Ministers were of the view that the future was a matter for the Audit Commission, that the Commission should start with a clean sheet of paper, and that its operations should not be constrained by the inheritance of a historical title – however honourable. So it was that the 'district auditor' disappeared from the Statute Book. But the Commission saw him as a fact of life. It saw the District Audit Service as its most important resource which could be most effectively used by preserving its identity. The historical decision was taken. The District Audit Service lives on.

J C NICHOLSON, CBE

Deputy Controller and Director of Operations of the Audit Commission since 1983. Before that, 30 years with District Audit including spells as Metropolitan District Auditor, Deputy Chief Inspector and the last head of the old Audit Service.

Illustrators

Claire Blackman

Is now on secondment to Vincent Square as
Assistant Project Manager; previously she
had spent the whole of her service in No
9AD, from her appointment in 1963 at
Maidstone, with a move in 1975 to
Canterbury. For many years she organised the
annual district dinners with great success,
and, to the delight of the guests, used her
artistic talents to decorate the menu cards.

Alastair Rankine

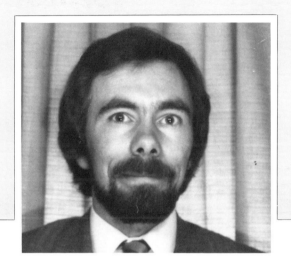

ALASTAIR RANKINE is a young qualified audit examiner who joined the District Audit Service in 1975 and works in London. His hobbies and interests range from photography and painting to winemaking, and, when he has time, cycling and country walking. For relaxation he enjoys music of all kinds.

Bob Kitson

BOB KITSON joined the Service in 1947 and is an SADA in the north-west. He is a talented cartoonist, contributing on a fairly regular basis to local newspapers. His other activities include playing and composing music and amateur dramatics.

Picture Sources

Title page
Photo: Royal Commission on the Historical Monuments
of England.

Chapter 1
1/1 Photo: Crown copyright. Reproduced with the
permission of the Controller of Her Majesty's Stationery
Office.
1/2 Photo: Crown copyright. Reproduced with the
permission of the Controller of Her Majesty's Stationery
Office, and the Advisory Committee of Works of Art in
the House of Commons.

Chapter 2
2/1 Illustration: Claire Blackman.
2/2 Illustration: Claire Blackman.
2/3 Photo: Illustrated London News.
2/4 Illustration: Claire Blackman.
2/5 Illustration: Claire Blackman.
2/6 Photo: Illustrated London News.
2/7 Photo: Illustrated London News.
2/8 Photo: Illustrated London News.

Chapter 3
3/1 Illustration: Claire Blackman.
3/2 Reproduction: HMSO.
3/3 Illustration: Claire Blackman.
3/4 Photo: Hulton Picture Library.
3/5 Photo: Source unknown.
3/6 Photo: Hulton Picture Library.
3/7 Photo: Daily Mirror.
3/8 Photo: R W Thirlwell.
3/9 Reproduction: The Observer.

Chapter 4
4/1 Illustration: Claire Blackman.
4/2 Photo: Illustrated London News.
4/3 Photo: Illustrated London News.
4/4 Illustration: Claire Blackman.
4/5 Illustration: Claire Blackman.
4/6 Photo: Illustrated London News.
4/7 Illustration: Claire Blackman.
4/8 Photo: Illustrated London News.
4/9 Illustration: Claire Blackman.
4/10 Illustration: Claire Blackman.
4/11 Illustration: Claire Blackman.
4/12 Illustration: Claire Blackman.

Chapter 5
5/1 Illustration: Claire Blackman.
5/2 Reproduction: Warwick Advertiser.
5/3 Reproduction: Warwick Advertiser.
5/4 Photo: TWM Griffith.

Chapter 6
6/1 Illustration: Claire Blackman.

Chapter 7
7/1 Illustration: Claire Blackman.
7/2–7/3 Reproduction; HMSO.
7/4–7/5 Reproduction by permission of the British Library.

Chapter 8
8/1 Illustration: Claire Blackman.
8/2 Reproduction: Express and Star Wolverhampton.

Chapter 9
9/1 Photo: Hulton Picture Library.
9/2 Illustration: Claire Blackman.
9/3 Photo: Hulton Picture Library.

Chapter 10
10/1 Photo: Source unknown.
10/2 Photo: A W Vaile.
10/3 Photo: A W Vaile.
10/4 Illustration: District Audit Society.

Chapter 11
11/1 Illustration: Claire Blackman.
11/2 Illustration: Claire Blackman.
11/3 Photo: A Long.

Chapter 12
12/1 Photo: L W Tovell.
12/2 Photo: A J Middleton.
12/3 Photo: Source unknown.
12/4 Illustration: Bob Kitson.

Chapter 13
13/1 Photo: Illustrated London News.
13/2 Photo: Illustrated London News.

Chapter 14
14/1 Illustration: Alastair Rankine.
14/2 Reproduction: Cliff Nicholson, CBE.
14/3 Illustration: Alastair Rankine.

Chapter 15
15/1 Photo: London Residuary Body.
15/2 Illustration: District Audit Society.
15/3 Photo: H Gwyther.
15/4 Photo: H Gwyther.
15/5 Reprodution: HMSO.
15/6 Photo: H R Mathieson.

Chapter 16
16/1 Illustration: Claire Blackman.
16/2 Illustration: Claire Blackman.
16/3 Illustration: Claire Blackman.
16/4 Illustration: Claire Blackman.

Chapter 17
17/1 Illustration: Bob Kitson.

Chapter 18
18/1 Illustration: Bob Kitson.

Chapter 19
19/1 Illustration: Claire Blackman.
19/2 Illustration: Claire Blackman.
19/3 Illustration: Claire Blackman.
19/4 Illustration: Claire Blackman.
19/5 Illustration: Claire Blackman.
19/6 Illustration: Claire Blackman.

Chapter 20
20/1 Illustration: Bob Kitson.
20/2 Reproduction: Daily Express.
20/3 Reproduction: The Mirror Group.
20/4 Reproductions: Evening Standard and The Mirror Group.
20/5 Reproductions: Times Newspapers, Sunday Express and Daily Telegraph.

Chapter 21
21/1 Photo: H Gwyther.
21/2 Photo: H Gwyther.
21/3–21/7 Photos: H Gwyther.
21/8 Photo: H Gwyther.
21/9 Photo: C G Trew.
21/10 Photo: H Gwyther.

Chapter 22
22/1 Reproduction: Sheffield Newspapers Ltd.
22/2 Illustration: Source unknown.
22/3 Reproduction: Sheffield Newspapers Ltd.
22/4 Reproductions: Daily Mail and The Times.
22/5 Reproductions: The Guardian and Sheffield Newspapers Ltd.
22/6 Reproduction: Times Newspapers.

Chapter 23
23/1 Photo: Alan Edmonds.

23/2 Illustration: Claire Blackman.
23/3 Illustration: Claire Blackman.

Chapter 24
24/1 Illustration: Bob Kitson.
24/2 Reproduction: Times Newspapers.
24/3 Illustration: Bob Kitson.

Chapter 25
25/1 Illustration: Claire Blackman.

Chapter 26
26/1 Illustration: Bob Kitson.
26/2 Illustration: Bob Kitson.

Chapter 27
27/1 Illustration: Bob Kitson.
27/2 Illustration: Bob Kitson.

Chapter 28
28/1 Illustration: Bob Kitson.
28/2 Illustration: Bob Kitson.
28/3 Photo: H Gwyther.
28/4 Photo: C G Trew.
28/5 Photo: C G Trew.
28/6 Photo: C G Trew.
28/7 R K Edwards.

Chapter 29
All illustrations: Crown copyright. Reproduced with the permission of the Controller of Her Majesty's Stationery Office.

Chapter 30:
30/1 Illustration: Claire Blackman.
30/2 Illustration: Bob Kitson.